Law,
Society,
and
Industrial
Justice

Law,

Society,

and

Industrial

Justice

Philip Selznick

with the collaboration of
PHILIPPE NONET *and* HOWARD M. VOLLMER

RUSSELL SAGE FOUNDATION   1969

PUBLICATIONS OF RUSSELL SAGE FOUNDATION

Russell Sage Foundation was established in 1907 by Mrs.
Russell Sage for the improvement of social and living
conditions in the United States. In carrying out its purpose
the Foundation conducts research under the direction of
members of the staff or in close collaboration with other
institutions, and supports programs designed to improve the
utilization of social science knowledge. As an integral part
of its operations, the Foundation from time to time
publishes books or pamphlets resulting from these activities.
Publication under the imprint of the Foundation does not
necessarily imply agreement by the Foundation, its
Trustees, or its staff with the interpretations or conclusions
of the authors.

© 1969
RUSSELL SAGE FOUNDATION
Printed in the United States of America
Library of Congress Catalog Card Number: 70–96114

Preface

The argument of this book was first sketched in a paper read at the 1957 meeting of the American Sociological Association; it was more fully stated at a Symposium on Business Policy sponsored by the Harvard Graduate School of Business Administration in 1963. Other commitments have obliged me to set the project aside several times; I am hopeful that the delay is offset by some gain in understanding. My view of law and authority has certainly benefited from the stirrings of the sixties, especially on the campuses, where there has been a quest for enlarged student rights and for the reconstruction of authority.

In the meantime, a number of graduate students, now colleagues, have worked on closely relevant topics. Howard M. Vollmer's *Employee Rights and the Employment Relationship* was published in 1960; Philippe Nonet prepared a master's thesis on *The Decline of Contract* in 1964; and Patrick J. McGillivray completed a dissertation on *Social Organization and Employee Rights* in 1966. C. Michael Otten's forthcoming study of private government on the campus reflects similar concerns. I am grateful for the collaboration of these colleagues, and for that of a number of other students who tarried for awhile to prepare a memorandum or a relevant term paper. Special thanks are due to Patrick J. McGillivray for reviewing the pattern of decisions in grievance arbitration, as reported in Chapter 4; and to Harvey Sacks, who helped me to understand the premises of American labor law.

I also wish to thank the Institute of Industrial Relations, University of California, Berkeley, where the study was initiated; and the Fund for the Republic, whose Trade Union Project helped support the survey reported in Chapter 5. Paul Jacobs was staff director of the Trade Union Project. He and I worked closely together at an early stage, and I should like to record here my deep appreciation for his help and friendship.

The data for Chapter 5 was gathered and analyzed, with my collaboration, by Howard M. Vollmer, who also helped on Chapter 3. Chapter 6 was prepared, with my collaboration, by Philippe Nonet. Nonet also helped in many other ways, and I am grateful to him for an intellectual fellowship that has truly been a high point of my experience as a teacher and scholar.

That association was made possible by the Center for the Study of Law and Society, subsisting on a grant from the Russell Sage Foundation. I extend thanks and greetings to all who have been connected with the Center, especially Leonard S. Cottrell of the Russell Sage Foundation, Vice-Chairman Sheldon L. Messinger, Mary Alden, Jerome E. Carlin, Caleb Foote, Sanford H. Kadish, Leo Lowenthal, David Matza, Frank C. Newman, Jerome H. Skolnick, and Elliot Studt.

As always, I am indebted to Gertrude Jaeger Selznick, for specific help on intellectual puzzles and for unflagging devotion to the examined life.

Philip Selznick

Berkeley, California
May, 1969

Contents

6. PUBLIC POLICY AND THE EMPLOYMENT RELATION 212

Regulation by indirection, 215
Voluntarism and passivity, 225
Private law public policy, 229

Part Three: The Emergent Law

7. PRIVATE GROUPS AND THE LAW OF GOVERNANCE 243

Public law and private law, 244
Due process asthe law of governance, 250
The concept of private government, 259

Part One | *Legal and Social Theory*

Chapter 1 | *Law, Society,*
and Moral Evolution

THIS IS A STUDY OF INDUSTRIAL ORGANIZATION, VIEWED
in the light of moral and legal evolution. "Moral evolution" is a somewhat
unfashionable phrase, but it can usefully denote the progressive clarifica-
tion of human ideals, and the enlargement of institutional competence to
serve them. Our concern is with a special ideal—the rule of law—and its
extension to the conditions of employment in modern industry.

The larger context of our inquiry is the embodiment of ideals in institutions, the infusion of group life with the aspirations and constraints of
a moral order. We take it for granted that this achievement, where it
occurs, is partial and incomplete; that it is often born of confusion and
sustained in struggle. We assume that to study the institutional embodiment of values we must look closely at the values themselves, at the characteristic ways they are elaborated and extended, and at the social circumstances that invite or resist them.

We begin, in Part One, with some relevant issues in legal and social
theory. Since the theme of the study is, in effect, legal "development,"
Chapter 1 treats the concepts of law and legality for the light they may
cast on that process.[1] Chapter 2 specifies the context more closely by reviewing some aspects of the law of associations, with special attention to
problems of legal cognition. We then turn, in Part Two, to the sociological
meaning of various developments that have received considerable atten-

---

[1] This chapter incorporates modified portions of the following essays by Philip Selznick:
"Sociology and Natural Law," *Natural Law Forum* 6 (1961), 84–108; "Sociology of
Law," *International Encyclopedia of the Social Sciences* (1968).

3

tion in recent years: the evolution of bureaucratic and other rational forms of organization; the rapid growth of collective bargaining and labor arbitration; the enlargement of governmental restraints on the authority of management. We also report on the attitudes of industrial workers toward procedural and substantive fairness. Chapter 7 returns to the more general issues of private government and emergent law. Our treatment is for the most part limited to the American experience.

A number of themes in the sociology of law have a central place in our discussion:

(1) the relevance of legal theory to private, non-state institutions;
(2) the nature of legality, and its social foundations;
(3) incipient and inchoate law;
(4) legal cognition, including the changing content and social function of legal abstractions;
(5) the relation between law and politics.

These general topics are explored in the course of a more pointed concern for the extension of the rule of law to industrial employment.

Law as Generic

If we are to study justice in industry, or in any other specialized institution, we must first be clear that law is found in many settings; it is not uniquely associated with the state. We need a concept of law that is sufficiently general to embrace legal experience within "private" associations, but not so general as to make law lose its distinctive character or become equivalent to social control.

Definitions and concepts.   Although we need an appropriate concept of law, we have no wish to argue for a special and restrictive definition; we do not propose stringent criteria to limit how the word "law" may be used. In our discussion we try to bear in mind the difference between how a term is defined and how we conceive a phenomenon.

In the logic of social inquiry, "concept" has a peculiar status. When we speak of the concept of totalitarianism or mass society or alienation or culture or socialization, we have in mind something more than a handy definition. The concept is open-ended, subject to debate and revision, accessible to empirical judgment. That is so because "concept" shades into "theory." Indeed, to explicate a concept is to state a theory.

Social science is best served when definitions are "weak" and concepts are "strong."[2] A weak definition is inclusive; its conditions are easily met.

---

[2] This point was suggested by Gertrude Jaeger Selznick.

A strong concept is more demanding in that, for example, it may identify attributes that are latent as well as manifest, or offer a model of what the phenomenon is like in a fully developed (or deteriorated) state. Accordingly, in what follows the word law is used in a way that is general enough to embrace all legal experience, however various or rudimentary. At the same time, law and legal process are understood as pointing to a larger achievement and a greater elaboration.

The centrality of authority. Contemporary jurisprudence is reasonably comfortable with law conceived as a generic phenomenon. This appears clearly in the writings of H. L. A. Hart and Lon Fuller.[3] Although they disagree sharply in other ways, both offer a theory of law detached from the concept of the state, that is, the organized political community. Moreover, both reject coercion as a touchstone of the distinctively legal.

Neither public government as usually understood nor "orders backed by threats" are central to the idea of law. Rather, *rule* and *authority* bring law into focus. A legal system is known by the existence of authoritative rules. Thus Hart argues that, in stepping "from the pre-legal to the legal world," a society develops special rules for curing the defects of a social order based on unofficial norms.[4] A regime of unofficial norms has a number of inherent limitations, including the difficulty of resolving uncertainties as to the existence or scope of a norm. In a pre-legal setting, no criterion or procedure is available for settling such issues. The distinctively legal emerges with the development of "secondary rules," that is, rules of authoritative determination. These rules, selectively applied, raise up the unofficial norms and give them a legal status.

It follows that a "rule is something more than an observed regularity of conduct, more also than a social prescription or norm. A rule is a special kind of norm—one that bears some warrant of validity.[5] It therefore tends to be formal, explicit, deliberately instituted. It is in some sense official.

The special work of law is to identify claims and obligations that merit official validation and enforcement. This may consist of nothing more than the establishment of a public record, say, of land holdings or clan prerogatives, invested with a special claim upon the community's respect as a guide to action. When institutions emerge that do this work we can speak of a legal order. These institutions need not be specialized. They

---

[3] H. L. A. Hart, *The Concept of Law* (Oxford: Oxford University Press, 1961); Lon L. Fuller, *The Morality of Law* (New Haven: Yale University Press, 1964).
[4] Hart, *op. cit.*, 91.
[5] As we use it at this point, "rule" does not necessarily carry a connotation of specificity; it includes authoritative "principles." On the significance of principles, see below, 26 ff.

may have no resource for coercive enforcement. It is essential only that their determinations affecting rights and duties are accepted as authoritative.

This approach may be compared with the sociological theory of Max Weber, who attempted to distinguish law from other modes of social control by offering a rather austere "operational" definition. Weber agreed that not every normative order is a legal order. The distinctively legal emerges when "there exists a 'coercive apparatus,' i.e., that there are one or more persons whose special task it is to hold themselves ready to apply specially provided means of coercion (legal coercion) for the purpose of norm inforcement."[6] A legal norm is known by the probability that it will be enforced by a specialized staff. Weber's definition is meant to exclude all value judgments in the assessment of what is or is not law.

Although he emphasized coercion, Weber was careful to point out that the latter may be psychological, not necessarily physical. The threat of physical force is not essential to legal action, for coercion may consist in public reprimand or boycott. This is important because Weber does not limit the idea of law to the political community, which may assume a monopoly of legitimate violence. His definition allows for what he called "extra-state" law, such as ecclesiastical law, or the law of any other corporate group binding on its members. So long as coercive means are available, exercised by a specialized staff within the group, the requirements for the existence of a legal order are fulfilled.

Weber's treatment seems very matter-of-fact and tough-minded. There is no reference to ideals or standards. Nevertheless, we should note that he speaks, not of coercion alone, but of a coercive "apparatus" and of "specially provided means for the purpose of norm enforcement." These qualifications are crucial, for Weber clearly does not mean that *any* group dedicated to the suppression of deviance becomes *eo ipso* an instrument of law. He must mean that such a group is specially *constituted*, that it acts authoritatively.

In much of his work, Weber saw quite clearly the intimate relation of the legal and authoritative. His theory of authority and legitimacy, for example, contrasts the charismatic, the traditional, and the "rational legal," thus placing law in a context of evolving forms of authority.[7] In that analysis, Weber assimilates fully developed law to a system of governance by

---

[6] Max Rheinstein (ed.), *Max Weber on Law in Economy and Society* (Cambridge, Mass.: Harvard University Press, 1954), 13.

[7] Max Weber, *Theory of Social and Economic Organization* (New York: Oxford University Press, 1947), Chap. 3.

rules. He sees the distinctively legal obligation as running to an impersonal order that exhibits a strain toward rationality. When Weber did not speak of the concept of law abstractly, but actually used it, especially in his theory of bureaucracy, he greatly modified the significance of coercion.

Of course, coercion is an important and often indispensable *resource* for law. But so is education, symbolism, and the appeal to reason. Coercion does not make law, though it may indeed establish an order out of which law may emerge. In the authoritative use of coercion, whether by private or public agencies, the legal element is not the coercion itself but the invocation of authority.

This point bears closely on the distinction between law and the state. We associate the state with coercion because it is the state, the organized political community, that has the main responsibilty for maintaining public order. Whether coercion used to that end is *lawful* is always an open question.

The view of law sketched here assimilates the theory of law to the theory of authority. This postulate governs both a minimal definition of law and a more elaborated concept. Rules of authoritative determination may take many forms and call upon many different resources. They may be blunt, crude, and "undeveloped." To bring law within the theory of authority does not require us to hold that only a "pure" or developed legal order deserves to be classified as such.

We should see law as endemic in all institutions *that rely for social control on formal authority and rule-making.* Law so understood is analytically distinct from the narrower view of public government, but it is also distinct from the broader idea of social control. The middle ground we seek is occupied by Fuller, for example, when he interprets law as "the enterprise of subjecting human conduct to the governance of rules."[8] The phrase "governance of rules" must be understood as shorthand for a system of order that contains specialized mechanisms for certifying rules as authoritative and for safeguarding rule-making and rule-applying from the intrusion of other forms of direction and control.

Fuller argues explicitly that law should not be equated with public government.

> A view that seeks to understand law in terms of the activity that sustains it, instead of considering only the formal sources of its authority, may sometimes suggest a use of words that violates the normal expectations of language. This inconvenience may, I suggest, be offset by the capacity of such a view to make us perceive essential similarities. It may help us to

---

[8] Fuller, *op. cit.*, 106.

see that the imperfectly achieved systems of law within a labor union or a university may often cut more deeply into the life of a man than any court judgment ever likely to be rendered against him. On the other hand, it may also help us to realize that all systems of law, big and little, are subject to the same infirmities.[9]

To equate law and the state impoverishes sociological analysis, because the concept of law should be available for study of any setting in which human conduct is subject to explicit rule-making; and when we deny the place of law in specialized institutions *we withhold from the private setting the funded experience of the political community in matters of governance.*

Law as a Realm of Value

To say that law is generic is a necessary first step in applying legal theory to specialized institutions. Our second step invokes the perspective of moral evolution. We want to ask what it means to "legalize" an institution, that is, to infuse its mode of governance with the aspirations and constraints of a legal order. To do this, we should first understand the view that law is intimately associated with the realization of values.

In the discussion of law there is an ever-renewed conflict between those who see it as a functional necessity and others who invest it with hope and promise. The former accept law as given, as fact, at best as an instrument of practical problem-solving. For the legal idealist, on the other hand, law connotes a larger moral achievement.

When law is conceived as a functional necessity, the focus tends to be on order and control. Law is summoned by elementary urgencies: keep the peace, settle disputes, suppress deviance. Authority pays its way, and redeems its coercive sins, if it can establish tranquillity, facilitate cooperative action, and uphold the mores, whatever they may be. This might be called the *minimalist* view of what law is and does. For it, "justice" is not a compelling symbol and at an extreme may even be scorned as the refuge of hopelessly muddled men.

It should be noted that order and control are values of a sort. They are certainly "things prized," and would satisfy almost any minimum definition of value, such as "the object of any interest." But order and control are values in a weak sense. They cannot of themselves sustain personal or group identity. They do not readily serve as vehicles of loyalty and commitment.

The alternative is to think of law as instituting a *kind* of order and a

---

[9] *Ibid.*, 129.

kind of social control. This approach asks more of a legal system and yields a richer sense of value. The contribution of law to social order is not lost, *but a closer concern for the continuum of means and ends appears.* Where there is fidelity to law, order is not to be purchased at any price. Rather, law imposes limits on social control. For example, the commitment of police to lawfulness is always to some extent a restraint on the means they can use to prevent crime or apprehend criminals.[10] The greater the self-consciousness about law, and the more law is looked to for the vindication of rights, the more apparent is a tension between law and order.

A normative concept of law, or of any similar phenomenon, turns attention from necessity to fulfillment. Instead of concentrating on the minimum functions of law, or on the minimum conditions that signify its emergence, the emphasis shifts to law's civilizing potential. A logically similar problem appears when the idea of "education" is discussed. A minimalist concept of education is content to equate it with the transmission of skills, including social skills, and of a received tradition. A more expansive and normative view embraces the contribution of education to moral sensibility.[11]

A superficially attractive way of resolving the conceptual ambiguity would restrict law, education, friendship, or literature in minimalist terms, then specify additional attributes that warrant the designation "good" law, "good" education, "good" literature, "good" friendship, and so forth. This solution has merit, but it is defective if the normative attributes are taken to be mere subjective preferences. For that lends an arbitrary cast to the phenomenon's "high state" or "excellence," as if this were a matter of likes and dislikes and had no intrinsic relation to the natural characteristics or the social dynamics of the institution or relationship. Although a definition of law should be spacious and inclusive, it ought to contain a theoretical warrant for treating at least a *strain* toward legal development as objectively grounded. This is accomplished when law is defined as a system of authoritative rules and decision-making.

A normative theory of law or friendship specifies *latent* values that inhere in the phenomenon. These values serve as resources for critical evaluation, not from the standpoint of the observer's preferences, but in

---

[10] See Herbert Packer, "Two Models of the Criminal Process," 113 *University of Pennsylvania Law Review* 1 (1964).

[11] For a discussion of normative concepts in social science, see Ernest Nagel, *The Structure of Science* (New York: Harcourt, Brace & World, 1961), 490–495; see also Gertrude Jaeger and Philip Selznick, "A Normative Theory of Culture," *American Sociological Review*, 29 (October, 1964), 653–669.

the light of the inner order of the phenomenon, including what the participants are likely to experience as deprivation or satisfaction.

We perceive latent values in the world of fact when we recognize, for example, that fatherhood, sexuality, leadership, friendship, and many other phenomena have a natural potential for "envaluation." This potential is not an abstract possibility but an empirical likelihood founded in conditions that are routinely generated by the experience or relationship. Biological parenthood, for example, is invested with value because the satisfactions associated with parenthood—satisfactions that are biologically functional—are not fully realized unless a guiding ideal emerges. Arbitrary social convention plays a part in this envaluation, but only a part. The same holds true for the dialectic of sex and satisfaction. The union of sex and love is by no means inevitable, but it is a value latent in human mating. That such values are subject to distortion, and are always incompletely realized, is not in itself a denial of their latency. On the contrary, to the extent that problems are set by such natural aspirations, whether or not they are fulfilled, their empirical significance is confirmed.

The transition from necessity to fulfillment has its echoes in contemporary social and psychological theory. "Functional analysis" is a way of studying social structure or personality by examining items of behavior or other social units for the work they do in sustaining or undermining a going concern or system. What is apparently or manifestly propaganda may be latently a way of contributing to group cohesion by keeping members busy; a mode of punishment sustains the common conscience; selective recruitment of administrative personnel undermines an established policy or bolsters a shaky elite. Functional analysis is most familiar in the study of personality where a great many items of perception and behavior become meaningful only when their contribution to the maintenance of personal adjustment, including neurotic adjustment, is understood.

In such interpretations, there is a strong and understandable tendency to identify what is required for the maintenance of a system with what is required for the *bare survival* of a group or individual. The very term "survival" suggests that what is at stake is the biological extinction of the individual or the complete dissolution of the group. In fact, however, systems may decay despite the continuity of individual or group life. If a man extricates himself from neurotic dependence on some other person or activity, then a system has changed. If an organization maintains its personnel and budget, and even its formal identity, but transforms its effective goals, capabilities, commitments, and role in the community, then too a system has changed. To be sure, some systems are indispensable if life is to exist at all; but other systems are required if a certain *kind* of life is to survive. In social science the most important analyses have to do not with the bare continuity of life but with certain kinds and levels of organization.

The idea that law connotes a special kind of order is implicitly accepted when we pay our respects to "the rule of law." In English *a* rule of law is a specific norm or guide to decision. The phrase is meant to be descriptive and value-free. But *the* rule of law is a more connotative and value-laden idea. It refers to aspirations that distinguish a developed legal order from a system of subordination to naked power.

The Ideal of Legality

The impulse to create a legal order is, in the first instance, a practical one. From the standpoint of the rulers, power is made more secure when it is legitimate; from the standpoint of the ruled, fears of oppression are allayed. Thus legalization is rooted in the problems of collective life. It is not, in its primitive forms, an expression of social idealism. It is obvious, moreover, that communities survive and even flourish without going very far toward legalization. We do not suppose that the values associated with law must necessarily be realized. Other values, for example, religious or aesthetic values, may define a world more appealing.

To understand what legalization entails for the life of a political community or a specialized institution, however, we should consider its ideal or developed state. In what follows we shall briefly explicate what is meant by "legality," which we take to be a synonym for "the rule of law."

The essential element in the rule of law is the restraint of official power by rational principles of civic order. Where this ideal exists, no power, including the democratic majority, is immune from criticism or entirely free to follow its own bent, however well-intentioned it may be. Legality imposes an environment of constraint, of tests to be met, standards to be observed, ideals to be fulfilled.

Legality has to do mainly with *how* policies and rules are made and applied rather than with their content. The vast majority of rules, including judge-made rules, spell out policy choices, choices not uniquely determined by the requirements of legality. Whether contracts must be supported by consideration; whether a defendant in an accident case should be spared liability because of plaintiff's contributory negligence; whether minors should be relieved of legal consequences that might otherwise apply to their actions—these and a host of other issues treated in the common law are basically matters of general public policy. For practical and historical reasons, a great many of these policy matters are decided by the courts in the absence of, or as a supplement to, legislative determination. In making these decisions, and in devising substantive rules, the courts are concerned with dimensions of justice that go beyond the ideal of legality. Legality is a part of justice, but only a part.

Nevertheless, there are times when the ideal of legality does determine the content of a legal rule or doctrine. This occurs when the purpose of the rule is precisely to implement that ideal, the most obvious illustration being the elaboration of procedural rules of pleading and evidence. In addition, principles of statutory interpretation, including much of constitutional law, directly serve the aim of creating and sustaining the "legal state." Some of these rules are "merely" procedural, chosen because some device was necessary, for which some other procedure might readily be substituted. Others are vital to the protection of just those substantial rights which the ideal of legality is meant to protect. These include primarily all that we term civil rights, the rights of members of a polity to act as full citizens and to be free of oppressive and arbitrary official power. Again, it is not the aim of this ideal to protect the individual against *all* power, but only against the misuse of power by those whose actions have the color of authority. Later we shall argue that in modern society we must extend our notions of who it is that acts "officially."

The effort to see in law a set of standards, an internal basis for criticism and reconstruction, leads us to a true *Grundnorm*—the idea that a legal order faithful to itself seeks *progressively to reduce the degree of arbitrariness in positive law and its administration.* By "positive law" we mean those public obligations that have been defined by duly constituted mechanisms, such as a legislature, court, administrative agency, or referendum. This is not the whole of law, for by the latter we must mean the entire body of authoritative materials—"precepts, techniques, and ideals"[12]—that guide official decision-making. Law is "positive" when a particular conclusion has been reached by some authorized body—a conclusion expressed in a determinate rule or judgment.

Plainly, positive law includes an arbitrary element. For him who must obey it, it is to some extent brute fact and brute command. But this arbitrary element, while necessary and inevitable, is repugnant to the ideal of

---

[12] See Roscoe Pound, *Jurisprudence* (St. Paul: West Publishing Co., 1959), II, 107: "Law in the sense we are considering is made up of precepts, techniques and ideals: A body of authoritative precepts, developed and applied by an authoritative technique in the light of or on the background of authoritative traditional ideals."

legality. Therefore the proper aim of the legal order, and the special contribution of legal scholarship, is to minimize the arbitrary element in legal norms and decisions. This objective may be compared to the scientific ideal of "reducing the degree of empiricism," that is, the number of theoretically ungrounded factual generalizations within the corpus of scientific knowledge.

If the reduction of arbitrariness is central to legality, three corollaries may be suggested:

1. **Legality is a variable achievement.** A developed legal order is the product of continuing effort and posits values that are always incompletely fulfilled. We can unblushingly speak of more or less legality, meaning nothing more obscure than that some systems of rules, and some modes of decision, are less arbitrary than others. A major topic in legal sociology is the study of empirical conditions that reduce or exacerbate the arbitrary element in making or applying rules. For example, studies of police discretion locate systematic sources of arbitrary decision in the handling of juveniles; "treatment" is seen as a cover for unsupervised control; the low visibility of decisions in administrative agencies tends to encourage self-serving discretion.

This is not to suggest that the notion of "arbitrary" is completely clear, or that it has a simple meaning. Rules are made arbitrarily when appropriate interests are not consulted and when there is no clear relation between the rule enunciated and the official end to be achieved. Rules are arbitrary when they reflect confused policies, are based on ignorance or error, and when they suggest no inherent principles of criticism. Discretion is arbitrary when it is whimsical, or governed by criteria extraneous to legitimate means or ends. All of this is a matter of degree. Few decisions are completely arbitrary, yet we may compare the more and the less.

The reduction of arbitrariness cannot be equated with the elaboration of formal rules and procedures. "Formal justice" equalizes parties and makes decisions predictable; it is therefore a major contribution to the mitigation of arbitrary rule. But legal "correctness" has its own costs. Like any other technology, it is vulnerable to the divorce of means and ends. When this occurs, legality degenerates into legalism. Substantive justice is undone when there is too great a commitment to upholding the autonomy and integrity of the legal process. Rigid adherence to precedent and mechanical application of rules hamper the capacity of the legal system to take account of new interests and circumstances, or to adapt to social inequality. Formal justice tends to serve the status quo. It therefore may be experienced as arbitrary by those whose interests are dimly perceived or who are really outside "the system."

Formal attributes of equality or certainty may run counter to the continuities of culture and social organization. One student of the role of British law in India has noted:

> The common law proceeds on the basis of equality before the law while indigenous dispute-settling finds it unthinkable to separate the parties from their statuses and relations. The common law gives a clear-cut "all or none" decision, while indigenous processes seek a face-saving solution agreeable to all parties; the common law deals only with a single isolated offense or transaction, while the indigenous system sees this as arbitrarily leaving out the underlying dispute of which this may be one aspect; the common law has seemingly arbitrary rules of evidence, which do not permit that which is well-known to be proved and that which is not can be proved; the common law then seems abrupt and overly decisive, distant, expensive, and arbitrary.[13]

The limits of formalism suggest that the reduction of arbitrariness requires a union of formal and substantive justice.

Properly understood, the concept of legality is more critical than celebrationist. To say that legality is a variable achievement is to leave room for the conclusion that, at any given time, the system of positive law is "congealed injustice."[14] An affirmative approach to legal values need not accept the defensive rhetoric of men in power. On the contrary, it offers principles of criticism to evaluate the shortcomings of the existing system of rules and practices.

2. Legality extends to administration as well as adjudication. Wherever there is official conduct, the possibility of arbitrary decision arises. That conduct may be far removed from rule-making or adjudication, at least in spirit or purpose. It may be a practical effort to get a job done. Yet the question of legitimacy—of power exercised *in the light* of governing norms—is always appropriate. Furthermore, the problem of arbitrariness is at issue whenever rights are determined, something that may occur quite incidentally, in the course of administrative decision and policy-making. Thus any official decision, whether it be a purchase, a hiring, a

---

[13] Marc Galanter, "Hindu Law and the Development of the Modern Indian Legal System" (mimeo.; prepared for delivery at the 1964 Annual Meeting of the American Political Science Association), 25. On the relation between formal and substantive justice, see Max Weber's discussion in Rheinstein (ed.), *Max Weber on Law in Economy and Society, op. cit.*, 224 ff.
[14] Howard Zinn, *Disobedience and Democracy: Nine Fallacies on Law and Order* (New York: Vintage Books, 1968), 4.

deployment of police power, or any other active effort to accomplish a defined social purpose, may be criticized in the name of legality.

It has been said that "reliance on the action of abstract rules governing the relations between individuals . . . is the essential basis of the Rule of Law."[15] That formulation is too sweeping, for it limits the legal ideal to the adjudicative mode. It precludes a law-governed, arbitrariness-minimizing sphere of administrative action.

In adjudication, whether conducted by an administrative agency or a court, there is a quest for and application of rules that are logically, if not historically, prior to the case at hand. It is not a rule tailored to the needs and circumstances of a particular plaintiff or defendant, with the idea of achieving a particular outcome. The same rule is applied to every member of a legally defined class of cases. A particular case cannot be handled, without risk to legality, unless it belongs to a category, unless it can be so classified that a general rule, applicable to the entire class of cases, can be invoked.

The application of general rules does not preclude "tempering justice with mercy," taking account of special strengths or weaknesses, or any other effort to adapt the administration of justice to the actual circumstances before the court or administrative tribunal. In principle, this is only a matter of specifying more closely the category to which the case belongs, often by combining a set of applicable concepts or doctrines, for example, that a contract made by a minor is voidable but that unjust enrichment will not be allowed. The only important criterion is: Would another litigant in the same circumstances be judged according to the same criteria?

Thus, in the determination of rights, "discretion" is compatible with the rule of law when it remains essentially judicial rather than administrative. Like any other discretion, judicial discretion involves a certain freedom of choice. The choice, however, is of a special kind. From among many possible ways of classifying the events at hand, the court selects that particular classification which will fix the rights and obligations of the parties. To this end, judicial discretion may carpenter doctrines and otherwise rework the legal materials. But the objective remains: Find a rule or a rule-set that will do justice in a special class of situations.

Administrative discretion is of another order.[16] The administrator (where

---

[15] F. A. Hayek, *The Political Ideal of the Rule of Law* (Cairo: National Bank of Egypt, 1955), 32.

[16] In his *Administrative Law Treatise* (St. Paul: West Publishing Co., 1958), K. C. Davis assimilates the administrative process to adjudication by defining an "administrative agency" as "a governmental authority other than a court and other than a

he is not really a judge) is also interested in diagnosing and classifying the world. But he properly looks to an end-in-view, the refashioning of human or other resources so that a particular outcome will be achieved. A judge becomes an administrator when his objective is to reform a criminal, avert a strike, or abate a nuisance. For then his aim is not justice but accomplishment, not fairness but therapy.

Administration may be controlled by law, but its special place in the division of labor is to get the work of society done, not to realize the ideals of legality. Adjudication also gets work done, in settling disputes, but this is secondary and not primary. The primary function of adjudication is to discover the legal coordinates of a particular situation. That is a far cry from manipulating the situation to achieve a desired outcome.

This line of reasoning suggests that administration, even in a developed legal order, is distinguished from adjudication by a weaker commitment to the ideal of legality. It does not follow, however, that legality is foreign to the ethos of administration. Its relevance appears in two ways. First, there is a common commitment to objective and impersonal decision-making. Second, administration can contain within it machinery that approximates adjudication when rights are affected.

Objective decisions call for *universalistic* rather than *particularistic* criteria of assessment—a distinction that is as subtle in logic as it is precarious in experience. The model of particularism is found in ties of common association—religious, political, kinship, friendship, even conspiratorial. The claim of a particular individual to be treated in a distinctive way is recognized. The prototypical case is nepotism. However, the nepotistic response may be made in the light of a general norm governing how one should treat a relative or friend. The tension is created by competing norms, not by a difference between decision in the light of what is general as distinguished from what is specific. The norm of particularism is subversive of objective and impartial judgment because it introduces extraneous, person-centered criteria of decision into settings where there should be a sovereignty of institutional purpose.

Universalism is as pertinent to administration as it is to adjudication. Universalism asks only that criteria of decision transcend the special interests of persons or groups. Situations may be dealt with according to the special requirements, and specific outcomes may be sought, but the integ-

---

legislative body, which affects the rights of private parties through either adjudication or rule-making" (I, 1). He suggests a distinction between the "executive process" and the "administrative process" (*ibid.*, 57). It seems better to maintain the more conventional usage and see administration as fundamentally task-oriented.

rity of official decision is retained so long as there is an objective relation between the course of decision-making and the requirements of institutional purpose. The official can then give reasons for his actions and expose them to criticism in the light of publicly acknowledged ends.

3. **Legality applies to public participation as well as to the conduct of officials.** If legality aspires to minimize the arbitrary element in law, then public participation must itself be subject to scrutiny and criticism. Positive law is a product of both will and reason; the mixture is variable and unstable. Although positive law cannot be *merely* an expression of social power, neither is it free of that element. The actions of an electorate and the decisions of a legislature may conform to procedural standards and yet contain strong arbitrary elements. Some statutes are passed under the heavy pressures of special interests or in a mood of panic, confusion, or unreason. And the quality of decision by a popular majority may be marred and distorted under conditions of collective excitement, irrelevant symbolism, or misinformation. When the public acts officially, or influences official conduct, it may do so arbitrarily. Legality recognizes the arbitrary element in law, and even protects some of those elements, such as the right of a legitimate decider to prevail for the time being despite some acting out of power or whim. But the larger aspiration of a community dedicated to law is to enlarge the role of reason and fairness in all public decision.

The general public contributes to legality, not only through the quality of democratic decision-making, but also insofar as it has the competence, and recognizes the duty, of criticizing authority. To be sure, there must be public respect for law, and appropriate self-restraint, but in a vital legal order something more is wanted than submission to constituted authority. A military establishment places very great emphasis on obedience to lawful commands, yet such a setting is hardly a model of institutionalized legality. So too, a conception of law as the manifestation of awesome authority encourages feelings of deference and is compatible with much arbitrary rule. In a community that aspires to a high order of legality obedience to law is not submissive compliance. The obligation to obey the law is closely tied to the defensibility of the rules themselves and of the official decisions that enforce them.

Thus understood, legality has a strong affinity with the ideal of political democracy. This is most readily manifest in democracy's dependence on limited governmental authority, and on the possibility of appeal, beyond majority will, for the protection of minority rights and the free creation of new majorities. But there is also an affinity of fundamental values—

above all, to the role of reason in official judgment. Legality does not require the machinery of democratic decision-making. But it does require that the civic participant be treated as a "legal man," a right-and-duty bearing entity invested with the presumption of competence and guaranteed access to tribunals that are committed to the impartial assessment of evidence and argument.

4. **Legality is an affirmative ideal.** The rule of law is a practical ideal, which is to say it rests in part on pessimistic premises regarding the nature of man and society. "Free government," wrote Thomas Jefferson, "is founded in jealousy, and not in confidence, it is jealousy, and not confidence, which prescribes limited constitutions, to bind down those whom we are obliged to trust with power; . . . in questions of power, then, let no more be heard of confidence in man, but bind him down from mischief by the chains of the Constitution."[17] The assumption is that no man, no group of men, is to be trusted with unlimited power. No amount of wisdom or good will can justify a transfer of untrammeled power to mortal men.

This view does not require the belief that any man, given the chance, would misuse power; rather, the premise is that there is a sufficient *risk* of such misuse to forbid *reliance upon* the idealism and good will of men in authority. Nor does Jefferson's pessimism necessarily deny that power and authority can be ennobling, summoning ordinary men to political and moral heights.

Legality begins as a principle of constraint, but it promises more than a way of moderating the uses of power. The "progressive reduction of arbitrariness" knows no near stopping-place. The closer we look at that process, the more we realize that it calls for an affirmative view of what it means to participate in a legal order, whether as citizen, judge, or executive. In its richest connotation, legality evokes the Greek view of a social order founded in reason, whose constitutive principle is justice.[18]

The Morality of Cooperation

We can better understand the human foundations of legality and the values it expresses, if we examine some relevant aspects of moral development. The latter must be understood as a natural process, a kind of matura-

---

[17] See E. D. Warfield, *The Kentucky Resolutions of 1798* (New York: G. P. Putnam's Sons, 1887), 157–158.
[18] See Werner Jaeger, "Praise of Law," in Paul Sayre (ed.), *Interpretations of Modern Legal Philosophers* (New York: Oxford University Press, 1947), 352–375.

tion. One phase of moral development is social and psychological—the reconstruction of the self, of interpersonal relations, and of orientations toward authority. Another phase is institutional—the creation of new social forms, new modes of participation, new ways of exercising authority.

The theory of moral development is hardly a well-established part of modern psychology and sociology. Nevertheless, a number of classic studies have dealt with this theme, and have done so in ways that are pertinent to the rule of law. Perhaps most closely relevant are the theories of Emile Durkheim, Jean Piaget, George H. Mead, and Max Weber. Durkheim and Piaget explicitly adopted a naturalist view of types and stages of morality, and they saw the import of their theories for conceptions of law and for modes of participation in the legal order.

In his *Division of Labor in Society*[19] Durkheim distinguished two types of social solidarity, "mechanical" and "organic," the latter representing a later stage of development. Mechanical solidarity is based on likeness and a sense of common identity. People are bound together by the fact that they have been brought up to act and think alike, follow similar life routines and share a "common conscience." The main source of cohesion is symbolic experience. This solidarity is "mechanical," Durkheim thought, because it resembles "the cohesion which unites the elements of an inanimate body, as opposed to that which makes a unit out of a living body."[20] Organic solidarity, on the other hand, is based on differentiation, analogous to a complex living body with specialized organs, each dependent on the others, and the whole dependent on the functional integration of the parts. Social differentiation makes people and groups interdependent; this outcome is organic solidarity.

In the stage of mechanical solidarity, social control through law is largely a matter of upholding the symobilic order. Group identity is reaffirmed by punishing deviants who violate what is sacred to the group. To enforce and reassert the common conscience, the community resorts to *punitive* law and *repressive* sanctions.

With the development of organic solidarity, another type of law becomes predominant. This is *restitutive* law, which is the law of cooperation. Its purpose is to restore social equilibrium by making a man whole, that is, compensating him for losses incurred when someone fails to discharge his lawful obligations. The classic branch of restitutive law is the

---

[19] George Simpson (trans.), *Emile Durkheim on the Division of Labor in Society* (New York: The Macmillan Company, 1933). First published in French in 1893.
[20] *Ibid.*, 130.

law of contracts. The contract is, wrote Durkheim, *"par excellence,* the juridical expression of cooperation."[21]

Each type of solidarity, and each of the two types of law, is associated with a distinctive "morality." Repressive law is a manifestation of communal morality and is suffused with the spirit of constraint. Restitutive law is the morality of cooperation; it binds together specialized groups or occupations, rather than whole communities. In organic solidarity Durkheim saw a rational basis for law and one that was compatible with personal autonomy.

Mechanical solidarity presumes that individuals are the same; organic solidarity presumes that they are different. "The first is possible only insofar as the individual personality is absorbed into the collective personality; the second is possible only if each one has a sphere of action which is peculiar to him; that is, a personality."[22] Thus restitutive law encourages autonomy as it facilitates cooperative action.

A strikingly similar model, using entirely different materials, was put forward by the Swiss psychologist Jean Piaget in *The Moral Judgment of the Child.* Piaget studied the responses of children to issues of punishment and fairness. He began with the premise that "all morality consists in a system of rules, and the essence of morality is to be sought for in the respect which the individual acquires for these rules."[23] As a result of this focus on rules, the theme of the study became the child's conception of justice.

Piaget distinguished two types of rules, coercive and rational. The former are based on respect for authority, and compliance is won by punishment. Characteristically, the child's obedience to a coercive rule does not depend on understanding its purpose. The rule is a received and external fact. Rational rules, on the other hand, are founded in a sense of fairness. mutuality, and respect for the ends the rule is meant to serve. A regime of coercive rules is a "morality of constraint"; a regime of rational rules is a "morality of cooperation."[24]

The two types of morality are stages on life's way. A first period, roughly until the age of eight, is characterized by submission to authority and externality of rules. It is a stage of "strict law,"[25] in which the bare fact of infraction, regardless of context or intent, warrants severe punishment. In

---

[21] *Ibid.,* 123.
[22] *Ibid.,* 131.
[23] Jean Piaget, *The Moral Judgment of the Child* (New York: Free Press, 1965), 13. First published in 1932.
[24] *Ibid.,* 335.
[25] See Pound, *op. cit.,* I, 382–406.

the second stage (ages nine to twelve) the commitment to retribution declines. There is a greater awareness of reciprocity, equal treatment, and mutual respect among peers, as well as an increased capacity to distinguish a just rule from one that is merely authoritative.

> [The younger children] do not attempt to understand the psychological context; deeds and punishments are for them simply so much material to be brought into some kind of balance, and this kind of moral mechanics, this materialism of retributive justice, so closely akin to the moral realism studied before, makes them insensible to the human side of the problem. . . . [C]hildren who put retributive justice above distributive are those who adopt the point of view of adult constraint, while those who put equality of treatment above punishment are those who, in their relations with other children, or more rarely in the relations between themselves and adults, have learnt better to understand psychological situations and to judge according to norms of a new moral type.[26]

In Piaget's theory moral evolution is marked by changes in personality, rules, and social relations. At stage one the child is "egocentric" rather than autonomous. He is basically a "loner," unable to engage in genuine cooperation; his play is characteristically mechanical and imitative; at the same time, he is dominated by respect for adult wishes. At this stage the child does not distinguish his own perspectives from the perspectives of others, and the psychological bases for criticism of authority have not been laid.

The transition to stage two sees the child increasing his freedom from adult constraint. He looks to the peer group for satisfaction and guidance. In the peer group an awareness of cooperation takes hold. Group participation encourages a more generalized, less egocentric approach to the world and, at the same time, helps the child to discover the boundaries that separate him from others. According to Piaget, cooperation presumes the participation of autonomous individuals, and as the child's own autonomy grows he gains respect for the autonomy of others. Thus the morality of cooperation is a morality of rational rules, interdependent activities, and autonomous individuals.

Piaget's two stages correspond closely to Durkheim's. Mechanical solidarity creates a morality of constraint; organic solidarity yields a morality of cooperation. Each posits a growth or rationality, social differentiation, and personal autonomy. On the other hand, in a lengthy commentary on Durkheim, Piaget argues that the French sociologist lost his early insight, expressed in *The Division of Labor in Society*, that there are two morali-

---

[26] Piaget, *op. cit.*, 267 f.

ties, one based on conformity to established norms, the other arising out of the necessities and opportunities of the division of labor. In his later writings on education, Durkheim seemed to recognize only one source of moral development—acceptance of authority.[27]

Of course, any theory of determinate "stages" of moral development is highly vulnerable, but more recent studies conducted to test Piaget's hypotheses have confirmed the basic findings, especially his theory that "the child's earliest morality is oriented to obedience, punishment, and impersonal forces, and that it progresses toward more internal and subjective values."[28] Some specific conclusions, such as the importance Piaget gave to the peer group in producing the morality of cooperation, have not been upheld.[29]

The idea that a morality of cooperation replaces a more primitive morality of constraint finds supportive resonance in the theories of George H. Mead, the American philosopher and social psychologist. The concept of moral evolution is less explicit in Mead's writings, but it is not far to seek. In *Mind, Self, and Society* Mead located moral development in the transition from a regime of "significant others" to a consciousness of the "generalized other."[30] The young child internalizes the attitudes and expectations of his parents and of other individuals who dominate his life. These significant others have a direct, personal impact on the child's conception of himself and of his world. Gradually, however, the child learns a different form of social participation. He begins to grasp the meaning of cooperation and to govern his actions by his understanding of group

---

[27] Saul Geiser suggests that the cleavage between Durkheim and Piaget is fundamental, and epistemological. For Durkheim, social facts are characterized by externality and constraint. "This postulate gives little weight to *subjective understanding* as a determinant of the nature of social objects, including rules. For Piaget, the child's understanding of the rules is crucial; it is this that changes in the course of psychological development." (Private communication.) At the same time, we should recognize that objective circumstances, including forms of cooperation, have much to do with the kinds of rules and sanctions that emerge in a given setting.

[28] Lawrence Kohlberg, "Development of Moral Character and Moral Ideology," in Martin L. Hoffman (ed.), *Review of Child Development Research* (New York: Russell Sage Foundation, 1964), 399.

[29] While holding to the idea of development, Kohlberg and other current students of moral growth are chary of determinate stages. They emphasize that the two moralities coexist and compete. In analysis, it is difficult to avoid the language of "stages," though they should not be applied mechanically, or taken as mutually exclusive progressions. See Roger Brown, *Social Psychology* (New York: Free Press, 1965), 241–242, 403 ff., 409. For a related analysis, see Jane Loevinger, "The Meaning and Measurement of Ego Development," *American Psychologist*, 21 (1966), 195–206. Seven "stages" or "milestones" of ego development are discussed, 198–200.

[30] George H. Mead, *Mind, Self, and Society* (Chicago: University of Chicago Press, 1934), 154.

activity. In time he can take the point of view of the group, not by mechanically following an assigned course of conduct but by recognizing how rules are related and how they contribute to the playing of a game or the achievement of a goal. The generalized other is this perspective of cooperative group life.

For Mead, moral evolution could be discerned (1) in the capacity for rational participation in rule-governed, organized social activity; (2) in the growth of personal autonomy, mitigating the over-determined, over-socialized self; and (3) in the enlargement of the self as parochial perspectives are overcome and the individual can adopt the standpoint of ever-larger communities and universal values. Here again, the interdependence of rational rules, cooperation, and personal autonomy is stressed.

At the institutional level, the most persuasive theories of moral evolution center on the emergence of rational forms of social organization. Here the major figure is Max Weber. Weber located that evolution in a determinate set of social processes, especially the rise of economic calculation and bureaucratization, and he kept close to the historical data. Weber would have resisted the notion that his historical sociology contains a theory of moral evolution, for he understood the ambiguities of rationality, and he was reluctant to compromise the "objectivity" of social science. Nevertheless, he did trace a pattern of change in which a received morality of constraint—traditional norms and forms of authority—was replaced by a new morality founded in the requirements of rational action. A basic feature of that morality was the reduction of arbitrariness in official conduct.

We shall have more to say about Weber's theory of rationality and legality in Chapter 3. At this point it may be noted that Weber's uneasiness about the moral worth of rationality was warranted, and points to an important limitation of his theory as a way of identifying the social foundations of legality. In his analysis of bureaucracy Weber adopted what Edmond Cahn once called the "official perspective."[31] Regularity and rationality were summoned by the needs of the administrative system, and the latter was typically a device for implementing the legitimate commands and policies of higher authority. Weber had no rich sense of group process, nor much feeling for psychological reality. He did not see rationality as the outcome of group conflict and accommodation within a framework of evolving, responsive purpose; nor did he fully appreciate the potential for human growth in self-affirming participation.

Other currents in the theory of organization, in some cases heavily influ-

---

[31] See Edmond Cahn, "Law in the Consumer Perspective," 112 *University of Pennsylvania Law Review* 1–21 (November, 1963).

enced by American pragmatism, have given great weight to the morality of cooperation. The writings of Mary Parker Follett and Chester I. Barnard, for example, insist that the efficient and effective organization must be viewed as a "cooperative system." In such a system authority is not self-justifying. It is founded in practical necessity, subject to reconstruction as new constraints and opportunities appear, disciplined by the "authority of the situation," and responsible to organizational purposes.

Miss Follett once wrote that administrative wisdom lies in depersonalizing the giving of orders, thus separating authority from domination:

> One *person* should not give orders to another *person*, but both should agree to take their orders from the situation. . . . Our job is not how to get people to obey orders, but how to devise methods by which we can best *discover* the order integral to a particular situation. When that is found, the employee can issue it to the employer, as well as the employer to the employee. This often happens easily and naturally. My cook or my stenographer points out the law of the situation, and I, if I recognize it as such, accept it, even although it may reverse some "order" I have given.[32]

In the morality of cooperation authority is situational, problematic, and responsive.

For Piaget, and for the American pragmatists, the morality of cooperation is the font of genuine rationality. Rationality is most securely based, and most fully achieved, if it emerges from below and is not merely a system imposed from above. How the morality of cooperation contributes to that end may be restated as follows:

1. Personal autonomy and competence. The individual is not a submissive, reactive participant in a regime of mechanical solidarity. He is capable of making his own assessments, transcending egocentric boundaries, and criticizing authority. He sees his obligation as deriving from personal and group requirements, and from his autonomously made commitments. In short, he is a responsible and rational actor.

2. Norms rooted in experience. In the morality of constraint the system of norms is received, pre-ordained, and prescriptive. Codes of conduct are transmitted by authority figures who claim unqualified deference. In such a system the paradigmatic legal act is the suppression of deviance.

The morality of cooperation, on the other hand, looks to norms that arise out of group experience. It is a morality of participation, of finding

---

[32] Henry C. Metcalf and L. Urwick (eds.), *Dynamic Administration: The Collected Papers of Mary Parker Follett* (New York: Harper & Row, Publishers, 1942), 59. Barnard's theory, in a sense less dynamic and less sensitive to the creative needs and potentials of lower-level participants, is contained in Chester I. Barnard, *The Functions of the Executive* (Cambridge, Mass.: Harvard University Press, 1938).

your own way, of meeting today's needs with today's resources. It is a philosophy of the present. The outcome of group learning may be a rediscovery of truths long since revealed, but the moral effect is to make each generation its own master. In the morality of cooperation the paradigmatic legal act is the reconstruction of received precepts to facilitate action and vindicate emergent rights.

3. Dialogue and problem-solving. Genuine cooperation is something more than the bare coordination of activities. Individual and group differences are recognized, not erased. And the reconciliation of those differences is not won by a demand for conformity. Rather, the guiding norm is joint problem-solving based on effective communication and openness to new perspectives. A problem-solving orientation in group affairs is not easily won, especially when authority and subordination are at stake. There must be a willingness to address issues on their merits, to make realistic assessments rather than conjure up imagined risks, to avoid standing pat on traditional thoughtways or prerogatives. The ethos of problem-solving is, therefore, strongly opposed to a morality of constraint, which imposes solutions and limits alternatives.

The congruence of a legal ethic and the morality of cooperation needs no laboring. If legality abhors arbitrary judgment and constraint, presses for justifications, invokes the authority of agreed-upon purpose, and values the competent participant, so too does the morality of cooperation. To be sure, not everything fits so neatly. One aspect of legality—legal continuity and the valuing of received precepts—is insecurely footed in a morality of cooperation. We shall return to that issue in a moment. At this point we may note some implications of the view that the morality of cooperation is a phase of human development, arises from personal and group experience, and is more than modestly congruent with the requirements of a developed legal order:

(1) The affirmative ideal of legality is no mere subjective preference. It rests on a natural foundation and has objective worth. It may lose out in competition with other values, or be blocked by the absence of congenial conditions, but the legal ethic finds its warrant in the contribution it can make to human growth and self-realization.

(2) If the morality of cooperation has the place we give it, then we may expect the emergence of legality—in explicit aspiration and institutional form, as well as in supporting circumstance—where rational forms of social organization prevail. Rational systems do not necessarily produce a full morality of cooperation, but they encourage it, the more so as the need

for effective participation grows. Moreover, the rationality of the system tends to diminish arbitrariness, including the authority of what is historically given, and to enhance the authority of purpose. When the ethic of cooperation makes sense historically as the preferred way of organizing human relations, a dynamic toward legality is created. For this reason, we see legalization as a peculiarly salient issue for the modern special-purpose organization.

(3) The two moralities suggest contrasting images of the legal order: (a) as a mechanism for upholding what is settled and established, and especially what is sanctified by tradition; (b) as a mechanism for problem-solving, guided by a commitment to rationality, personal autonomy, and rather general social ideals. The former encourages the use of law to enforce conformity and resist change; the latter sees law as a resource for facilitating change while maintaining core values.

The Emergent Polity

It is obvious that the two moralities, and their legal correlates, persist and compete. There is no question of a morality of cooperation fully supplanting a morality of constraint, if only because no enduring social system can entirely dispense with received precepts. With the ascendance of the morality of cooperation, however, *the received precept is generalized.* The authoritative starting-point shifts from the specific norm to the more general concept or ideal, from the prescriptive regulation to the guiding principle.[33]

In his lectures on the growth of the law, Cardozo took it for granted that "principles," no less than specific rules or judgments, are part of the law:

> "The general body of doctrine and tradition" from which the judgments derived, and "by which we criticize them" [here he was quoting Pound] must be ranked as law also, not merely because it is the chief object of our study, but because also the limits which it imposes upon a judge's liberty of choice are not purely advisory, but involve in greater or less degree an element of coercive power. . . . What permits us to say that the principles are law is the force or persuasiveness of the prediction that they will or ought to be applied. Even when the conclusion upon a special state

---

[33] The transition from due process conceived as a set of fixed norms to a "flexible" due process illustrates this point. See below, 251–252. See also John T. Noonan, Jr., "*Tokos and Atokion*: An Examination of Natural Law Reasoning Against Usury and Against Contraception," 10 *Natural Law Forum* 215–235 (1965), tracing a similar shift in Catholic doctrine.

of facts is in doubt, as in the case of the manufacturer of the Buick car, there is little doubt that the conclusion will be drawn from a stock of principles and rules which will be treated as invested with legal obligation. The court will not roam at large, and light upon one conclusion or another as the result of favor or caprice. This stock of rules and principles is what for most purposes we mean by law.[34]

Cardozo accepted Justice Holmes' view that law is revealed in the prediction of "what the courts will do in fact," but he added the civilizing emphasis that the *grounds* of the prediction, when confirmed, should be considered part of the law. The explication of principles that guide judicial decision is a discovery of law, not in the strict sense of positive law, but as part of a larger body of authoritative materials. We should also note that Cardozo, in the passage just quoted, speaks of principles that "ought to be" applied, thereby suggesting that legal principles are something more than empirical summaries of what judges do.

Even a cursory look at the legal order will remind us that a great deal more is included than rules. Legal ideas, variously and unclearly labeled "concepts," "principles," and "doctrines," have a vital place in authoritative decision. "Detrimental reliance," "attractive nuisance," "reasonable doubt," "exhaustion of remedies," "agency," are among the many familiar concepts which purport to grasp some truth and provide a foundation for the elaboration of specific rules. In addition, of course, there are even more general ideas stating the necessary conditions of "ordered liberty" or that guilt is individual rather than collective. It would be wrong to speak of these as merely a "source" of law; they are too closely woven into the fabric of legal thought and have too direct a role in decision-making.[35]

If principles and concepts are in some important sense part of the law, it does not follow that the legal world is a heavenly city of abstract ideas. On the contrary, the development and application of these materials requires a continuing assessment of human situations. The transition from general principle to specific rule requires a confrontation of social reality. *Ex facto ius oritur*—the law springs from the fact. The maxim reminds us that a preoccupation with ideas and ideals, however essential to the legal process, will be sterile indeed if it is not supplemented by more pragmatic and empirical concerns.

One way of seeing the interplay of principle and fact in law is to take

---

[34] Benjamin N. Cardozo, *The Growth of the Law* (New Haven: Yale University Press, 1924), 36 f., 43.
[35] See Roscoe Pound, "Hierarchy of Sources and Forms in Different Systems of Law," 7 *Tulane Law Review* 475–487 (June, 1933); also Graham Hughes, "Rules, Policy and Decision-Making," 77 *Yale Law Journal* 411–439 (January, 1968).

seriously the difference between general values and specific norms. Science as an enterprise may be known by ideals of rigor and self-correction, but the norms of proper inquiry must vary with the content and maturity of the discipline. Democracy seeks the rational, self-preserving consent of the governed, but under certain circumstances maximizing the number of voters, or relying on techniques of direct rather than representative government may undermine rather than further the democratic ideal. The norms derive, not from the ideals of the system alone, but also from knowledge of what men and institutions are like. Only thus can we know what norms are required to fulfill the ideal.

The same logic applies, and with special force, in the legal order. The concept of legality does not settle the rules of pleading, evidence, or judicial discretion. Legality is a master ideal, not a specific set of injunctions. This ideal is to be realized in history, not outside of it; and history makes its own demands, offers its own opportunities. Even when we know the meaning of legality we must still work out the relation between general principles and the changing structure of society. New circumstances do not necessarily alter principles, but they may and do require that new rules of law be formulated and old ones changed.

In this perspective, the achievement of legality is seen as the refinement of basic principles, their application in depth, and their extension to new social settings. As this evolution takes place, however, *the line between the legal and the political is blurred.* Indeed, that line is obscured at two points: (a) when law emerges and (b) when its distinctive mission is fulfilled. For the legal order stands midway between "power politics" and "polity." In its early stages law emerges from and depends upon the assertion of power and the contest of wills; it confirms the outcome of the struggle and, at the same time, provides a moderating framework and a sublimating symbolism. In dialectical imagery, force is the thesis, law the disciplining antithesis. But as a system of discipline law has its own shortcomings. Standing alone, it cannot fulfill its own promise as an affirmative ideal. The latent historical outcome—the renewing synthesis—is the absorption of legal ideals into the political order and, at the same time, the creation of supportive institutions, values, and modes of thought. Law *aufgehoben* is polity achieved.

This somewhat old-fashioned way of putting things may gain in relevance and clarity if we consider a specific setting—the modern university. In recent years there has been a growing concern for "legalization," that is, for reducing the arbitrariness of official action and for recognizing or reconceiving the rights of students and faculty.[36] The main impetus usually comes from below, in the form of more or less militant self-assertion by the legally disprivileged; but the trend also reflects a bureaucratic impulse and a sensitivity to cultural change. The immediate effect is formalization. Rules are promulgated to specify rights and obligations, thus limiting administrative discretion and putting potential rule-violators on notice. Having made what they conceive to be a transition to rule-governed administration, the university officials congratulate themselves—and await obedience.

Unfortunately for the administrators' peace of mind, the quest for law generates new aspirations and more comprehensive goals. Once the rules become problematic, authority is in disarray. There is a demand that the rules be legitimate, not only in emanating from establishing authority, but also in the manner of their formulation, in the way they are applied, and in their fidelity to agreed-upon institutional purposes. The idea spreads that the obligation to obey has some relation to the quality of the rules and the integrity of their administration. A critical spirit emerges which insists that decisions be justified and that channels be available for effective review and the hearing of grievances. When discipline is imposed, it is demanded that due process be protected, including the right to be heard by an independent body, and to raise the invalidity of a rule as a defense. All aspects of making and administering rules are to be scrutinized and pitilessly compared with the legal ideal.

As awareness expands and the dialogue is pressed, issues of academic "law and order" merge into larger questions of governance. Attention turns to the distinctive nature of the academic polity. What are the forms and limits of student participation? How is such participation affected by the administrative structure of the university, especially the prevalence of viable, semi-autonomous units? What are the possibilities of creating an academic community in which the morality of cooperation may prevail? Does not that morality suggest an ultimate transcendence of strict law and of machinery founded in distrust? What is the relation between academic governance and the life of the mind?[37]

These queries suggest that polity is ultimately a union of procedural and substantive values. To be sure, effective civic participation, and authority chastened by law, are necessary conditions for polity. But *a* polity is always

---

[36] See below, 266 ff.
[37] See Caleb Foote, Henry Mayer, and associates, *The Culture of the University: Governance and Education*, Report of the Study Commission on University Governance, University of California, Berkeley (San Francisco: Jossey-Bass, 1968).

a definite human community. It must have, therefore, a historicity and commitment of its own. The values of the community may be enriched and safeguarded by the evolution of law, but law is the servant of polity, not its master. It follows that legal procedures and rules are not self-justifying, even if they are offered as extrapolations from the ideal of legality. The contributions they make, and the costs they exact, must be assessed in the light of substantive ends.

Legitimacy in depth.   The evolution of legality, and the transition to polity, are made manifest in the theory of legitimacy. Legitimation can begin in a quite primitive fashion. It may mean little more than unconscious acceptance of someone's authority because he is thought to have communication with the gods, or special magical powers, or because he belongs to a noble family. Respect is won because public sentiment supports some concept of the rightful power to lead and to decide. There need not be any awareness of the habit of thought involved, nor surely any self-consciousness regarding the abstract connection between exercised authority and an underlying principle of legitimacy.

Many regimes properly classified as legitimate retain a very large amount of arbitrary rule. But legitimacy carries the lively seed of legality, implanted by the principle that reasons must be given to defend official acts. For reasons invite evaluation and evaluation encourages the development of objective standards. At the same time, implicit in the fundamental norm that reasons should be given is the conclusion that where reasons are defective authority is to that extent weakened and even destroyed.

A primitive legitimacy speaks only to the *gross* justification of a claim to hold office. The relevant writ is *quo warranto*, which runs against the usurper. At this stage, once the right to rule is established, an estoppel is raised against the critic. His duty is to submit to what he himself has accepted. This Hobbesian premise carries a portent of things to come, but it falls short of a developed legality. Legality gains strength and focus as the criterion of legitimacy is extended *in depth*, used to query *particular* acts and policies.

Some principles of legitimacy are more competent than others to sustain a posture of criticism. If power is justified on the basis of hereditary succession, for example, it is difficult to find the leverage for calling officials to account. The same may be said of any principle of legitimacy that amounts to a laying on of hands, a transfer of authority justified only by the certification of its source. The "democratic" conferral of unlimited powers by plebiscite is a case in point. So too is government by a university or other administrator on whom plenary authority has devolved.

The development of legality requires a richer doctrine of justification, one that permits appeal to public purpose and to the moral commitments of the community. But once that road is taken, *the principle of legitimacy shades into a political philosophy.* The polity becomes the touchstone, not the legal order treated as a realm apart.

In the Aristotelian view, polity is the "right" constitution, in that it is organized for the common good rather than for parochial interests. As the highest form of human association, polity presumes civic competence, justice, moderation, and rational consensus. However, as Barker has noted, polity meant something more than "constitution" as we use the term. "A 'constitution,' in our sense of the word, is not a way of life. The *politeia* was; and it was thus something more—if also, in legal precision, something less—than a constitution."[38] A polity is a political community, if by that we mean a community capable of offering a "public life" to its citizens. It is a moral unity and, at the same time, a mode of participation and of social organization.

As polity evolves, the legal order expands in scope and depth. A primitive polity cannot readily look beyond "law and order" narrowly conceived— restraint of violence, husbanding of authority, protection of minimal rights. A more advanced polity can register and give effect to broader and more subtle concepts of public responsibility; new energies may be summoned for the assertion of rights and the critique of authority; more risks may be taken in the quest for a more responsive and more inclusive legal system.

This evolution may be observed in constitutional development, for there is a close connection between the concept of a "living" constitution and that of "emergent polity." A living constitution is subject to interpretation in the light of social needs and circumstances. Its authoritative clauses are given new content as new understandings and necessities emerge. But this does not reduce the constitution to a handy barometer for registering social forces or the changing sentiments of judges. A living constitution can rise to the height of the times, not by mindless adaptation but by progressive fulfillment of its own premises. Those premises are the premises of polity.

Law contributes to polity by (1) enlarging constitutional consensus and (2) multiplying the avenues of civic participation. As concepts of due process, representative government, equal protection of the laws, and freedom of association and public expression are expanded, the latent object of the constitution appears: the attainment of full citizenship. One result

---

[38] Ernest Barker, *The Politics of Aristotle* (London: Oxford University Press, 1948), lxvii.

of this awareness is the assignment to government of an affirmative duty to remove social obstacles to civic participation, whether or not they are of its own making. A related outcome is the fading of the boundary between "state" and "society."

Incipient and Inchoate Law

In applying the evolutionary perspective of the foregoing analysis to the sphere of industrial justice, we do not mean to suggest that legal development is a pristine process, or that there is anything inevitable about it. The "unfolding" of latent values, where it appears, depends on favorable historical circumstances; it is mediated by political contention. On the other hand, legal *development*, as distinct from legal *change*, is not an arbitrary vector of happenstance forces. The emergence of a law-governed setting has its own logic, its own name and nature.

The argument to follow sees legal development as incipient, problem-solving, and inchoate. This perspective helps bridge the gap between a normative theory of law, which centers on latent values, and the more stringent perspective of sociological realism.

The anti-formalist posture of legal sociology encourages interest in the problem-solving practices and spontaneous orderings of business or family life. While this approach has tended to depreciate formal law, and has been indifferent to legal ideals, it just as easily supports an emphasis on the *emergence* of formal law out of the realities of group life. Incipient law may be created by a stabilized public sentiment or pattern of organization; it refers to a compelling claim of right or a practice so viable and so important to a functioning institution as to make legal recognition in due course highly probable. Thus some of the private arrangements worked out in collective bargaining (to be discussed in Chapter 4), especially seniority rights and protection against arbitrary dismissal, may be seen as incipient law.

Nevertheless, the location of incipient law cannot rest solely on the prevalence of a practice or even the urgency of a claim; two parallel assessments are required. First, the social viability of the practice in question—its functional significance for group life and especially for new institutional forms—must be considered. Second, the contemporary evolution of relevant legal principles must be assessed to see whether the new norm can be absorbed within the received but changing legal tradition. Thus incipient law is not based on abstract postulates; nor does it reflect the moral preferences of the observer. Incipient law is emergent *positive* law, responsive to, and made possible by, particular social circumstances.

In this perspective, some law is seen as latent in the evolving social and economic order. For example, the trend toward strict liability for harm caused by defects in manufactured goods (weakening or eliminating the need to prove negligence) reflects changing technology, both in manufacture and distribution, as well as the increased capacity of large firms to absorb the attendant costs either by increasing productivity or by passing them on to the general public. Similarly, the growing importance of large-scale organizations carries with it the likelihood that new claims of right will emerge, based upon a new perception of organizational membership as a protectable status.

For legal scholars, there should be nothing strange or alien in a concept of incipient law. A great deal of legal inquiry is devoted to tracing the emergence of new rules and principles. Although most of this work deals with acts and opinions of legislatures, courts, and other official agencies, some of it does rely on factual assessments of institutional change. It may be said, indeed, that the monitoring and midwifery of incipient law is one of the chief offices of legal scholarship.

An incipient legal change tends to be manifested in inchoate law. Inchoate law is unordered and unsystematic, often based on *ad hoc* but convergent pronouncements. Instead of a clearly enunciated authoritative principle, there may be many diverse evidences, coming from a variety of official voices, that new claims are being recognized, new powers or expectations affirmed. Thus inchoate law is something more than incipient law. The latter is mainly an attribute of social practice and belief; the former is an attribute of law itself.

Admittedly, the study of incipient and inchoate law does not necessarily entail a preoccupation with distinctively legal values. Many changes in substantive law, although based on a pattern of social and economic evolution, may appear to be neutral, so far as the integrity of the legal order is concerned. We do not mean to suggest that principles of legality are on the agenda whenever the topic of legal and social change is explored. Legality may hover in the background, if only because the capacity of the system to adapt and to meet new challenges is at issue, but it need not be in the foreground of inquiry.

In this study legality does have a central place, for our concern is with the capacity of special-purpose organizations to "establish justice." At the same time, we recognize that the legal potential, if it exists, is to be found in the social dynamics of the institutions themselves. We can therefore accept the dictum of Ehrlich that "the center of gravity of legal development lies not in legislation, nor in juristic science, nor in judicial decision, but in society itself."[39]

---

[39] Eugen Ehrlich, *Fundamental Principles of the Sociology of Law* (Cambridge, Mass.: Harvard University Press, 1936), xv.

Chapter 2 | *The Quest for a Law of Associations*

TO EXTEND THE RULE OF LAW IS TO BUILD IT FIRMLY into the life of society, to make the master ideal of legality a true governor of official conduct. If this is to come about, political and legal theory must lend a hand. It can do so by fashioning concepts and doctrines to bridge the gap between new social realities and the received legal tradition.

In contributing to that effort, students of law and society are confronted with a special intellectual problem: how to bring legal ideals to the "private" sector of community life. That sector includes autonomous groups and enterprises not formally part of government but exercising a sometimes powerful dominion, often deeply influencing the achievement of full citizenship in a moral commonwealth. The issue is: Can we justify, within the framework of legal theory, the application to private organizations of principles hitherto restricted to public government?

That question sets the theme of our study, and an answer to it will be attempted in Chapter 7. At this point, we shall discuss some of the broader problems of industrial jurisprudence within which issues of law and private power must be set. These problems have to do with the competence of Anglo-American law to grasp the associational reality of industrial life. An adequate theory of associations is a legal as well as a scientific necessity. And the experience of the law, in its quest of such a theory, can help reveal the emerging issues and the legal potential.

Although the law of associations is not recognized as a distinctive, systematically developed branch of the Anglo-American legal system, there is a very large body of relevant rules and concepts. The phrase "law of associations" is sometimes used, but it is more often avoided as overly general and fraught with ambiguity. The usual practice is to distinguish "business associations," mostly incorporated, from all other groupings, such as trade unions, churches, social clubs, and fraternal organizations, mostly unincorporated.[1] This distinction has a rough utility, but it is less than satisfactory. Problems of sociological classification press hard upon the legal categories.

Whatever its form or purpose, the large private organization has set still-unresolved problems for the legal order. How shall the place of such groups in the political community be defined? By what means and to what extent shall the organization be held responsible for its acts? How can the law take account of the association's inner order? How shall the rights of members, and others affected, be conceived and protected? As the answers to these questions are framed, the law's logic-in-use becomes a testing ground for political and social theory.

If industrial justice is bound up with the law of associations, this is to some extent a commentary on the changes that have taken place in the social significance of property and contract. In the stark vision of economic individualism, the lone protagonist found his protection in the enforcement of promises and in the vindication of vested property interests. But today property and contract have weakened as legal resources for the defense of personal freedom within the economic order. This is so in part because the large enterprise—the "representative social institution"[2] of modern life—has brought with it new modes of belonging and dependency. It has undercut the worth of contractual freedom and has lessened the significance, even for the middle-class man, of traditional forms of property, notably the ownership of chattels and land.

Furthermore, property and contract were never dependable resources for the dispossessed. When "society" and "polity" were exclusive clubs, the dependent mass of city workers and rural laborers hardly counted. For them, the claims that could be built on property and contract meant little. With the enlargement of civic participation, this hitherto voiceless population begins to be heard. Although the old forms and the old actors remain, a new and dominant figure takes center stage. His claims must re-

---

[1] But see Zechariah Chafee, Jr., "The Internal Affairs of Associations Not for Profit," 43 *Harvard Law Review* 993, 1008 (1930), where an argument is offered for giving the law of associations not for profit "its natural place beside the law of business corporations and partnerships."

[2] Peter F. Drucker, *The Concept of the Corporation* (New York: Mentor Books, 1964), 18–19.

flect the true condition of modern life, which is to say, the condition of Administered Man.

Associations and Freedom

From the standpoint of social policy, the law of associations has had three basic commitments:
(1) *to sustain the vitality of the group structure of society;*
(2) *to regulate group action in the interests of the community as a whole;*
(3) *to protect the rights of individuals who encounter the power of the organized group.*

The first of these commitments has drawn its main strength from the celebration of political liberty and economic individualism. Although the right of association is not explicitly preserved in the United States Constitution, the Supreme Court has largely upheld the dictum of Tocqueville that "the most natural privilege of man, next to the right of acting for himself, is that of combining his exertions with those of his fellow creatures and of acting in common with them. The right of association therefore appears to me almost as inalienable in its nature as the right of personal liberty."[3] The philosophy of laissez faire, claiming the freedom to pursue economic activity without leave or hindrance, added greatly to the sense that the formation of voluntary private groups is a necessary ingredient of a free society. To be sure, the doctrine of criminal conspiracy was used against trade unions in the early nineteenth century, and effective organization was long hampered by a fearful and unfriendly judiciary, but this anomaly yielded in due course to the more general consensus.

The "vitality of the group structure of society" is, however, a more comprehensive value than freedom to associate. If the latter alone is basic, then the association-in-being is ancillary, prized only because without it there would be no instrument of effective speech, petition, worship, or economic action. But associations contribute to freedom in other ways as well. The autonomous organization, intermediate between the state and the individual, provides a haven of protection and a vehicle of meaningful participation. It lends texture to the commonwealth, a texture that can sustain autonomous sources of social identity, train alternative leaders, curb pre-

[3] Alexis de Tocqueville, *Democracy in America* (New York: Alfred A. Knopf, Inc., 1956), I, 196. See Robert A. Horn, *Groups and the Constitution* (Stanford, Calif.: Stanford University Press, 1956); also David Fellman, *The Constitutional Right of Association* (Chicago: University of Chicago Press, 1963).

cipitate action, and restrain the hand of government. A polity is impoverished when it strips the individual of his group attachments and leaves him naked before a central authority. And the group structure of society, as a system of power, generates countervailing forces to moderate the influence of any single power bloc. These are the enduring truths of pluralist doctrine.[4]

In asserting the intrinsic value of private institutions, pluralism had two important limitations. First, greatest emphasis was placed on a *minimalist* view of the free society. A viable group structure of society was perceived as necessary for maintaining the bare bones of liberty, and especially for building barriers against the total state. This aspect of pluralism does not assure, however, that higher aspirations will be served. Second, the classic pluralists took as their model the historically validated, person-centered unities of community, church, and guild. It remained unsettled to what extent the modern bureaucratic organization could be a genuine vehicle of social participation.

In recent years we have seen a transition from preoccupation with freedom *of* association to a concern for freedom *in* associations. This renewed awareness stems from a realization that the private organization can be more oppressive than the state.[5] The loss of a job, or the right to pursue a profession, or the opportunity to continue one's education, may be far more hurtful than a term in jail. When these deprivations are inflicted arbitrarily, and there is no recourse, a gap in the legal order exists. We become more sensitive to that gap when the decisions are made by organizations that seem large, powerful, and impersonal, and by men who have the look of an officialdom.

The rise of new centers of potential oppression may be less important

---

[4] We have in mind especially the writings of Tocqueville, Lamennais, and Hauriou in France; the English pluralists Figgis, Laski, and Cole; and the perspective of Otto von Gierke in Germany. For a sympathetic review of major ideas in this tradition see Robert A. Nisbet, *The Quest for Community* (New York: Oxford University Press, 1953), esp. Chaps. 10 and 11. A more jurisprudential treatment may be found in Frederick Hallis, *Corporate Personality: A Study in Jurisprudence* (London: Oxford University Press, 1930).

[5] Of course, some of the proponents of the modern democratic state, such as Rousseau, were keenly aware of this potentiality. Dicey pointed out that a body "created by combination—a natural corporation, if the expression may be allowed—whether a political league, a church, or a trade union, by its mere existence limits the freedom of its members, and constantly tends to limit the freedom of outsiders." He argued that the nineteenth-century individualists never dealt with this problem satisfactorily, a failing which was "closely connected with the tendency of all individualists to neglect the social aspect of human nature." A. V. Dicey, *Law and Public Opinion in England in the Nineteenth Century* (London: Macmillan and Company, Ltd., 1952), 154, 158. First published in 1905; second ed., 1914.

than (1) the changing aspirations of the community and (2) the opportunity to do something about them. Subordinate and dependent men have always been treated badly by their masters. The contemporary situation is different in this, that new expectations are penetrating areas hitherto closed to scrutiny or immune to challenge; and modern organizational settings make possible new ways of asserting claims and institutionalizing victories.

A striking example of rising expectations is found in a recent book by a young Catholic priest.[6] Pressing *aggiornamento* on a new front, Father DuBay analyzes authority in the church and concludes that democracy must have a place within it:

> The problem of the responsibility of the layman will hardly be solved without giving him the freedom to participate on every level of church government. We can hardly expect a man to do his best *for* an organization unless he is given a share of freedom to operate *within* it. Church structures should manifest the fact that the layman is a subject of the church, not an object of it. . . . There is need for immediate access to grievance machinery and court hearings for all church members. Freedoms of expression and assembly must be carefully defined and protected if the church is to evolve solutions for rapidly increasing problems. . . . Our goal would certainly include the writing of a constitution for the church, one which clearly protects the rights of all by defining them and setting limits on the exercise of authority.[7]

A similar impulse is manifest in higher education and among the poor in their dealings with welfare agencies. What were once considered sacred precincts, where administrative officials could act as they saw fit, are increasingly exposed to the demand that arbitrary decision-making be abated. As earlier in the growth of trade unionism, these awakenings are more properly seen as responses to new self-conceptions, and to new opportunities, than to new oppressions.

Whatever its source may be, the concern for freedom *in* associations has required a fresh assessment of the large organization, including its potentialities as well as its dangers. That assessment suggests, for example, that there is a convergence between the large voluntary association and the large administrative organization.

The chief feature of the "administrative organization" is its capacity to mobilize sustained energies. Its "members" are usually employees. In a free society most employees in most organizations can quit if they wish, but

---

[6] William H. DuBay, *The Human Church* (New York: Doubleday & Company, Inc., 1966).
[7] *Ibid.*, 163, 165, 166.

usually we do not think of workers or staff personnel as "voluntary" members. This is so because employment is usually compelled by economic necessity; it is not the free expression of personal inclination or commitment. Moreover, this kind of membership presumes the acceptance of administrative discipline.

Theoretically, a "voluntary association" is formed by the joinder of mutual interests, not by the purchase of deployable energies. An "interest group," whether religious, economic, political, or recreational, is usually voluntary in that sense. It brings together people who characteristically retain effective freedom to withdraw at will or to vary their contributions. In such groups democratic forms are likely to emerge, both to sustain legitimacy and to encourage participation. Thus the voluntarism of the "voluntary association" is warranted by special attributes of adherence, participation, and control.

The voluntary association changes its character when two conditions occur: (a) the establishment of a sizable administrative staff, and (b) the emergence of a dependent constituency. A paid staff has a "multiplier effect," for it makes possible coordinated and sustained effort; and it creates a vested interest in the organization's continuing existence. Often enough, the members become a resource to be developed by the administrative staff; or they become customers, purchasing the services of headquarters personnel. As the staff increases in number and competence, it becomes the central feature of the organization and the members become a clientele. In effect, the voluntary association creates and maintains an administrative organization, either by a system of private taxation, as in the case of many interest groups, or by putting the paid staff to work producing goods or services for sale on the market, as in the case of the business firm with multiple shareholders. Either way the voluntaristic basis of the organization weakens as the effective enterprise, carried forward by the administrative organization, gains the capacity to perpetuate its existence.

A more subtle convergence is seen when the voluntary members, though not employees, become dependent on the organization. When this occurs the members must bow to discipline. Economic dependency occurs in trade unions, and in professional associations that control licensing or other privileges, such as the opportunity to serve on a hospital staff. Students and similar clineteles are "captive" in varying degrees, and the effective rendering of services, if nothing else, requires considerable discipline and commitment. Dependency may also be emotional, or reflect total absorption in a tight community, as in some forms of political or religious affiliation. Dependency limits freedom of adherence, thus diminishing the felt necessity to win consent; it deepens commitment, thus increasing both the salience of membership and the significance for the individual of the way administrative authority is exercised. In this way, freedom yields to constraint, and the line between the voluntary association and the administrative organization is blurred.[8]

This convergence invites us to think of the large organization *as a generic phenomenon*, a locus of authority, commitment, dependency, and power. It is the reality of this nexus, regardless of the form in which it is cast, that poses problems of freedom and civic participation.

As a theory of the social foundations of freedom, pluralism rests its hopes on civil antagonism. It sees in group conflict a benign disorder, framed only by quite general purposes and minimal restraints. A crucial assumption of this theory is that the political community embraces a broad range of interests and that these interests are largely self-generating and self-sustaining. In other words, the theory postulates that the social energy for group organization will be forthcoming.

In the special-purpose organization, the chances that a viable group life will emerge, sustained by "natural" interests, are much more limited than in the more comprehensive community. If the special purpose is taken seriously, and activities are coordinated, then that purpose largely determines the internal structure of the organization. Although it is true that any big enterprise is an "organization of organizations," the subgroups are designed and ordered in the light of economic and administrative criteria. Thus pluralism has a limited worth as a guarantor of even minimal freedom in the special-purpose organization.

This does not mean that internal pluralism can be entirely discounted. On the contrary, the division of labor within an enterprise very often creates centers of energy and commitment, transforming a technical unit into a unity of persons and a locus of value. Interest groups within large organizations range from small informal groups of workers to the major department capable of summoning its own loyalties. (For the wise top administrator, this is an opportunity as well as a risk.) Associations that are federated or made up of local branches also have potentials for internal pluralism. As in the larger community, the pluralism of special-purpose

---

[8] This is a latent conclusion of Robert Michels' *Political Parties: A Sociological Study of the Oligarchical Tendencies of Modern Democracy* (New York: Free Press, 1949). His "iron law" applies best to action organizations that require permanent staffs. For a related analysis, stressing the way members of a voluntary association become "managerial resources," see Philip Selznick, *The Organizational Weapon* (New York: Free Press, 1960), Chap. 1.

organizations can protect the individual and provide him with meaningful affiliations. At least he has a choice between identification with the parent organization or with the subgroup to which he is assigned. In considering organizational resources for the restraint of arbitrary power, it is important to hold on to the pluralist perspective. The more complex and multi-purpose the organization—that is, the closer it approximates a comprehensive community—the greater the likelihood that internal pluralism can make a contribution to an environment of relative freedom.

Pluralism's positive attitude toward the corporate group has never been fully accepted in modern political philosophy. The main opposition has come from those who upheld the integral sovereignty of the modern state and feared that autonomous unities would be, in the words of Thomas Hobbes, "lesser Common-wealths in the bowels of a greater, like wormes in the entrayles of a naturall man."[9] A corollary theme sees the corporate group as a threat to the individual. If the association is a locus of value, then loyalty, subordination, and status will seem attractive conditions of the human spirit; the defense of individuality, nonconformity, and vested personal right will weaken. This threat is sometimes phrased as a "new feudalism."[10]

One contemporary response is the theme of W. H. Whyte, Jr.'s, *The Organization Man.*[11] There it is argued that the individual should avoid giving too much of himself to the large organization, especially the benevolent, soul-suffocating business enterprise. He can preserve his freedom only through a measure of alienation:

> He must *fight* The Organization. Not stupidly, or selfishly, for the defects of individual self-regard are no more to be venerated than the defects of cooperation. But fight he must, for the demands for his surrender are constant and powerful, and the more he has come to like the life of organization the more difficult does he find it to resist these demands, or even to recognize them.[12]

Similarly, Clark Kerr has argued that associations of limited function, correspondingly restrained in the demands they make upon the individual, are most congenial to a free society. "The organization which seeks to encompass the totality of the life of the individual can subject him to its control as no limited-function organization can. An organization with

---

[9] *Leviathan* ("Everyman's Library" [London: J. M. Dent & Sons, Ltd., 1914]), 177.
[10] See Roscoe Pound, "The New Feudal System," 19 *Kentucky Law Journal* 1, 14f. (1930); also Charles A. Reich, "The New Property," 73 *Yale Law Journal* 733, 768ff. (1964).
[11] New York: Simon and Schuster, Inc., 1956.
[12] *Ibid.*, 404.

limited functions and limited rules can require only limited commitments from its participants."[13] In this perspective the organization is a necessary evil to be approached warily and embraced without ardor.

Limited commitment is indeed a kind of safeguard. It reduces exposure to potentially arbitrary action and preserves to the person alternative sources of satisfaction. And yet the commitments that inescapably remain may be of great importance to the individual. His organization member-ship—above all, his right to do a job—may be his most valuable property. The question is not whether the individual can minimize demands upon him by limiting his commitments. It is rather, can individual rights in associations be fully protected without some concept of meaningful membership?

Furthermore, the idea of limited commitment, though consistent with the minimalist perspective of pluralism, surrenders the one redemptive aspiration of that political philosophy—the hope that through significant membership in corporate groups the individual's relation to the larger com-monwealth can be extended and enriched. Such an aspiration may have little relevance to the narrowly conceived enterprise founded on unskilled or casual labor. But as these conditions become the exception rather than the rule, and as the potentials of large organizations change in other ways, it seems likely that old hopes will be renewed, perhaps to be transformed into urgent demands.

The Corporate Entity

In attempting to grasp and govern the reality of association, a major con-ceptual resource of the law has been the idea of a corporation. The history of this idea strikingly displays the ambiguities of legal cognition. Both law and sociology need a theory of the corporation, but the legal order has its own problems and constraints. It must do more than fashion a concept useful for describing and analyzing a recurrent phenomenon. In developing an official way of perceiving the world, the law must *control the policy im-plications* of its theory.

This constraint has had the following effect: In enforcing accountability, and in specifying privileges and powers, the legal theory of corporations has stressed the *dependent* reality of corporate existence, especially as being the product of authoritative definition; and it has focused attention on *some* participants and relationships, neglecting the social and legal sig-

---

[13] Clark Kerr, "Individual Rights in an 'Organization Society'" (Address to the Los Angeles Bar Association, May 28, 1959; mimeo.).

nificance of others. These selective concerns have sharply limited the congruence of legal and sociological perspectives.

A sociological theory of the corporation would pay little attention to the words of art or the technical procedures that create the formal status of incorporation; and it would cut across the distinction between voluntary associations and administrative organizations. It would be more concerned with (a) the emergence of institutions and (b) the compelling realities of internal social structure. A number of contemporary writers have taken this sociological tack. They have invoked the idea of "institution," at least implicitly, and have reconstructed the theory of corporations by taking account of a broad spectrum of internal social facts, especially the way power is amassed, justified, distributed, and used.[14]

In sociology the term "institution" may refer to a group or to a social practice, to the Republican party or to the secret ballot. This ambiguity is more apparent than real. Whether it be a group or practice, a social form becomes institutionalized as, through a process of social growth and adaptation, it takes on a distinctive character, competence, or function, and becomes charged with meaning as a vehicle of group identity or a receptacle of vested interests. Characteristically, an institution is not an expendable instrument for the achievement of narrowly defined goals. It is valued for the special place it has in a larger social system and for the way it serves the aspirations and needs of those whose lives it touches. As a result, the institution is not readily dispensable. It usually serves more than one goal or interest. It endures because persons, groups, or communities have a stake in its continued existence.

The existence of an institution is inescapably a relative matter and one of degree. Groups and practices are more or less institutionalized, that is, more or less expendable, more or less infused with value, more or less imprinted with a special character or competence, more or less tied to an effective social base, more or less preoccupied with maintaining themselves as "going concerns."[15] Institutionalization is relative in that, for example, a government agency may be a locus of commitment and value for its staff, or for a special constituency, yet may be conceived and handled in quite narrowly instrumental terms by the larger system of which it is a part.

The emergent, system-forming nature of institutions has several implications for legal theory:

---

[14] See below, 65 ff.

[15] For further discussion of institutionalization see Philip Selznick, *Leadership in Administration* (New York: Harper & Row, 1956); also Leonard Broom and Philip Selznick, *Sociology* (New York: Harper & Row, 1968), 215–218.

1. Rights are claimed for the system.   If institutions are outcomes of historical growth and represent, as it were, congealed commitment, they inevitably have lives of their own. They are "organisms," not by fiat of a romantic imagery, but simply because forces are set in motion that will prize and protect the institution as a going concern. When people are committed to a social system they claim for it, rather than for themselves as individuals, the status of a rights-bearing entity. It may be necessary on other grounds to reduce these group claims to individual claims, or to deny legal status to the institution, but the social reality producing the claim depends on empirical credentials, not legal ones.

2. There is a demand for legal cognition of the nature of the institution.   As going concerns, institutions have determinate attributes. These attributes are not settled by formal definitions. Rather, the nature of an institution is known by its mission and its competence, its commitment to and capacity to perform a social function. Distinctive competence is in turn bound up with the social structure of the agency—the roles and relationships, the norms and values, that comprise an operating social system. Types of institutions have characteristic structural attributes and requirements, and the law of associations is continually pressed to develop ideas that fit these realities. If legal theory obscures or distorts the true character of the institution, those who have a stake in it will feel that their legal claims are precarious and that they live under the threat of arbitrary judgment.

3. There is a strain toward public accountability.   As a narrow functional group becomes institutionalized, it tends to take on the perspectives, and incorporate the goals and interests, of those who have mixed their own lives with its history. What may have begun as a purely private effort to mobilize resources for particular ends becomes in time a captive of the broader interests that have become implicated in its existence. Sociologically, if not legally, there is a movement from private to public responsibility whenever leadership loses full freedom to manipulate resources and becomes accountable to the interests of others and to the enterprise itself as a continuing system. This result is not always welcomed. Indeed, a great deal of managerial effort is devoted to blocking and overcoming the drift toward institutionalization, with its attendant broadening of responsibility and dilution of power. But the more enduring the organization, and the larger the scale and scope of its activities, the more likely is it that the strain toward public accountability will be manifest.

No clear line of demarcation exists between institutional and pre-institutional states. As we have indicated, institutionalization is a kind of social change; its outcome is variable and relative. This is not a conceptual flaw; it inheres in the processual, emergent nature of social reality. To the extent that the law requires clear distinctions, not as analytical categories but as descriptions of palpable groups or persons, the sociological phenomenon is troublesome and recalcitrant.

Thus institutionalization sets problems for the legal system. It calls for recognition of claims founded in the reality of association. Yet no sure guide or limit is offered. Vexing though this may be, legal theory cannot avoid the underlying issues. For example, a recent discussion of the public obligations of corporations criticized the view that "the corporation is an institution separate from its existence as a vehicle for the business interests of its shareholders,"[16] with its corollary that the managers owe fiduciary obligations to the institution rather than, or at least in addition to, the shareholders. This would make it proper for corporate managers to spend the firm's money for the welfare of employees or the community, and to do so in good conscience. The author asserts that "the concept that the corporation is a *public* institution [emphasis supplied] is not necessary in order to justify most publicly motivated acts. Pursuit of public obligations is not inconsistent with the 'old' view that the fiduciary obligations of managers are owed to the shareholders."[17]

As others have before him, Professor Ruder sees a risk that untrammeled discretion will be granted to corporate managers if they are conceived as free to pursue their own concepts of public welfare, responsible only to a vague and fluctuating constituency. "If the standard of sound management practice becomes merely that of the public good, limitless 'legitimate' uses for corporate funds other than shareholder welfare will be possible."[18] At the same time, "reliance upon traditional profit maximization theory does not amount to a rejection of modern day notions of corporate responsibility. Within the confines of the business judgment rule there is ample opportunity for expenditure of corporate funds upon worthwhile public welfare measures. The only limitation is that corporate policy must be reasonably related to long-term corporate benefit."[19]

Clearly the operative phrase is "long-term." Maximization of profit is to remain the lodestar of business activity, but the demand for immediate

---

[16] David S. Ruder, "Public Obligations of Private Corporations," 114 *University of Pennsylvania Law Review* 209, 212 (1965). Reference is to the argument in E. Merrick Dodd, Jr., "For Whom Are Corporate Managers Trustees?" 45 *Harvard Law Review* 1145 (1932).

[17] Ruder, *op. cit.*, 212–213.

[18] *Ibid.*, 226.

[19] *Ibid.*, 223.

returns may be countered by invoking a statesmanlike responsibility for the long run. Note that reference is made to long-term *corporate* benefit, not shareholder interest. This would justify concern for any constituency important to the well-being of the enterprise. But even if the aggregate of shareholders is the point of reference, it is clear that these are not determinate individuals. As Kenneth Boulding has said, "responsibility to anonymous and abstract stockholders . . . can easily be translated into responsibility for the organization itself."[20]

We need not here consider whether the principle of long-term benefit can provide adequate legal recognition for the social responsibilities of business.[21] For our purposes, the important point is that *decision-making in the light of long-run benefits presumes a concept of the institution.* The enterprise as a going concern, as a relational entity, becomes the focus of policy and strategy. This has nothing to do with formal incorporation. It has to do with all the empirical requirements of organizational survival, including survival as a certain *kind* of organization. These requirements become operative goals. The more complex the enterprise and the more numerous its hostages to fortune, the more attenuated is the relation between the operative goals of management and the distinctive interests of shareholders.

If the corporate enterprise is in some sense an institution, it does not follow that it thereby becomes a *public* institution, if by that we mean an agency invested with significance for an entire community. We have suggested that all institutionalized groups exhibit a strain toward the public. But this may mean only that the members become a collective constituency, *a* public to whom leaders are accountable for the management of the enterprise. As the category of "members" is enlarged, the sense of public accountability is extended.

The sociological approach, which sees institutions as emergent realities, is understandably uneasy with the "concession" and "fiction" theories of the corporation.[22] The concession theory states that organized groups have only such *legal* status as the law has conceded to them; the fiction theory insists that corporations do not exist at all save as creatures of legal artifice. The views attract each other, for if the corporation is a mere fiction it cannot "have" any rights or powers, or assert any claims, beyond those granted to it. A well-known formula is Chief Justice Marshall's dictum in the

---

[20] "A Look at the Corporation," *The Lamp*, Standard Oil Co. of New Jersey, New York, 1957.

[21] See Dodd, *op. cit.*, 1156–1157, where the principle of long-term benefit is explicitly rejected.

See Roscoe Pound, *Jurisprudence*, (St. Paul: West Publishing Co., 1959), IV, 222 ff.

Dartmouth College case: "A corporation is an artificial being, invisible, intangible, existing only in contemplation of law. Being the mere creature of law, it possesses only those properties which the charter of its creation confers upon it either expressly or as incidental to its existence."[23]

We shall not offer here yet another review of an "endless problem."[24] It is sufficient to say that the institutional perspective is quite compatible with a more selective policy-oriented concept of the corporation. There is no challenge to sociological realism in a legal policy that reserves to government the power to determine which groups under what conditions should be granted the special benefits of formal incorporation, such as limitation of liability, collective acquisition of property, or the capacity to sue and be sued by members and outsiders. Similarly, if the formal attributes of a legally recognized corporation are stressed, for the purpose of specifying and limiting privileges or powers, or as a way of questioning how much reality of association lies behind the formal device, there can be no sociological complaint.[25] Thus understood, the concession and fiction "theories" are constructs of policy, not of cognition.

Nevertheless, the restrictive connotations of the concession and fiction theories have hampered the capacity of legal doctrine to take full account of associational life. They have encouraged very indirect and sometimes tortured lines of reasoning when the courts have sought to recognize the capacity of an association to act as a unit, and be treated as one, despite the want of formal incorporation.[26] The status of incorporation has often been taken as an attribute of social reality rather than as something to be granted under determinate conditions, including *de facto* conditions of association as well as *de jure* qualification under a corporations statute. The issue of formal qualification has tended to cloud and dominate the quest for legal cognition of the large-scale organization in modern society.

A corollary is the tendency to see the business corporation as essentially a union of shareholders. Max Radin encouraged this way of thinking when he spoke of the corporation as "a verbal symbol, a mathematical expression. It is quite unnecessary for these patient people who feel that they would rather, in any given case, enumerate the several million stockholders

---

[23] *Dartmouth College v. Woodward*, 4 Wheaton 518, 627 (1819).
[24] Max Radin, "The Endless Problem of Corporate Personality," 32 *Columbia Law Review* 643 (1932).
[25] See Roscoe Pound's discussion of the practical import of the concession and fiction theories. *Jurisprudence*, IV, 260.
[26] See E. Merrick Dodd, Jr., "Dogma and Practice in the Law of Associations," 42 *Harvard Law Review* 977 (1929).

of the American Telephone and Telegraph Co. than say briefly and concisely, 'Tel. and Tel.' "[27] This approach, which treats the corporate device
as a mere convenience, has an attractive simplicity. But is it sufficiently
faithful to the social reality of the large corporation?

The historic preoccupation with what the corporation "*is*" *as a legal
entity* deeply affects how the law perceives the institution *as an empirical
reality.* The relation between legal entity and empirical reality has not been
overlooked, but most of the discussion has centered on the specification
of factual conditions that have, or should have, *de jure* consequences for
corporate status.[28] This includes (a) the conditions under which a "*de
facto* corporation" exists: where it is shown that a going concern existed
in fact, the courts may recognize a corporate entity, at least for some purposes, despite a failure of formal qualification; as a result, the responsibilities and benefits of incorporation, such as liability to the entity for
obligations contracted, or limited liability of shareholders, may be protected; (b) the conditions under which the courts may "pierce the corporate
veil," that is, disregard formal incorporation and hold individuals personally liable or, perhaps, treat a cluster of interlocking corporate units as a
single business entity; usually this means that incorporation was indeed "a
mere business device with no reality of association."[29] These and similar
assessments help to mitigate the view that legal recognition of corporate
status is a matter of arbitrary definition. They sustain John Dewey's point
that to speak of a corporation as a legally conceived "right-and-duty-bearing
unit" is not to deny that there are "properties which any unit must ante-
cedently and inherently have in order to be a right-and-duty-bearing
unit."[30] But the discussion still gives center stage to what is or is not a
legally distinct cooperative system.

The question of corporate status, however, is only one of the problems
posed for the law by the fact that an organized entity exists, acts, and has
social consequences. The benefits of formal corporate status are obviously
of great practical importance, especially in facilitating the amassing of resources sufficient to establish a large-scale going concern. They are not
indispensable, as the history of some large firms, such as the Ford Motor
Company, and of associations such as churches and trade unions, has
shown. But even when the issue of corporate status is determined, there

---

[27] Radin, *op. cit.*, 658.
[28] See Adolf A. Berle, Jr., "The Theory of Enterprise Entity," 47 *Columbia Law Review*
343 (April, 1947).
[29] Pound, *Jurisprudence*, IV, 260.
[30] "The Historic Background of Corporate Legal Personality," 35 *Yale Law Journal* 655,
658 (April, 1926).

remains a large number of other questions regarding the structure of the enterprise and its role in the community. These questions, and the legal answers they evoke, do not depend on recognized corporate status. They reflect the existence of a *system-in-being* with respect to which legal rules and policies need to be framed.

Berle has stressed that "the enterprise, and not the incorporation papers, is the true entity."[31] If that is so, then a legal theory of the association must take account of the true requirements of a viable enterprise, its true constituents, its true obligations. Beyond corporate "personality" and its attendant problems lies an expanding horizon of policy concerns. Given the empirical reality of association, how shall its internal life be ordered? how shall authority be exercised? who are the members?

These questions look to the factual conditions of institutional life. They presume that the association has a life and character of its own. From this it does not necessarily follow that an association's claim to autonomy must be recognized. That conclusion, associated with the English pluralists, may be justified on other grounds, but it cannot be based solely on the reality of associations. A more general issue is the integrity of legal cognition, the capacity of the law to recognize, for example, that the large, enduring enterprise is something more than an association of shareholders.

It may well be that when the law is sensitive to the prior reality of associational life it also tends to see the association as a source of self-generated value and commitment, hence as a bearer of rights that are more recognized than created by law. The thought that this may be so probably underlies that aspect of pluralist doctrine which offers the reality of groups as an argument for autonomy. But a realistic theory, while committed to taking account of the factual conditions of group existence, may just as well serve a policy of stringent regulation. The question of what to do about group reality is not settled when that reality is affirmed.

In the quest for a jurisprudence of associations, the classic issue of what constitutes a legal entity yields to problems of greater urgency and relevance. Above all, there has been a need to shift attention from the association conceived as *any* purposive grouping, of whatever size or texture, to the organization that is a sufficiently significant center of power, or locus of value, to invite rule-making in the interests of the organization itself, of its constituent elements, and the community. A fundamental premise of the new perspective is that the nature and composition of the corporate

---

[31] "Theory of Enterprise Entity," 358. For a discussion of "enterprise" law, reporting the German experience and debate, see Michael P. Fogarty, *Company and Corporation— One Law?* (London: Geoffrey Chapman, 1965).

group is not taken as fixed by legal definition. Rather, it is something to be learned in the course of legal experience.

Of all the subjects of that learning, none is more important than the problem of membership. In the still-dominant view, the shareholder is the true member of the corporate entity. This follows from the imagery of *a voluntary association of principals* as the empirical basis of corporate existence. But this approach runs counter to an institutional theory of the corporation. Thus a recent writer who has adopted that theory concludes:

> A concept of the corporation which draws the boundary of "membership" thus narrowly is seriously inadequate. It perpetuates—and presses to a logical extreme—the superficial analogy of the seventeenth century between contributors to a joint stock and members of a guild or citizens of a borough. The error has more than theoretical importance because the line between those who are "inside" and those who are "outside" the corporation is the line between those whom we recognize as entitled to a regularized share in its processes of decision and those who are not.
>
> A more spacious conception of "membership," and one closer to the facts of corporate life, would include all those having a relation of sufficient intimacy with the corporation or subject to its power in a sufficiently specialized way.[32]

The appeal for a "more spacious" concept of membership recalls Chester Barnard's suggestion, in a classic work on the theory of organizations, that our thought should not be constrained by common-sense definitions of organizational boundaries.[33] He thought of organizations as "systems of cooperative activities" and preferred to think of "contributors" rather than members. Thus customers and suppliers would be included. A disposition to expand the roster of participants is manifest whenever attention is cen-

---

[32] Abram Chayes, "The Modern Corporation and the Rule of Law," in Edward S. Mason (ed.), *The Corporation in Modern Society* (Cambridge, Mass.: Harvard University Press, 1959), 41. For pertinent discussion in Britain, see K. W. Wedderburn, *Company Law Reform*, Fabian Tract 363 (London: Fabian Society, 1965). Wedderburn warns against promoting an "unreal unity" of workers and management, but suggests that, in addition to experiments with works' councils, legal recognition of workers' interests might take the form of widening requirements affecting disclosure. "The time is past when our blood can be made to run cold at the thought of crossing the wires of company law and 'master and servant' law. If the creditor who lends cash to the company is entitled to disclosure, so is the employee who brings his labour and his security to the enterprise." (p. 15). See also Norman Ross, *The Democratic Firm*, Fabian Research Series 242 (London: Fabian Society, 1964), p. 25: "It is clear that in the reformed firm all contributors of labour services and of what is generally known as equity capital must in law be members of the firm." For a Liberal view, see George Goyder, *The Responsible Company* (Oxford: Basil Blackwell, 1961), Chap. XII, "The Participating Company."

[33] Chester I. Barnard, *The Functions of the Executive* (Cambridge, Mass.: Harvard University Press, 1938), 76–77.

tered on empirically given operative systems rather than on formally defined units.

In Barnard's theory, *activities* are coordinated, not whole persons or groups. This emphasis helped to expand and generalize the notion of formal organization. But it also offers a clue to the distinction between "contributors" and "members." The former are involved segmentally, as participants in discrete though often repetitive transactions. The latter are implicated as more nearly total persons or groups. This means that the individual or group is so far involved in the system, so dependent on it, that a relation of subordination develops. To be a member is to be subject to the authority of the system, though the exercise of that authority may be obscured by the rhetoric and ritual of market transactions.

In the experienced world, the corporate entity "is" what we learn about it as we note its effects and try to deal with it. Out of this inquiry more than one model must emerge, reflecting both the special problems being considered and the peculiar attributes of a business, a university, or a welfare agency. If our main concern is the fate of individuals in bureaucratized settings, we may want to think of the institution as a potential nexus of humanizing relationships, of warmth, intimacy, and self-fulfillment. But we may also want to see it as a potential body politic,[34] as a legal order struggling to be born.

Contract and Association

The individualist bias of modern political and legal doctrine has diminished the perceived reality of both persons and groups. The person becomes an abstract individual, his special identity lost in the egalitarian, competitive-market imagery of the free man. The group is a composite of individual ties and relationships. In keeping with that perspective, nineteenth-century judges gave a prominent place to the emergent law of contracts.[35] Contract was thought of as a kind of legal atom, the building-

---

[34] See Earl Latham, "The Body Politic of the Corporation," in Mason (ed.), *op. cit.*
[35] On the extension of the sphere of contracts see A. V. Dicey, *op. cit.*, 150 ff. Dicey points out that "the substitution of relations founded on contract for relations founded on status was for individualists generally, and especially for Benthamite liberals, the readiest mode of abolishing a whole body of antiquated institutions, which presented, during the eighteenth century, a serious obstacle to the harmonious development of society. Hence individualistic reformers opposed anything which shook the obligation of contracts, or, what is at bottom the same thing, limited the contractual freedom of individuals" (p. 151). The assumption is that legislation, e.g., usury laws, impairing the obligation of contract would have as its main effect the limitation of the terms of contract as freely bargained by individuals.

block of larger structures. The freely contracting individual, creating relations of his own making, was the paradigm of legal man.

The preeminence of contract impeded the evolution of a law of associations, for two reasons. First, the contract model was nominalist in spirit. It reduced group reality to the acts and relations of determinate individuals. Second, contract attenuated the meaning of social participation. The idea of a person in his wholeness, and in his potential as a group member, lost its hold on the legal imagination. The new jurisprudence could more comfortably apprehend a fragmented act of will.

The continuing appeal of the contract model is easy enough to appreciate. As it developed in the nineteenth century, the law of contracts embodied values of freedom, equality, self-government, and legal competence. Contract law was to be liberating and facilitative, a channel for the release of energies. It also contained a rights-endowing symbolism. If an express or implied contract is found, legitimate expectations may be inferred. A contract is an instrument of reciprocal obligation. Hence, if the association is a bundle of contracts, there is doctrinal basis for defining the obligations and prerogatives of all participants, including those who hold authority.

The history of the law of contract well illustrates what Holmes called "the paradox of form and substance in the development of law."[36] In legal history there is a persistence of abstract formulas whose content changes as the law adapts to new social realities. The law, wrote Holmes, "is forever adopting new principles from life at one end, and it always retains old ones from history at the other, which have not yet been absorbed or sloughed off."[37] While much the same may be said of all intellectual traditions, the tension between what is received and what is newly learned is poignant in a discipline that has a special commitment to authoritative materials, for the law seeks legitimacy as well as truth. By drawing upon already-legitimated concepts or principles to deal with new situations, the integrity of law can be protected while social transition is eased.

As an abstract idea, contract stands for the voluntary but conditional assumption of legal obligation. So general a formula, however, embraces very significant differences among types of contracts. Perhaps most important is the difference between contracts of *submission or adherence*[38]

---

[36] Oliver Wendell Holmes, Jr., *The Common Law* (Boston: Little, Brown and Company, 1881), 35.

[37] *Ibid.*, 36.

[38] The "contract of adherence" should be distinguished from the "contract of adhesion." The former posits a continuing relationship, the latter may be quite transitory, but is one-sided, with no opportunity for bargaining.

and contracts of *limited commitment*. This distinction is implicit in Weber's discussion of "status contracts" and "purposive contracts."[39]

The status contract is a voluntary agreement for the creation of a continuing relationship, especially one that affects the "total legal situation" of the individual:

> By means of such a contract a person was to become somebody's child, father, wife, brother, master, slave, kin, comrade-in-arms, protector, client, follower, vassal, subject, friend, or, quite generally, comrade. To "fraternize" with another person did not, however, mean that a certain performance of the contract, contributing to the attainment of some specific object, was reciprocally guaranteed or expected. The contract rather meant that the person would "become" something different in quality (or status) from the quality he possessed before.[40]

Such a contract is voluntary at its inception, but once the act of adherence occurs, the relationship is governed by preexisting rules or by the authority of a dominant partner. The conditional element of the contract is attenuated because only a *general* reciprocity is expected. Characteristically, there is a waiver of specific duties, at least on one side. The commitments accepted are general and diffuse; they are not premised on explicit consent to particular obligations.

The purposive contract is the characteristic legal institution of an exchange economy. It is a contract made to complete a specific transaction or to further a discrete objective. Only a tenuous and temporary association is created. The purposive contract is infused with the spirit of restraint and delimitation: open-ended obligations are alien to its nature; arms-length negotiation is the keynote.

The contract of adherence, on the other hand, is the gateway to permanent association. Such a contract fits the requirement and the ethos of a status-based society:

> In the really feudal centuries men could do by a contract, by the formal contract of vassalage or commendation, many things that can not be done now-a-days. They could contract to stand by each other in warfare "against all men who can live and die"; they could (as Domesday Book says) "go with their land" to any lord whom they pleased; they could make the relation between king and subject look like the outcome of agreement; the law of contract threatened to swallow up all public law. Those were the golden days of "free," if "formal" contract. . . .[41]

---

[39] Max Rheinstein (ed.), *Max Weber on Law in Economy and Society* (Cambridge, Mass.: Harvard University Press, 1954), 105.

[40] *Ibid.*, 106.

[41] Sir Frederick Pollock and Frederic William Maitland, *The History of English Law Before the Time of Edward I* (Cambridge, England: Cambridge University Press, 1952), II, 233.

But this comment is offered in a context that emphasizes "the late growth of a law of contract" in English law. The underlying contrast is, again, between the voluntary assumption of a status and the formation of a transitory arrangement for limited, reciprocal performances. The status contract is associational and prescriptive; its significant symbols are "bond" and "obligation." The purposive contract is atomistic and self-determining; its significant symbols are "freedom" and "consensus."

The tension between association and contract is revealed when we examine some of the premises of the modern law of contract:[42]

1. Voluntarism in depth. This first feature is also the most general. It lends sense and support to the more specific elements of the law of contract. Voluntarism means that the parties decide for themselves (a) whether a relation between them should be established and (b) what the terms of that relation should be. The arrangement is voluntary in that private persons freely assume obligations not otherwise required by law. The law of contracts enters mainly to certify and enforce those obligations, secondarily to set limits on who can make a valid contract and what subject-matters are barred. In the classic view, such limitations are minimal, for example, for the protection of children, the restraint of fraud, and the prohibition of involuntary servitude. The leitmotif is freedom and the premise is that a mature man is the best judge of his own interests.

The contractual relation is voluntary "in depth" because consent extends beyond an initial act of association or adherence. In principle, the entire relationship is suffused with a legitimacy born of consent. Contract presumes "agreement"; its validity depends on proof of a "meeting of minds." Whatever is not agreed to remains in an unordered world so far as the parties are concerned.

The premises of voluntarism strain against the reality of human association. Association bespeaks *commitment, open-endedness,* and *structure.* Whereas contract presumes a world of independent, roughly equal actors who achieve their objectives by making determinate arrangements with predictable outcomes, association undermines predictability and proliferates obligations. Voluntarism is weakened when the true "transaction" is the creation of a system of cooperation.

2. Limited commitment. The application of voluntarist doctrine to contract law has been marked by a preference for clearly delineated promises. This reflects (a) the historic reluctance of the courts to lend them-

---

[42] See M. Hauriou's discussion of the tension between contract and "institution" in *Principes de Droit Public* (Paris: L. Lanoge and L. Lenin, 1910), Chap. V.

selves to speculative claims or to assume new burdens of interpretation; (b) the basic image of economic transactions as casual, fungible, and market-oriented; and (c) the wish to preserve the freedom of the parties to clarify for themselves the scope of their agreement.

If contract is bottomed on consent, then what the parties actually agreed to should determine what their responsibilities are. Ideally, contractual commitments are specific rather than diffuse; they are determinate, not open-ended. That is why contract as a legal device is so well adapted to the market economy. The obligor knows what he is getting into and can calculate his costs. He can maximize his freedom to make alternative decisions under changing economic conditions.

The principle of limited commitment is upheld by a number of legal policies. Most important is the quest for consensual specificity. Evidence will be sought of what the parties had in mind, and where there is a written document the language of the agreement will have preeminent authority. In addition, of course, contractual rights and duties are limited to the *period* of the agreement. And the law of contracts has been restrictive in the remedies it has made available, the only one really in the spirit of contract being an action for compensatory damages.

The principle of limited commitment loses force, however, when a continuing relationship is contemplated, or when one is established willy-nilly. A businessman heedful of his reputation, mindful of future sales, or otherwise dependent upon his customer or supplier, is reluctant to insist on contractual specificity or to invoke contractual remedies:

> Disputes are frequently settled without reference to the contract or potential or actual legal sanctions. There is a hesitancy to speak of legal rights or to threaten to sue in these negotiations. Even where the parties have a detailed and carefully planned agreement which indicates what is to happen if, say, the seller fails to deliver on time, often they will never refer to the agreement but will negotiate a solution when the problem arises apparently as if there had never been any original contract.[43]

Of course, a relationship may be contractual in nature even where there is little reliance on legal sanctions. Nevertheless, a preference for negotiation, and acceptance of cancellation as a normal cost of doing business, suggest that trust and continuity often have more practical worth than arms-length reciprocity and limited commitment.

In a cooperative system consensual specificity—detailed planning by

---

[43] Stewart Macaulay, "Non-Contractual Relations in Business: A Preliminary Study," *American Sociological Review*, 28 (February, 1963), 61.

prior agreement as to the obligations of each party—may do more harm than good:

> Even where agreement can be reached at the negotiation stage, carefully planned arrangements may create undesirable exchange relationships between business units. Some businessmen object that in such a carefully worked out relationship one gets performance only to the letter of the contract. Such planning indicates a lack of trust and blunts the demands of friendship, turning a cooperative venture into an antagonistic horsetrade. Yet the greater danger perceived by some businessmen is that one would have to perform his side of the bargain to its letter and thus lose what is called "flexibility." Businessmen may welcome a measure of vagueness in the obligations they assume so that they may negotiate matters in light of actual circumstances.[44]

A zeal for specifying obligations in advance tends to close relations rather than open them, undermines trust, and limits contributions.

Furthermore, a fully planned relationship has a *static* quality. The situation of the parties at the time the bargain was struck governs the agreement for its duration. It is difficult, in strictly contractual terms, to take account of a dynamic relationship, in which the needs and contributions of the parties may change, or to establish the capacity of the new entity to deal with new situations. When terms are "frozen," and interpreted as fully explicating the scope of the agreement, there is little leeway for adaptation and growth. A contract that forms a going concern must be, in some sense, a "living" document. In that case, however, the specificity of the agreement is less highly prized.

3. Mutuality. If contract is a way of releasing human energies by making private arrangements more secure, it is also a principle of order. The law of contracts presumes that the parties have established a viable and largely self-enforcing system, a system founded in self-interest and reciprocity. Thus the idea of exchange, with its corollary of mutually dependent duties, is fundamental to the theory of contract.

From a legal standpoint mutuality has a double significance. First, a finding of exchange is a condition of legal validity. In principle, there must be consideration on each side. The gratuitous promise will not be enforced. This requirement is often reduced to a formality, but it remains important at the doctrinal level and is always available to the courts for application in an appropriate context.

A more important significance of mutuality is found in how the law handles a breach of contractual duty. When one party fails to perform the

---

[44] *Ibid.*, 64.

other has two remedies available. If the failure is material, he may be justified in refusing to carry out his part of the bargain; and he may seek compensatory damages in a lawsuit. The overriding policy of the law is that the contractually established balance of interests is to be upheld. Reciprocity redeemed will make a man whole.

Thus in the contract model, the contributions of one party are made in consideration of the contributions of another. Each accepts certain obligations in return for a balanced personal advantage. The model applies rather neatly to a simple exchange, *when each party can have his own end-in-view*. But if the contract creates a pattern of cooperation for the achievement of *common ends*, then an insistence on full reciprocity may be self-defeating. If rewards depend on the success of the joint effort, it may be necessary to modify significantly the principle of mutuality. Reciprocity is never completely eliminated, but it tends to be overshadowed by dependency and rational coordination. In the world of practical problem-solving, who needs whom and who can do what come to be more pressing bases of decision than issues of commutative justice. As the employment relation has evolved, for example, the employee's formal freedom to quit is in many settings greater than the employer's freedom to dismiss.

It has been pointed out that in many areas of social life reciprocity is a "starting mechanism" for the creation of new relations that must be interpreted in their own terms.[45] The principle of *quid pro quo* is a universal ground of obligation, but it is not the only one. It is most effective when the independence of the parties outweighs in importance the union they have formed. An alternative ground of obligation is the assumption of responsibility for a family or other going concern. While usually both principles—reciprocity and "assumpsit"[46]—coexist and reinforce each other, exchange is most compelling in the absence of a fuller social integration. As commitment to the social system deepens, so too does the idea that a social role is instinct with obligation, an obligation not wholly dependent on the dutiful conduct of others.

As applied in contract law, the principle of reciprocity lends legitimacy to retaliation as a way of life; undermines obligation by encouraging the view that one party is relieved from his duties whenever the other violates

---

[45] See Alvin W. Gouldner, "The Norm of Reciprocity," *American Sociological Review*, 25 (April, 1960), 161–178.

[46] In English legal history a man's failure to perform what "he undertook" (*assumpsit*) was an early ground of obligation. Legal recognition of this responsibility, apparently at first independent of reciprocity, fed into the emerging law of contracts. See Theodore F. T. Plucknett, *A Concise History of the Common Law* (Boston: Little, Brown and Company, 1956), 637–650.

his own commitments; and makes rules vulnerable because, on grounds of reciprocity, any infraction becomes an occasion for questioning their existence. These tendencies are hostile to a form of organization that transcends immediate interests and encourages long-run cooperation.

This aspect of mutuality points to the most important limitation of the contract model as a way of dealing with the reality of sustained cooperation: the ever-present threat of dissolution. Ideally, in accord with the principle of limited commitment, a contract is made in contemplation of its termination. The underlying assumption is that the parties are free to withdraw and make new, more beneficial arrangements once their minimal commitments are fulfilled.

4. Boundedness. "Privity of contract" is a policy of the common law that only the parties to a contract may claim its benefits or be required to meet its obligations. This follows from the voluntarist view that contract is a private, delimited arrangement. Those who form the contract speak only for themselves. At the same time, they should be free of interference from others only indirectly concerned. A break in the wall of privity occurred with the recognition of "third party beneficiary" contracts, agreements that provide for benefits to persons who did not participate in the exchange of promises or acts that formed the basis of the agreement. Such "strangers" may sue the promisor if he breaches the contract to their detriment. The specter of privity was also raised (and overcome) in the "product liability" cases, since no promises had been made by the manufacturer to the ultimate consumer.[47]

The doctrine of privity brings to bear the atomist and subjectivist spirit of the law of contract. The Roman idea that a contract is the formally manifested agreement of independent wills has encouraged a quest for definite parties. Since it is will and intention that is expressed, it is important to know who the parties are and what interests they have if ambiguities are to be assessed. This way of thinking is not helpful when the agreement is associational in nature. It inhibits the recognition of new corporate realities because it overstresses the legal integrity of the *initiating* parties. The subjectivist bias presses for ascertainment of who willed what. It is reluctant to recognize that what may have begun as an isolated bargain struck may come to implicate others, creating expectations so well founded that in time the law must deal with them.

Sustained cooperation tends to diminish the determinateness of the parties. To further the common effort, new relationships are established,

---

[47] See William L. Prosser, *Handbook of the Law of Torts* (St. Paul: West Publishing Co., 1955), Chap. 17, "Liability of Contracting Parties to Third Persons."

60   *Legal and Social Theory*

new dependencies and vested interests accepted. Over time, the "true" participants may include other parties, such as trade unions or creditors, who did not share in forming the original agreement. As a result, the principle of privity, which presumes that a contractual relation is bounded and isolable, comes to seem wanting in realism. Although it is true that enduring association tends to create islands of exclusiveness, thus limiting freedom of entry, that exclusiveness is *emergent*. It is not necessarily restricted to the specific parties who initially "willed" the arrangement.

A more radical weakening of privity occurs when the social consequences of private, contractual cooperation are serious and manifest. Then the actors lose their innocence and the systems they form can no longer be thought of as isolated. The contractual relations become subject to prescriptive regulation. In one form or another, a wider outside interest becomes a party to the agreement.

To the extent that continuity and concerted effort are prized, each element of the contract model is subject to attrition and distortion. The movement is from limited to diffuse commitment, from reciprocity to interdependence, from mutuality to unilateral obligation, from equality to subordination, from privity to openness, from self-regulation to external constraint. The outcome is that the logic of adherence regains its relevance and vitality.

The limitations of contract are clear enough when continuing relationships, of whatever kind, are to be understood. But the idea of *association* has more definite connotations: membership, division of labor, authority. When these attributes emerge, or must be fostered, the need for a new model, going beyond contract, becomes acute.

The tension between contract and association is explored more pointedly in Chapter 4, in connection with a discussion of the collective bargaining agreement. We there consider the idea of a "constitutive" contract, and the importance of a concept of government for interpreting such agreements. At this point, however, we should take note of two more general criticisms that may be made of contract doctrine as a foundation for the law of associations. These are (1) the limits of contract as an instrument of self-government; and (2) the emergence of status.

(1) The idea of contract as "unofficial self-government" has wide currency. The formation of contracts is presented as a kind of self-help, a legally provided opportunity for private parties to establish working relationships and govern their own affairs:

[Not enough has been said] about the process whereby a couple of lawyers bring two militantly hostile parties together in an office, adjudicate their disputes, draw a decree or statute called a contract to govern their conduct for the next ten years, and thereafter administer the law they have written in a way that will sensibly and faithfully carry out the legislative intent.[48]

But in the normal case self-regulation by contract is a weak form of government. A contract may establish determinate obligations, which may indeed be law for the parties, without creating a governing authority. Government presumes that some rule and others obey. *Self*-government tempers that relationship but does not eradicate it. Moreover, the establishment of a government is not a contract between principal and agent. The authority of an agent may be as narrowly defined as the principal may wish, but governmental authority has an irreducibly comprehensive character. That is so because government has inherent responsibility, and at least a minimum of implied authority, to protect the welfare of the corporate group, taking account of its changing circumstances and adaptive needs. As a corollary, there is always some open-endedness in a government's claim upon the commitments of citizens or members.

For these reasons, the governmental model is difficult to square with the premises of the purposive contract. There may be mutuality, consensus, and limited commitment in a politically organized community. But the mutuality is not evenly balanced, the consensus is not specific, the commitments are, at best, only relatively limited. As we have suggested earlier, the spirit of contract had much to offer in sustaining the voluntarist foundations of government; but the concept of contract cannot of itself provide an adequate theory of authority or of emergent law.

(2) When Maine stated his famous "law of progress"—"the movement of the progressive societies has hitherto been a movement *from Status to Contract*"[49]—he explicitly qualified it in several ways. The words "progressive" and "hitherto" suggest that he was offering a generalization about the emergence of modern society and was not arguing that all social organization must move in one direction only, from status to contract. Furthermore, he clearly had in mind the relative decline of kinship as a principle of social organization. Maine carefully restricted the term status to the social and legal attributions that derive from and "to some extent are still coloured by, the powers and privileges anciently residing in the

---

[48] David Cavers, "Legal Education and Lawyer-Made Law," 54 *West Virginia Law Review* 180 (1952).
[49] Sir Henry Sumner Maine, *Ancient Law* (London: Oxford University Press, 1931), 141.

Family."[50] Status was to refer to "these personal conditions only" and not "to such conditions as are the immediate or remote result of agreement."[51]

In thus qualifying his thesis, Maine showed a remarkable prescience. He evidently understood that there might be some status outcomes of "agreement," although to say so would require a broadened meaning of status. It will be recalled (see page 54) that Weber and others clearly recognized the importance of the "status contract" in the pre-modern era. More recent history suggests that a form of status can emerge out of the purposive contract, too, when the latter is in fact a vehicle of enduring organization.

Sociologists usually *define* status in a rather general and uncomplicated way, for example, as "a person's social position." However, the *concept* of status contains unexplicated theory; it therefore has a denser meaning. Most important are the associated ideas of social rank and social identity. Although there may be status without ranking, social positions tend to be differentially rewarded and esteemed, and a system of *fixed* statuses is especially likely to emphasize rank and use many devices for maintaining distinctions of place and privilege. A similar logic applies to the relation between status and social identity. From the standpoint of the person, a social position may be transitory and segmental, therefore incapable of fixing a social identity; but the fixing of identities is a characteristic kind of work done by a stabilized system of statuses.

Both sociologically and legally, the idea of status evokes the "person," not the abstract individual. Status suggests *salient differentiation*, not equality. That is why Maine associates status with the "law of persons." Indeed, historically, the law of persons *was* the law of status. It dealt with all those relations that could be said to create a legal identity: slave, serf, servant, ward, infant, wife, cleric, citizen, king. All these were statuses recognized by law. Each clothed the individual with salient disabilities or privileges. If the law of persons is not a vital category in today's common law, this reflects the decline of status as a central concern and guiding idea.

Contract strains against the idea of the person. Therefore contract principles lose authority as status emerges in organizational life. Only a concept of membership as status can bring the person back into legal focus. We shall return to that problem, and its relevance for the law of governance, in Chapter 7.

---

[50] *Ibid.*
[51] *Ibid.*

Power and Property

If the concepts of corporation and contract fail to grasp the reality of association, so too does that other shibboleth of legal man in his economic relations—the idea of private property. Like contract, property has played an ambiguous role in legal development affecting freedom and organization. On the one hand, the right to private property creates an unfettered sphere of action, an island of privacy, a foundation of personal independence and group autonomy; and the concept of property is a way of distinguishing what is settled and substantial from what is ephemeral, elusive, or dependent on the will or grace of another. As a vested right, property is an anchor of protection against uncompensated taking, whether by public or private agencies. Property rights are thus a source of security in an otherwise uncertain world.

Yet the received notion of property has limited legal cognition; it has hindered the development of a theory adequate to deal with the internal ordering and external effects of modern economic organization. Although Anglo-American law displays a greater flexibility than other systems in its approach to property,[52] that idea still carries restrictive connotations:

(a) The concept of property is possession-oriented and thing-centered. This is a question of legal imagery, not of abstractly correct definitions. Students of jurisprudence recognize that property rights are created and sustained by relations among legal actors, not by the connection between owner and thing owned. To be an owner is to have rights against others. Moreover, the "thing owned" may be any economic benefit, remote from material objects, and might even include a vested interest in the largess of government programs.[53] But the validity of these conclusions, suggesting an abstract and flexible concept of property, should not obscure the social fact that for a long time "property" has evoked "man seized of what is his own." Although earlier forms of property were heavily influenced by the relational and fiduciary perspectives of family organization and feudal tenure, the new property of the post-feudal world, largely commercial and industrial, reunited *persona* and *res*. The legal imagination was captured by John Locke's model of lonely, resolute, pioneering man appropriating material objects through toil and binding his self to his possessions.

---

[52] See O. Kahn-Freund, "Introduction," Karl Renner, *The Institutions of Private Law and their Social Functions* (London: Routledge and Kegan Paul, Ltd., 1949), 18–24; W. Friedmann, *Law in a Changing Society* (Berkeley and Los Angeles: University of California Press, 1959), 66 ff.

[53] See Charles A. Reich, "The New Property," 73 *Yale Law Journal* 733 (1964).

(b) Property is individual-centered. In seventeenth-century theory, the right to private property was founded in the postulate that the individual has a proprietary right in his own person.[54] Appropriation of economic goods was justified by the requirements of individual survival and integrity. In 1932 it could be said that "in the annals of the law property is still a vestigial expression of personality and owes its current constitutional position to its former association with liberty."[55] Although many legal changes have attenuated the perceived bond between property and personal liberty, property still finds its moral and cognitive significance in the justification and definition of private rights, not in the framing of social purpose and social responsibility.

(c) Property is domination-centered. "The owner," wrote Holmes, "is allowed to exclude all, and is accountable to no one."[56] The owner is *dominus*, master of his entitlement. Although the law may set limits, the spirit is one of exclusive and unlimited control.

Power over things and control over possessions are prominent themes in the litany of property, but *authority* is not. The concept of property hides more than it reveals about the phenomenon of authority, despite the fact that in its early history *dominium* was closely associated with power over persons, that is, members of the Roman household.[57] Gradually, according to Noyes, personal relations were differentiated from the master's *dominium* over things, including slaves.[58] In modern history "intra-familial power has remained to some extent a power over persons but has ceased to be property; inter-familial power has remained property but has ceased to be a power over persons."[59]

The claim to exclusive and unlimited control has done most to dim the legal perception of how property is organized and what human values are at stake. The main counter to that claim was, from ancient times, the idea of stewardship, that is, property held as a trust for the common good. But ownership as stewardship, though deeply rooted in a philosophical and religious tradition, yielded to the triumphant ethos of capi-

---

[54] For a recent analysis, see C. B. Macpherson, *The Political Theory of Possessive Individualism: Hobbes to Locke* (London: Oxford University Press, 1962), 143, 197 ff.
[55] Walton H. Hamilton, "Property—According to Locke," 41 *Yale Law Journal* 864, 878 (1932).
[56] O. W. Holmes, Jr., *op. cit.*, 246.
[57] C. Reinold Noyes, *The Institution of Property* (New York: Longmans, Green and Co., Ltd., 1936), 78.
[58] *Ibid.* "The eventual exact coverage of the word *dominion* in late Roman law, if it can be said to have arrived at exactitude, covers the relation of the master of the house only to the slaves and to non-human objects, animate and inanimate."
[59] *Ibid.*, 428.

talism. There occurred an "intellectual passage from the conception of private property as secondary and contingent to the conception of it as ultimate and absolute."[60] The imagery of absolute dominion has been served by both individualism and thing-centeredness: The former limits the apparent reach of power, and therefore makes it more palatable; and things can assert no claim of right.

These historic connotations of property have made it a stumbling block for the law of associations. When commerce and industry are perceived as the use and disposition of private property, there is no encouragement to legal scrutiny of the social structure that lies behind the economic act. The reality of social organization is obscured. Three aspects of that reality strain against the received doctrine:

1. Subordination. After a century of study and strife, we have yet to give adequate legal recognition to the sociological argument of Karl Marx that property creates a system of power:

> An industrial army of workmen, under the command of a capitalist, requires, like a real army, officers (managers), and sergeants (foremen, overlookers), who, while the work is being done, command in the name of the capitalist. . . . It is not because he is a leader of industry that a man is a capitalist. The leadership of industry is an attribute of capital, just as in feudal times the functions of general and judge were attributes of landed property.[61]

Marx understood, and discussed extensively, the significance of cooperation for capitalist production.[62] He saw in administrative coordination a major source of capitalist productivity and therefore, in his terms, of "surplus value." To him the enterprise was indeed an association, but not as a union of shareholders. It was as an organization of labor and of industrial command.

Marx's critique was carried forward, with more attention to jurisprudential issues, by the Austrian socialist Karl Renner.[63] Renner's study, first published in 1904 and revised in 1929, anticipated many current lines of thought regarding law and industrial organization. His larger concern

---

[60] Henry Scott Holland, "Property and Personality," in Charles Gore (ed.), *Property: Its Duties and Rights* (London: Macmillan and Co., Ltd., 1915), 181. Holland notes that this transition was mediated by a subtle change from claims against the property-owner as founded in justice to appeals based only on charity, conscience, and goodwill. "This appeal to charity, whenever it is greatly in evidence, is a sure signal that things have got wrong. It always means that the individual right is treated as absolute in itself, and has escaped out of its proper subordination to the demands of justice" (p. 180).
[61] Karl Marx, *Capital: A Critique of Political Economy* (New York: The Modern Library, 1906), 364, 365.
[62] *Ibid.*, Chap. XIII, "Cooperation."
[63] *Op. cit.*, above, fn. 52.

was to show how property as a legal abstraction maintains a formal continuity while radical changes occur in the ordering of economic life. He argued that the "functions" of a legal idea change with alterations of the "economic substratum." At the same time, the formal continuity screens the unacknowledged function.

With Marx, Renner emphasized the role of property in creating and disguising the subordination of workers:

> We see that the right of ownership thus assumes a new social function. Without any change in the norm, below the threshold of collective consciousness, a *de facto* right is added to the personal absolute domination over a corporeal thing. . . . It is the power of control, the power to issue commands and to enforce them. . . . Thus the institution of property leads automatically to an organization similar to the state. Power over matter begets personal power. . . . Property, from a mere title to dispose of material objects, becomes a title to power, and as it exercises power in the private interest, it becomes a title to domination.[64]

The capitalist's power of command was buttressed by the employment contract, which gave the worker a nominal freedom but sealed his subordination to him who owned the means of production.[65] In Renner's theory, the employment contract is a *Konnexinstitut*, a complementary or satellite legal institution. The satellite institution gives effect to the true social function, the operative significance, of the right to private property.

2. Socialization. Another *Konnexinstitut* in the realm of property is the law of business association.[66] The legal opportunity to create an enterprise fund by combining many investments transforms the social meaning of property. Individual property becomes collective ownership. The individual's title becomes in fact "a mere debt of a certain kind." This argument has since, of course, been fully developed.[67] The fragmentation of corporate ownership, and the concomitant separation of ownership and control, have brought a new era of private power. *Dominium* passes from the *de jure* owner of shares to a *de facto* managerial group that is largely self-perpetuating and even legally free of direct shareholder

---

[64] *Ibid.*, 107, 117.
[65] See below, 134 ff.
[66] Renner, *op. cit.*, 217 f.
[67] Notably in A. A. Berle, Jr., and Gardiner C. Means, *The Modern Corporation and Private Property* (New York: The Macmillan Company, 1933); A. A. Berle, Jr., *The 20th Century Capitalist Revolution* (New York: Harcourt, Brace & World, Inc., 1954); A. A. Berle, Jr., *Power Without Property* (New York: Harcourt, Brace, & World, Inc., 1959).

control. Although the shareholders may claim residual assets in case of liquidation, the true owner of enterprise property is the enterprise itself. And power is in the hands of those who conduct its affairs.

The transition from individual to collective property is a form of socialization, for group interests are made controlling and rights are vested in a going concern. Individual ownership is tamed, limited, and subordinated to institutional goals. Nevertheless, the group property is still *private* and to that extent asserts a claim to autonomy, which is to say, freedom from legal supervision. The rise of private, collective ownership creates a crisis of credibility; it is no longer possible to justify unfettered control on the ground that property is individual-centered and therefore has a limited reach and a personal significance. Furthermore, collective ownership invites scrutiny of the inner order of the enterprise, especially the way power over persons is generated and used.

3. Concentration. Collective ownership has aggregated wealth and has placed it at the disposal of organizations that are immortal and know no boundaries. With the help of modern corporation law, which permits maximum flexibility in the setting of business goals, and subject to only modest anti-monopoly restraints, collectively owned private enterprise holds a dominant position in the economy. Although the degree of concentration has apparently been stable for some time, it remains that "the one hundred-and-thirty-odd largest manufacturing corporations account for half of manufacturing output in the United States. The five hundred largest business corporations in this country embrace nearly two thirds of all nonagricultural economic activity."[68]

Each of these roads from private property to social power has distinctive characteristics and effects. Subordination speaks to an internal transformation of *dominium*, the control over things, into *imperium*, the right of sovereign command; socialization of property produces a new agency of *dominium* and places its traditional justification in doubt; concentration has to do with the capacity of that new form to impose its will on the surrounding environment. All of these changes create a demand for restraint and accountability, for countervailing institutions, and for a conception of the organization that yields a theory of authority.

One way of mitigating subordination is to recognize in law a *membership right in a going concern*. This would be, in Pound's classification, an "interest of substance," one of "the claims or demands involved in the

---

[68] Edward S. Mason (ed.), *The Corporation in Modern Society* (Cambridge, Mass.: Harvard University Press, 1959), 5.

individual economic life."[69] Pound includes "continuity of employment" as an interest of substance,[70] and this interest is sometimes treated as a property right in a job.[71] This claim, when it is made, is more self-protective than assertive. The job is not a capital resource for the employee who "owns" it, neither is it a personal possession to be changed or disposed of at will. In the usual case, the right to a job embraces two defensive claims: (1) seniority and (2) freedom from arbitrary dismissal, discipline, and discrimination in hiring.

Seniority does have the color of a traditional property right, for it vests in a specific individual the right to claim a continuing economic benefit.[72] A similar, though collective, right is asserted when a craft union has, in effect, possessory rights in job assignment,[73] or when a union resists plant relocation or technological change because of the attendant destruction of jobs. The job, or the set of jobs, becomes an object of quasi-ownership. Freedom from discriminatory hiring, however, or from wrongful discipline or dismissal, does not presume a vested right. Employment may be refused on proper grounds; layoff or dismissal may result from economic stringencies or even from faulty management decisions. The right is against *arbitrary decision*; it is not a claim to the job itself.

Membership rights are best perceived as status rights.[74] The emergence of a right to continuity of membership, and to protection of membership privileges, is a phase of the modern transition from contract to status:

> Formerly based upon contract, the labour relationship has now developed into a "position," just as property has developed into a public utility. If a person occupies a "position," this means that his rights and duties are closely circumscribed, the "position" has become a legal institution in character much like the fee of feudal times. The "position" comprises the claim to adequate remuneration (settled by collective agreement or works rule), the obligation to pay certain contributions (for trade unions and insurance), the right to special benefits (sickness, accident, old age, death) and finally certain safeguards against loss of the position or in case of its loss.[75]

---

[69] Pound, *Jurisprudence*, III, 28.
[70] *Ibid.*, 233–235.
[71] See Frederic Meyers, *Ownership of Jobs: A Comparative Study* (Los Angeles: Institute of Industrial Relations, University of California, Los Angeles, 1964).
[72] For further discussion of seniority, see index references below.
[73] On collective job rights, see Patrick McGillivray, *Social Organization and Employee Rights* (unpublished Ph.D. dissertation, Department of Sociology, University of California, Berkeley, 1966), Chap. 2.
[74] See below, 271–273.
[75] Renner, *op. cit.*, 121.

As Kahn-Freund points out,[76] the feudal analogy should not be taken too seriously. There are many obvious differences between the status of employee and of feudal tenant, notably the unilateral right of the employee to quit for any reason, though perhaps with notice. Renner understood that "this development to 'establishment' and 'position' has affected only a part of property and labour and even this only partially. . . . The ultimate direction of this change is clearly determined and its results are unequivocal, but they have neither undergone theoretical analysis, nor have they entered common consciousness."[77]

The recognition of status rights can provide a platform for the defense of the individual against arbitrary interference with his right to hold a job or with the special privileges he has won. But status rights cannot be equated with property rights, because the concept of property has only a tenuous hold on the social reality of membership. This is the clear conclusion to be drawn from the history of legal efforts to base membership rights in voluntary associations on claims to property.

In suits against trade unions, churches, and other voluntary associations for alleged wrongs against a member, the courts have sometimes relied on property to establish a protectable interest. Such a finding was encouraged by the peculiar history of equity jurisdiction, which required the finding of a property interest if equitable remedies were to be granted. (Without equity jurisdiction, there could be no "specific," nonmonetary relief, such as court order for reinstatement of a member wrongfully expelled.) However, the thing-centered connotation of property plagued the courts in these cases and inhibited recognition of the true interests at stake. The courts responded to this difficulty, first, by expanding the idea of property so as to make it, in some cases, "virtually meaningless,"[78] for example, when one court concluded that "the unimpeded exercise of the functions of elective office, such as membership on the executive board of a labor union, is a right so fundamental as to be deemed the equivalent of a property right."[79] Second, the courts have tended to abandon both the property theory of membership rights and the property-interest basis of equity jurisdiction.[80]

---

[76] *Ibid.*, 170.
[77] *Ibid.*, 122.
[78] Joseph R. Grodin, *Union Government and the Law: British and American Experiences* (Los Angeles: Institute of Industrial Relations, University of California, 1961), 63.
[79] *Bianco v. Eisen*, 75 N.Y.S. 2d 914 (Sup. Ct. 1944), quoted in Grodin, *op. cit.*, 63.
[80] On the attenuation of the rule restricting equity jurisdiction to property rights, see William Q. de Funiak, *Handbook of Modern Equity* (San Francisco: University of San Francisco Press, 1950), Chap. VIII.

So property fades as a meaningful basis for sustaining the substantive rights of members. Contract fares no better. Although the courts have long looked to a contract theory for justification of members' claims, in fact, as discussed above, the premises of contract run counter to the reality of association. To deal with that reality, the courts have had to depart from contract principles.[81] They have struck down unfair rules, even though such rules were otherwise considered terms of a putative contract and therefore binding even if unfair or harsh; and they have required the member to look to internal tribunals for interpretation of rules instead of allowing direct recourse to the courts, as they would in an ordinary dispute over the provisions of a contract.

Chafee argued that the true basis of legal protection is a *relational interest*:

> The member's relation to the association is the true subject matter of protection in most cases where relief is given against wrongful expulsions. The wrong is a tort, not a breach of contract, and the tort consists in the destruction of the relation rather than in a deprivation of the remote and conjectural right to receive property. Although this theory of a relation as the basis of relief receives practically no support in judicial opinions, the reasons outlined in the preceding discussion indicate that it is the correct explanation of the decisions.[82]

It is easy enough to conceive of relational interests as legally protectable substantive rights,[83] and to do so without invoking the notion of property. "Relational interest" must be interpreted broadly, however, and made equivalent to "status," if it is to serve as a basis for protecting the full range of membership rights. The relational-interest approach may suffice to sustain a claim against wrongful expulsion or against interference by third parties. But the law of associations requires a more pointed concept of the *nature* of the relation at stake. Above all, it must recognize as crucial the individual's encounter with organizational authority.

A theory of authority is required, not only by the fact of subordination, but by the socialization of ownership and the concentration of power. All of these developments have undermined the social acceptance of unfettered domination. In one form or another, the principle of stewardship, of fiduciary responsibility, is being reasserted. The issue goes beyond legitimacy. The problem is not to justify great and autonomous power but to

---

[81] See Zechariah Chafee, Jr., "The Internal Affairs of Associations Not For Profit," 43 *Harvard Law Review* 993, 1001–1006 (1930).
[82] *Ibid.*, 1007.
[83] See Leon Green, "Relational Interests," 29 *Illinois Law Review* 406–490, 1041–1057 (1935).

temper that power in the light of public policy, and to do so without stifling managerial freedom or destroying institutional autonomy. This requires that external control be geared to the reconstruction of the association's inner order, especially the way authority is generated, sustained, and renegotiated.

The reconstruction of authority is sometimes phrased as the emergence of a "corporate conscience." Berle has argued that the large modern corporation is a "nonstatist political institution, and its directors are in the same boat as public office-holders."[84] Corporate power, based on domination-centered private property, is in many areas theoretically absolute, but in practice is responsive to countervailing power and to criticism that may affect public standing and respect. "Limiting customs" grow up to restrain corporate power, as in the relation between the large manufacturer and franchised dealers; and there is a sensed unease when the corporation is called on to sift out employees who are "security risks." Berle sees these developments more as potential than as achievement. They are "a tropism in the emerging corporate system."[85] There is hope, he suggests, for corporate recognition that unlimited power is unacceptable in the American constitutional system.

> So, it seems, the corporations have a conscience, or else accept direction from the conscience of the government. This conscience must be built into institutions so that it can be invoked as a right by the individuals and interests subject to the corporate power.[86]

In this perspective the corporate conscience, such as it is, is a historical outcome, a product of institutional adaptation. There is an underlying assumption that, in a world of collective property and corporate organization, stewardship is once again a relevant idea. It is not so much that stewardship is morally appealing, for that might always have been so. Rather, stewardship *of a certain kind and degree* makes sense historically. It is sustained by the compelling necessities of institutional life. It finds a practical warrant in what the firm "of institutional size" can do, and in what it must do.

The following chapters may be read in part as a quest for the corporate conscience: its origins, its locale, its sustaining forces, its legal implications, its troubles and limits. It will be quickly evident, however, that we have had to go beyond the corporate managers as individuals to con-

---

[84] *The 20th Century Capitalist Revolution*, 60.
[85] *Ibid.*, 81.
[86] *Ibid.*, 113f.

sider the organization as a whole. What is at stake is the capacity of the institution to do justice. That competence is located in the attributes of a social system, conceived as an arena within which authority is exercised and rights are asserted. To grasp the nature of that system, and to draw the legal conclusions, is the major task of a law of associations.

Part Two | *Social Foundations of*

Industrial Justice

Chapter 3 | *Management and Governance*

IN THIS CHAPTER WE EXPLORE THE CONTRIBUTION OF administrative rationality to industrial justice. Two major topics are considered: (1) the quest for orderly management and (2) the managerial need to take account of human needs and aspirations. The first topic takes us into a discussion of bureaucratic and post-bureaucratic rationality. The second is seen in the administrative logic of "human relations." We conclude with a consideration of the interplay of legal, political, and human-relations values.

Rationality, Legality, and Managerial Self-restraint

Among the master trends of modern history, none has been more widely noted than "the bureaucratization of the world." If kinship, fealty, and contract were representative modes of social ordering in earlier centuries, today the principle of *rational coordination* dominates the scene. This principle finds a natural habitat in the large, centrally governed administrative organization. While rational coordination can and does go on in smaller settings, often with greater effectiveness, it is the effort to run a large enterprise that produces the characteristic social form we call bureaucracy.

The term bureaucracy has borne both honorific and pejorative connotations. Modern social science has attempted to maintain a posture of

75

neutrality, equating bureacracy with officialdom, whatever may be the positive or negative correlates of bureaucratic rule or circumstance.[1]

Here we are concerned with the significance of bureaucracy for managerial self-restraint, especially as that bears on the emergence of a rule of law in personnel administration. To explore this problem, we must give some attention to the idea of bureaucracy itself. What can the theory of bureaucracy tell us about the relation between rationality and legality? What conclusions may we draw for the evolution of industrial justice?

Max Weber's treatment of bureaucracy foreshadowed its relevance for the theory of private government. He characterized bureaucratic authority, in its fully developed state, as "legal-rational," thus suggesting a special connection between the internal administration of a special-purpose organization and the character of a legal order.[2] This interpretation is central to our thesis and therefore merits close inspection.

For Weber the rise of modern bureaucracy was but a part of a larger social process—the rational reconstruction of human institutions. He saw rationalization as the decisive feature of modernity, the key to ineluctable change in economics, politics, law, and cultural life. Rationality brought with it a pervasive "disenchantment," an erosion of those bonds and symbols that had limited man's capacity to see the world as freely manipulable. In the new age, old unities could be sundered, fragmented, and rearranged to serve the purposes of autonomous and self-confident men.

This is not to say that Weber looked with optimism upon the drift of history, or that he saw rationality as a simple phenomenon. On the contrary, he knew that a commitment to rational forms and orientations would tend to depersonalize the world; and the machinery it created might well crush the spirit. Furthermore, rationality has its own dilemmas, and these set continuing problems for modern institutions. One that Weber emphasized repeatedly was the tension between "formal" and "substantive" rationality.[3]

---

[1] For a recent effort to associate the concept of bureaucracy with an inherent pathology, see Michel Crozier, *The Bureaucratic Phenomenon* (Chicago: University of Chicago Press, 1964).

[2] See Max Weber, *The Theory of Social and Economic Organization* (New York: Oxford University Press, 1947), 328 ff. Also, H. H. Gerth and C. Wright Mills, *From Max Weber: Essays in Sociology* (New York: Oxford University Press, 1946), Chap. VIII; Reinhard Bendix, *Max Weber: An Intellectual Portrait* (Garden City, N.Y.: Doubleday & Company, Inc., 1960), Chap. XIII.

[3] See Weber, *op. cit.*, 184–186; also Max Rheinstein (ed.), *Max Weber on Law in Economy and Society* (Cambridge, Mass.: Harvard University Press, 1954), xlviii, 61 ff. For a related view, see Karl Mannheim, *Man and Society in an Age of Reconstruction* (New York: Harcourt, Brace & World, Inc., 1949), 51 ff.

A system is rational when it applies calculable means, in accordance with objective standards and general rules, to the achievement of determinate ends. It is *formally* rational when explicit criteria of efficiency or logic, including a legal or even religious logic, govern the choice and organization of means. Thus formal rationality, though it contributes to substantive outcomes, speaks mainly to the internal state of the system. A system is *substantively* rational when it is effectively articulated to social or human purpose.[4] Cost accounting contributes to the formal rationality of the business enterprise; it does not guarantee that the social ends of economic activity will be fulfilled, or even that the proper strategic decisions, from the standpoint of the enterprise, will be made. Legal decisions may be rigorously controlled by internal criteria of validity, yet substantive justice, as defined by the society, may be wanting.

It was formal rationality that caught and held Weber's attention. He had no illusions about substantive outcomes, but he was fascinated by the tendency of modern society to objectify the idea of rationality, to make the word flesh by embodying it in enduring activities and agencies.

Weber's approach was evolutionary, in a broad and undogmatic sense of that hard-used term. He was mainly interested in distinguishing the modern from the pre-modern. He saw in bureaucracy *the emergence of rationality as an attribute of a system.* Thus Weber was not imposing a "rational model" on human affairs. To him the coming of rationality was a historical process—always problematic, always dependent on congenial circumstances, always bearing with it unintended social effects.

The main features of bureaucracy, more or less as Weber saw them, may be summarized as follows:

1. An explicit purpose. Theoretically, a knowable end is a necessary ingredient of "formal" organization, the genus of which bureaucracy is a species. Indeed, it is the purposive character of the group that most clearly marks it as "a system of consciously coordinated activities or forces of two or more persons."[5] Conscious coordination has to be *for* something. Furthermore, the more explicit the purpose, the greater is its capacity to serve as a premise of decision-making and as an instrument of control. The explicit purpose helps hold the bureaucrat accountable

---

[4] Mannheim adds the thought that substantive rationality is an act "which reveals intelligent insight into the inter-relations of events in a given situation" (*op. cit.*, 53). A man who is only a cog in a machine, unaware of the ultimate end of his work, or how it fits into the whole, may be part of a "functionally rational" system, but substantive rationality is lacking. This suggests that the categories of formal and substantive rationality may also be applied to the internal analysis of systems.

[5] C. I. Barnard, *The Functions of the Executive* (Cambridge, Mass.: Harvard University Press, 1938), 73.

for his actions and provides him with guidelines for the improvement of administration.

An important difference between the bureaucratic and pre-bureaucratic modes lies in this objectivity of purpose. In pre-bureaucratic organization, the administrative staff takes its cue from a leader to whom personal loyalty is given. The purposes of the organization are the personal aims of the leader. "Organizational ends are predominantly the private, subjective ones of their respective heads, not public, 'objective' ones."[6] As such, they do not contribute to formal rationality.

In his most direct analysis, Weber hardly mentioned the place of purpose in bureaucracy. He simply takes it for granted that bureaucratic organization is a rational instrument subordinate to given ends. Yet Weber's neglect of purpose has a certain point. For him bureaucracy was not a dynamic institution committed to solving problems and attaining objectives. He saw it rather as a relatively passive and conservative force preoccupied with the detailed implementation of previously established policies. In such a setting purpose lacks creative significance. It is not in the foreground of bureaucratic awareness.

2. A determinate hierarchy.   The most visible feature of the bureaucratic landscape is the array of echelons. As a way of attaining efficiency and effectiveness, bureaucracy places its bets on authoritative channels of communication and control, authoritative allocations of responsibility. This creates the bureaucratic phenomenon par excellence—the "sphere of competence." Defined spheres of competence are the basic units of the organization. The effort to coordinate them yields the familiar hierarchical pattern.

Bureaucratic hierarchy is, therefore, more than a formal chain of command. It is an arrangement of parts that have an integrity and continuity of their own. The parts are offices, not persons. It is the office that is vested with authority, not the incumbent.

The alternative to bureaucratic hierarchy is a more flexible, *ad hoc* form of organization. Assignments of work and authority are not allowed to crystallize as fixed spheres of competence. The person holding the office is more important than the office itself. Paradoxically, these attributes appear in both pre-bureaucratic and post-bureaucratic stages of development. The pre-bureaucratic leader insists that the administrative staff be personally dependent upon him. He senses the tension between effective personal command and the creation of legally competent officials.

[6] William Delany, "The Development and Decline of Patrimonial and Bureaucratic Administrations," *Administrative Science Quarterly*, 7 (March, 1963), 466.

Assignments are made on the basis of personal qualities. Authority is not formally delegated to subordinate offices but merely invested in individuals, to be held at the pleasure of the chief. In post-bureaucratic organization the same flexibility is sought, but by other means.

3. **An officialdom.** The rise of bureaucracy has been accompanied by the emergence of "the official" as a social role. Much of Weber's discussion has to do with the distinguishing features of an officialdom. Among these is the commitment to a full-time career. One who undertakes official duties while continuing a private occupation or holding an independent social status lacks full commitment to the organization. It is difficult to summon his continuing loyalty or obedience. By contrast, the official is wholly dependent on the organization, though not upon any specific leader of it. To reinforce this organizational dependency, the official is appointed, not elected. He does not have an independent constituency. His appointment, however, is by impersonal process; it is not an act of grace or favor. The official thus appointed, and thus committed, does not exploit the organization for his personal benefit. He finds his reward in a relatively stable salary and in professional prestige. Therefore, ideally, his compensation is divorced from the fluctuating fortunes of the enterprise.

In professional management, impersonality is an ideal of conduct and an instrument of technical administration. "Above all," wrote Weber, "bureaucratization offers the optimal possibility for the realization of division of labor in administration according to purely technical considerations, allocating individual tasks to functionaries who are trained as specialists. . . . 'Professional' execution in this case means primarily execution 'without regard to person' in accordance with calculable rules."[7] Impersonality is sustained by the application of objective criteria in recruitment and promotion. Whether the criteria stress merit or seniority, they do not depend on uniquely personal qualities or relationships.

The principle of professional management looks to *expertise* as the foundation of decision-making and authority. When the official is appointed, he accepts the obligation to act on the basis of his special knowledge and training. "Bureaucratic administration means fundamentally the exercise of control on the basis of knowledge."[8]

4. **Governance by rules.** Weber stressed administration according to "calculable rules" as "of paramount importance for modern bureaucracy."[9] The bureaucrat's main commitment is to an impersonal order, a system

---

[7] Rheinstein, *op. cit.*, 350.
[8] Weber, *op. cit.*, 339.
[9] Gerth and Mills, *op. cit.*, 215.

of rules that limits his own discretion and which he must apply in an even-handed way. In speaking of *calculable* rules, Weber was emphasizing that modern administration seeks to make decisions as objective as possible, eliminating whatever is subjective and irrational. A calculable rule is, in the first instance, a dependable rule. But it is more than that. It is also "intellectually analyzable,"[10] and based upon rational assessment of organizational aims and resources. Self-serving decision-making, as in nepotism, however dependable, would not meet the test.

In the theory of bureaucracy rule-governed decision is not an end but a means. It is a way of maximizing rationality *under certain conditions.* Therefore the question is always open: How rational is the rule? Weber did not dwell upon this problem. Given his historical perspective, he was content to note that a system of impersonal rules, grounded in technical aims and expertise, was a notable achievement compared to the rampant traditionalism and person-centered administration of an earlier era.

Weber's identification of bureaucracy with rational organization is subject to some qualification, and we shall return to that issue presently. At this point we wish to call attention to one striking feature of the bureaucratic model, with its stress on objectivity and impersonality. *In theory, bureaucratic administration is the antithesis of arbitrary rule.* Bureaucracy formalizes every facet of decision-making and in doing so sets an ideal of limited discretion. The official *qua* official is not free to hire his relatives or to express his personal prejudices. He is called upon to resist every choice that is, from the standpoint of the system, an arbitrary intrusion of alien standards or interests.

In Weber's model rational assessment of objective purposes, and fidelity to rule, are basic norms of official conduct. He also said that "in principle a system of rationally debatable 'reasons' stands behind every act of bureaucratic administration, that is, either subsumption under norms or a weighing of ends and means."[11] It follows that the bureaucratic decision is open to criticism in the light of established rule and explicit purpose.

This strain toward controlled, non-arbitrary decision is the underlying phenomenon which justifies Weber's conception of bureaucratic authority as "legal-rational." As we have argued above,[12] the ideal of legality stimulates a quest for the progressive reduction of arbitrariness in rule-making and administration. This reduction proceeds as the rational component of law is enlarged. Bureaucratic administration, as Weber saw it, com-

---

[10] Weber, *op. cit.*, 361.
[11] Gerth and Mills, *op. cit.*, 220.
[12] See Chap. 1, p. 12.

bines the legal impulse to reduce arbitrariness with a supporting commit-ment to rationality as a master ideal.

"Bureaucratic rule was not and is not the only variety of legal authority, but it is the purest."[13] In thus stressing the intimate relation of legality and bureaucracy, Weber had two things in mind. First, he saw bureauc-racy as an instrument of *public* law, the vehicle by which that law be-comes increasingly objective and rational, therefore more closely approxi-mating what Weber thought of as the pure type of legal authority. The modern *Rechtsstaat*, he would say, finds its genius in bureaucratic ad-ministration.

Second, he glimpsed a more general relation of bureaucracy and law, one that had to do with modern bureaucracy as a type of organization, whatever its purposes or its auspices. It was clear to him that bureaucracy could be private as well as public. "Bureaucracy, thus understood, is fully developed in political and ecclesiastical communities only in the modern state, and, in the private economy, only in the most advanced institutions of capitalism. . . . It does not matter for the character of bureaucracy whether its authority is called 'private' or 'public.' "[14]

Thus the "legality" of bureaucratic authority does not necessarily de-rive from the public status of the agency or enterprise. It is founded in the internal life and order of the association. Bureaucratic authority is "legal" because (a) its legitimacy is of a special kind—warranted by rational principles, justified by its contribution to the organization; and (b) it is committed to rule-governed decision-making, with all that entails for the quality of the rules themselves, for the nature of the delegation, for objective recruitment and assignment, for equal treatment of like cases, for the visibility of norms, for appeal to authority as a paradigm of official conduct, for the elaboration of principles of criticism. *The source of these attributes is internal; the dynamic they create calls forth the ideals of legality.*

Although the essentials of bureaucracy as a legal order are stated by Weber, we should bear in mind that he shared a continental and Roman perspective on law and authority. In that view authority takes on a heavy, somber note and law is fundamentally a system of command. If "cor-rectness" is a keynote, so too is obedience. The whole is stuffy, pompous, and uninviting. Weber's image of law does not reflect the critical, search-ing, dynamic character a legalist ethos can have. This limited conception

---

[13] Gerth and Mills, *op. cit.*, 299.
[14] *Ibid.*, 196–197.

of the legal may account in part for Weber's ultimate dislike of bureaucratic organization.[15]

If bureaucracy obeys an inner impulse to create a legal-rational order, it does not follow, of course, that the impulse is always manifest in reality. The idea of bureaucracy is dispositional. It identifies a phenomenon that has significant latent potentialities. Just how much of this potentiality will be fulfilled depends on environing circumstances. In a heavily status-oriented community, or in a society where any official job is a high prize, an emerging bureaucracy will have mixed features, to say the least. In a totalitarian setting, where bureaucratic organization is supervised, stretched, and pummeled by political agencies, the rational-legal potentialities will be frustrated.[16] On the other hand, if the theory is correct, we should expect the latent disposition to make itself felt as these constraints are attenuated or removed.

The history of industrial management shows many evidences of a strain toward internal legality. With the decline of family management in industry, for example, the justification for authority is more and more referred to claims of competence, service, and rational principles of administration. The historic significance of this transition is the rise of self-restraint as a hallmark of enterprise management.

Pre-bureaucratic management was typically one-man rule. The dominant figure resisted delegation of authority and was inclined to make as many decisions as possible on his own. The relation between the "big boss" and his staff was personal and he expected unreserved loyalty and obedience. In the bureaucratic setting authority is more impersonal, more systematic, more limited, and more effectively delegated. Respect is shown for authority based on technical competence. And all officials, including top management, accept a framework of established rules. In this sense, bureaucratic authority is "constitutional."

---

[15] "This passion for bureaucracy, as we have heard it expressed here, is enough to drive one to despair. It is as if in politics the spectre of timidity . . . were to stand alone at the helm; as if we were deliberately to become men who need 'order' and nothing but order, who become nervous and cowardly if for one moment this order wavers, and helpless if they are torn away from their total incorporation in it. . . . [T]he great question is therefore not how we can promote and hasten it, but what can we oppose to this machinery in order to keep a portion of mankind free from this parcelling-out of the soul, from this supreme mastery of the bureaucratic way of life." From a speech by Weber (1909), included as Appendix I, J. P. Mayer, *Max Weber and German Politics* (London: Faber and Faber, Ltd., 1943), 127–128.

[16] See Reinhard Bendix, "Bureaucracy," *International Encyclopedia of the Social Sciences* (New York: Free Press, 1968), 212; also *Work and Authority in Industry* (New York: John Wiley & Sons, Inc., 1956), Chap. 6; Franz Schurmann, *Ideology and Organization in Communist China* (Berkeley: University of California Press, 1966).

In many firms having professional management the principle of command is modified. Ultimate authority is still at the top, and directives are issued down the line, but there is a greater emphasis on consultation. At least within the officialdom itself, those whose work may be affected by an impending decision are given a chance to be heard. This is not democracy, in the sense of majority rule, but the base of managerial decision is broadened to take advantage of the professional expertness and practical knowledge that exists at lower levels of the organization. At the same time, the legitimacy of decision, as based on rational assessment taking account of all that should be considered, is strengthened.

The pre-bureaucratic business leader was impatient with formal rules and procedures. He liked to keep his accounts in his hat and to run the organization from day to day without clear-cut policies. Much was done in accordance with tradition—"this is the way we always do it"—or by improvisation to fit the requirements of the moment. The intuitive understanding derived from one man's experience, often a rich experience, was the foundation of decision-making in the enterprise.

The bureaucratic way is directly contrary. Systematic procedure based on "sound management principles" is the ideal. Rules and policies are developed to guide decision-making in all phases of activity. Men are hired in accordance with criteria worked out by personnel specialists; they are trained, assigned, and supervised according to specified routines. Tradition is never its own justification but is subject to question and revision by experts in organization planning and human engineering. A "web of rules" governs behavior at all levels of the enterprise, although the specificity of the rules may vary considerably.

> The web of rules becomes more explicit and formally constituted in the course of industrialization. At the very early stages, the very notion of a rule may be alien, and individual incidents are confronted without regard to their more general implications. The continuing experience of the same work place, the growth in size, the same workers, and the emergence of managerial staff tend to result in customs and traditions which begin to codify past practices. . . . Some rules may later emerge which anticipate problems rather than merely summarize past decisions. The statement of the rule then becomes more formal and elegant, particularly as specialists are developed in rule-making and administration.[17]

Detailed rules also existed in the early days of the factory system, but at that time the rules mostly applied to the discipline of the work force

---

[17] Clark Kerr, J. T. Dunlop, F. H. Harbison, and C. A. Myers, *Industrialism and Industrial Man* (Cambridge, Mass.: Harvard University Press, 1960), 198–199.

rather than to other policies and practices of management. The worker was subject to very close supervision, and was required to abide by many regulations governing his conduct both on and off the job. At a later stage rules become protective as well as restrictive; they apply to management as well as to the worker.

The elaboration of formal rules creates expectations regarding the consistency and fairness of official action. The formal rule is a kind of commitment, as suggested in the following comment by an industrial relations executive:

> Our plant rules are not formalized by being reduced to writing. We have avoided this, for to do so would possibly make them subject to negotiation with the union. Not having written rules has strengthened rather than weakened the unilateral authority of management in this regard. This is a fact, not wishful thinking.[18]

Thus what might seem to be an instrument of managerial power—the establishment of a rule—is viewed as a mixed blessing, if not worse. The rule is double-edged, limiting both the rule-maker and the potential offender. At the same time, as we know, rule-making cannot be avoided. Unlimited managerial discretion has its own great costs. Rules and formal organization liberate management to exercise discretion where it is most needed and can be most fruitful.

It follows that the bureaucratization of American industry[19] should be a major source of self-restraint. For bureaucracy brings with it a flowering of "personnel policy" and a concomitant elaboration of rules and procedures. Such regulations limit the arbitrary exercise of managerial prerogative. To a large degree, the inhibitions are self-imposed, for without consistent policies and procedures administrative rationality cannot be achieved. Motivated by a concern for efficiency, managers have been impelled to tame and temper their own authority. By incorporating objective standards in rules, the rule-makers bind their own hands.

Progressive management celebrates the "policy method" of administration. Explicit statement of organizational aims and basic methods is seen as a prophylactic against opportunistic, *ad hoc* decision-making. A National Industrial Conference Board study stressed the need for principled decision-making, and saw that this entailed managerial commitment and self-restraint:

---

[18] Bureau of National Affairs, *Disciplinary Practices and Policies*, Personnel Policies Forum Survey No. 42 (Washington, D.C.: Government Printing Office, 1957), 2.
[19] See Bendix, *Work and Authority in Industry*, Chap. 4; also Orme W. Phelps, "A Structural Model of the U.S. Labor Market," *Industrial and Labor Relations Review*, 10 (April, 1957), 402–423.

Is a policy a promise? While it is not a legal obligation, which can be enforced by the courts, policy has the backing of management's integrity. If management means what it says, and a policy is worthless without this premise, employees can consider a policy statement as a declaration which gives them the right to expect the performance of, or forbearance from, certain acts. Policy commits management at all levels to make all decisions in view of announced purposes.[20]

Thus policies create legitimate expectations, which are further supported by the rule that policy statements should be in writing:

Unless policies are written, they cannot be regarded as firm commitments. There is always the opportunity to hedge a little, to make a slight exception, to depart just this once in the interests of expediency. Probably herein lies the reluctance on the part of some to formulate actual policy. Top management, whether consciously or not, wants to leave itself an "out." It is not ready, actually, to adhere in all instances to its basic beliefs. If there is no thought of evasion, why *not* put the intent into writing? If the belief is of value, the believer will appreciate the assistance of the written word in making clear the intent.[21]

Of course, the commitment is to a general formula, not to detailed rules or procedures. But a policy, though necessarily framed in broad terms, must have a definite content and fully convey top management's intent or aim. A meaningful policy is an effective tool for designing *and criticizing* specific rules or procedures.[22]

Personnel policies have two main functions. They establish the premises of managerial decision. And they create an environment of secure expectations. Security of expectations, in turn, is a basic ingredient of fairness:

From the standpoint of employees, the outstanding advantage of personnel policies is fairness—the fact that they assure equal treatment for all employees. . . . Policies serve as a written Bill of Management—a statement of civil liberties in corporate practice. Human beings want to know the conditions under which they are hired. . . . Policies protect the employee against the supervisor who shows partiality, or is otherwise unjust. . . . The employee knows what to expect if he gets a new boss, or is transferred to a new department or to a new plant, and "knowing the score" is a constant source of satisfaction. He has freedom from fear; he can relax and attend to his job.[23]

This statement contains some hyperbole, and its very existence is evidence

---

[20] Geneva Seybold, *Statements of Personnel Policy*, Studies in Personnel Policy No. 169 (New York: National Industrial Conference Board, 1959), 6.
[21] *Ibid.*
[22] See above, 28, on the relation between principles and rules.
[23] Seybold, *op. cit.*, 16 f.

that many managers need to be convinced. Nevertheless, it shows how normative administrative theory strains toward the ideal of internal legality.

Knowledge-based, systematic procedure has become, indeed, an increasingly compelling standard for modern management. In the personnel field, this is reflected in the greater use of job evaluation and job description, as well as formalized rules and personnel regulations. For example, one study was able to compare several samples of industrial firms with respect to their personnel practices.[24] Of a 1947 sample of 325 firms, 46 per cent had written personnel policies; a 1952 sample of 628 firms showed 67 per cent.[25] There were also increases in the use of job analysis and other personnel research procedures.

Another survey in 1951 of personnel practices in 600 southern industrial plants reported roughly comparable conclusions. This survey is of special interest because comparisons are available by plant size and unionization, as well as by industry. Plants of 100–500 employees were classified as "small" and plants having more employees were classified as "large." In nonunion firms having personnel specialization (a full-time personnel worker and/or an organized personnel department), 56 per cent of the small plants and 77 per cent of the large plants reported the use of job evaluation. In unionized firms 54 per cent of the small plants and 69 per cent of the large plants used job evaluation.[26] These data indicate that increased size of an enterprise, in both the presence and absence of unionization, is associated with increased use of systematic procedures.

The Bureau of National Affairs reported in 1957 that about three out of four companies studied had written plant rules outlining personnel policies and practices.[27] And among the forty-four large firms in the San Francisco Bay area we studied in 1958,[28] over 80 per cent had formalized

---

[24] William R. Spriegel and Alfred G. Dale, *Personnel Practices in Industry*, Personnel Study No. 8 (Austin: Bureau of Business Research, University of Texas, 1954). "It should be emphasized that the survey is not a sampling of American business as a whole, nor is it the intention of its authors that it should be so construed. The listing of respondents represents a selection of firms known or believed to have well-developed personnel policies. Within the limits dictated by this selectivity, an attempt was made to preserve a reasonable balance in the pattern of company locations, sizes and types" (p. 9f.).
[25] *Ibid.*, 39.
[26] H. Ellsworth Steele, William R. Myles, and Sherwood C. McIntyre, "Personnel Practices in the South," *Industrial and Labor Relations Review*, IX (January, 1956), 248.
[27] Bureau of National Affairs, *Disciplinary Practices and Policies*, 1–2. Based on responses from a panel of 160 "top personnel officials in all types of companies, large and small, in all branches of industry and all sections of the country."
[28] See below, 103.

written personnel regulations. The personnel director of one of these companies commented:

> We believe we have developed increased understanding with our employees over the years. In connection with increased understanding, we believe in this company that rules are necessary to any game, whether you are talking about football, baseball, or employee relations. The larger a firm becomes and the more employees you have, the more rules of procedure you need in order to try to keep personnel policies uniform.

Whatever the effectiveness of these procedures in improving the quality of personnel decisions, they do contribute to a style of administration that is specialized, expert-minded, and rule-governed.

Another indicator of limited managerial discretion is the widespread acceptance of seniority as a criterion of decision. Almost all collective bargaining contracts in industrial plants have seniority provisions, and these have been fairly readily granted, at least with respect to the regulation of layoffs. More important for this discussion is the prevalence of seniority in *nonunion* firms. The study of southern industries, referred to above, found that seniority in "promotion, layoff, and rehire" was used in over 80 per cent of the nonunion companies having personnel specialization, and in about 99 per cent of the unionized companies.[29] Personnel specialization (having a full-time personnel worker and/or an organized personnel department) has a significant effect on this as well as other personnel practices. When small plants (100 to 500 workers) were compared with respect to the presence or absence of personnel specialization, it was found that among nonunion plants *without* personnel specialization 64 per cent used seniority; where specialization was present 84 per cent applied that criterion.

A later study (1964) comparing 309 union and 672 nonunion firms in the Southeast found seniority widely used in nonunion plants. In the sample as a whole, 85 per cent of the union and 60 per cent of the nonunion companies reported that seniority was an important factor in promotion.[30] The authors add:

> The wide use of seniority in nonunion plants deserves comment. To be sure, managers pointed out that in these plants seniority is used less rigidly and for more restricted purposes than in union plants. Also, many personnel men in organized plants reported that they carry a continual struggle to win proper consideration of worker qualifications for promotion and

---

[29] Steele, Myles, and McIntyre, *op. cit.*, 248.
[30] H. Ellsworth Steele and Homer Fisher, Jr., "A Study of the Effects of Unionism in Southern Plants," *Monthly Labor Review*, 87 (March, 1964), 267; also, "Plant Size and Personnel Practices in the Southeast," *Alabama Business*, 36 (March 15, 1966), 2–5.

to keep the way open for promising young men to rise in the company. But even in nonunion plants, the principle of seniority receives support because it "reduces headaches" and "helps to avoid charges of favoritism."[31]

Thus, even so important a limitation on discretion may be welcomed as a contribution to orderly management. Although management may not initiate the seniority rule for fear of creating vested rights, its willingness to concede the point reflects a need for objective criteria that can be applied easily, systematically, and with beneficial effects on employee morale. A management spokesman has said: "In the worker's mind, seniority is an impersonal standard which minimizes possible employer discrimination and favoritism in matters affecting the worker's job. For this reason, employers' policies regarding the seniority principle represent one of the cornerstones of sound labor-management relations."[32]

Among nonunion firms that have a seniority rule for layoffs, most do not accept "straight" or unqualified seniority.[33] Formally, and to some extent in practice, seniority is qualified by consideration of merit, family status, and hardship. Nevertheless, the difficulty of establishing accurate yardsticks for assessment of individual cases seems to result in a falling back on length of service as the main criterion:

> Two compelling reasons are cited for strongly emphasizing seniority even where policy calls for consideration of other factors first. One of these is the company's inability to prove ability differences except where it is extremely evident on the basis of work record. The second is the employer's somewhat natural feelings of responsibility and loyalty for those employees who have been with the company for a long time. Several cooperators [respondents] with recent layoffs indicate that they gave greater weight to seniority than previously anticipated. When it actually came down to specific layoffs, they found that deviations from straight seniority were kept to a minimum.[34]

In some cases, the unqualified seniority rule for layoffs is based on a concern for the integrity of personnel evaluation as a continuing function:

> Whether a layoff situation is the proper time to deprive an employee of his job because of low ability or poor physical condition is seriously questioned by several cooperators.

---

[31] Steele and Fisher, "Unionism in Southern Plants," 268.
[32] National Association of Manufacturers, "Current Industrial Seniority Practices: A Survey," *Management Review*, 36 (February, 1947), 84.
[33] John J. Speed and James J. Bambrick, Jr., *Seniority Systems in Nonunionized Companies*, Studies in Personnel Policy No. 110 (New York: National Industrial Conference Board, 1950), 5.
[34] *Ibid.*, 9.

One executive points out that in his opinion the transfer or discharge of subaverage workers should be handled on a continuous basis. He feels that the inefficient producers should be replaced as they become known and not carried along until the layoff ax falls. . . .

An executive in an eastern manufacturing concern echoes these sentiments. While no layoffs have occurred as yet in his company, he points out that a constant awareness of the straight seniority system and its implications must be maintained. Straight seniority is workable, he says, as long as day-by-day decisions during full employment are sound. . . .

Another company following straight seniority feels that if ability precedes seniority at layoff time, a tempting opportunity is afforded supervisors to unjustifiably "clean house." Previous layoff experience convinced this top management that "line supervisory personnel were most anxious to take advantage of layoffs to weed out their poorer workers and retain those whom they considered to be superior." However, this company felt that such action might be unfairly discriminatory and lead to endless arguments and grievances. As a result, top management endorsed a straight seniority policy at layoff time except where written records could clearly justify exceptions.[35]

These comments suggest that a keen sense of professionalism in personnel relations may be compatible with a "mechanical" procedure when the latter is an integral part of a rationalized system of personnel practice.

The case for seniority in promotions is weaker than for layoffs. Industrial employees commonly are more interested in job security than in job advancement and managements are more likely to be concerned with competence and merit in promotions than in layoffs. Nevertheless, the quest is for *objective* criteria to supplement the seniority rule. The personnel director of a prominent can manufacturing company stressed this point when he said: "We follow seniority strictly in layoffs. In promotions we follow seniority plus ability—but the problem is how to define and evaluate ability."[36]

While the seniority rule is an obvious restriction on management's free choice, the introduction of other objective standards for promotion has, in principle, the same effect. The National Association of Manufacturers has endorsed the trend toward development of objective techniques for measuring employee abilities:

It is vital to the development and maintenance of good human relationships that the factors used to qualify length of service be measured in as objective and equitable manner as possible. To do so, management should

[35] *Ibid.*, 6.
[36] From an interview (1958).

develop adequate techniques, including the best use of employee records, job descriptions, merit rating plans, [and] supervisory appraisal ability.[37]

The practical obstacles are great, and the tests devised may leave much room for arbitrary discretion. But the commitment to procedural regularity seems clear.

Another source of managerial self-restraint is the formalization of procedures for the administration of industrial discipline. Formal rules promise equal treatment; they define expectations; they tend to specify the limits of authority. These restraints are inherent in governing by rules and industrial management is not excepted from them. As already indicated, a great many business firms have written personnel regulations in the form of "plant rules." Many other companies operate under rules that are as well known to employees, even though they are not in written form. The outlook for the future was summarized by one personnel executive as follows:

> I see a continuing trend toward specifying and tightening disciplinary policies. Employees like to have a tight-run ship. They like to know that their supervisor will take the same action each day. They like to have rules and to have a part in creating them. They expect their discipline to be fair.[38]

Management discretion in this area tends to be limited in several ways. First, to spell out what is *not* allowed by implication leaves other forms of conduct free of managerial control, or at least places a special burden on management to show why control should be imposed. Second, explicit formulation of rules invites critical assessment of them. There will be pressure to legitimate rules by showing their practical necessity. If a company attempts to make rules that go beyond the commonly accepted requirements of the employment relation, or run counter to the employees' own assessments of what the work situation demands, considerable difficulty in enforcement may be expected.[39] Third, personnel policy recoils from a crude application of punitive sanctions. Some gradation of offenses and penalties is recognized by many firms as important to sound management.[40]

In the unionized sector of industry, a major mechanism for invoking rules and protecting the rights they create is the grievance procedure.

---

[37] National Association of Manufacturers, *Seniority*, Information Bulletin No. 20 (New York, 1955), 7.

[38] From an interview with a paper products company personnel manager (1958).

[39] See Alvin W. Gouldner, *Patterns of Industrial Bureaucracy* (New York: Free Press, 1954), esp. Chaps. 9–10.

[40] Bureau of National Affairs, *Disciplinary Practices and Policies*, 2–4.

This depends to some extent on bureaucratization: In non-factory employment, notably in the building trades, systematic grievance procedures are less fully developed.[41] But among unionized firms that have a stable workforce the institution is widely prevalent.[42]

It has been said that the grievance procedure "is the feature of the labor agreement most difficult to duplicate in nonunion personnel .management."[43] There is some reason to believe, however, that grievance procedures are gaining a greater foothold in nonunion firms. In 1954, a National Industrial Conference Board study pointed out that only 21.5 per cent of companies studied had formal grievance procedures for nonunion hourly personnel and only 8.6 per cent had such procedures for nonunion salaried personnel.[44] However, the 1962 survey of southern companies, mentioned above, reported that 54 per cent of the nonunion firms had formal grievance procedures, compared to 97 per cent of unionized firms.[45] In commenting on "the wide use of grievance procedures by nonunion plants," the authors note:

> Some of these plants, it is true, have retained the practice from organized days. As the manager of a unionized spinning and weaving mill declared, "I've found from thirty-two years of experience that without such procedures management would not hear about certain grievances until they reached a dangerous stage." He would keep the grievance procedure, but without the arbitration step, even if his plant went nonunion. Similarly, the personnel manager of a large metal-working plant stated, "Under the union relationship, if a man has a grievance, it comes up; it doesn't lie festering." Personnel men in some unorganized plants seek to avoid unionization by establishing practices which reduce or resolve worker grievances.[46]

Among nonunion companies, the presence of personnel specialists was positively correlated with the proportion of plants having formal grievance procedures.[47]

---

[41] See Van Dusen Kennedy, *Nonfactory Unionism and Labor Relations* (Berkeley: Institute of Industrial Relations, University of California, 1955), 38f.
[42] See Bureau of National Affairs, *Disciplinary Practices and Policies*, 9. See also Rose T. Selby and Maurice L. Cunningham, "Grievance Procedures in Major Contracts," *Monthly Labor Review*, 87 (October, 1964), 1125–1130.
[43] Phelps, *op. cit.*, 418.
[44] National Industrial Conference Board, *Personnel Practices in Factory and Office*, Studies in Personnel Policy No. 145 (New York, 1954), 56, 109.
[45] Steele and Fisher, "Unionism in Southern Plants," 264.
[46] *Ibid.*, 265.
[47] *Ibid.* For other reports on nonunion settings, see J. J. Bambrick, Jr., and J. J. Speed, *Grievance Procedures in Nonunionized Companies*, Studies in Personnel Policy No. 109 (New York: National Industrial Conference Board, 1950); Bureau of National Affairs, *Grievance Procedures for Unorganized Employees*, Personnel Policies Forum Survey No. 49 (Washington, D.C.: Government Printing Office, 1958).

In both unionized and nonunion industry, modern personnel policy has had to take account of trade-union demands and achievements. Therefore, it is difficult to sort out the "pure" effect of managerial self-restraint. It is evident that "the large unorganized industrial firm, especially the exceptional nonunion firm in an organized area or industry, is always under heavy pressure to conform to the pattern laid down in union-management agreements in other sections of the industry or in related industries."[48] On the other hand, the logic of management has its own imperatives, manifested in a commitment to explicit policy, systematic procedure, and the maintenance of organizational equilibrium. The premises of modern personnel management are by no means completely alien to the policies of trade unions. This is a chief social foundation of labor-management accommodation.

Although bureaucracy as we have come to know it does have inherent sources of self-restraint, there are two fundamental limitations upon its capacity to make decisions in the spirit of legality:

(1) The enterprise is not mainly in the business of dispensing fairness. Its primary obligation, as seen by the responsible leaders, is to ensure survival and growth by getting a job done. This commitment to the task at hand competes for resources with the auxiliary work of personnel management. The latter cannot be guaranteed a high priority. There is always a risk that "sound personnel policy" will be given short shrift when other demands are pressing.

(2) Bureaucratic authority is not easily checked and challenged from below. Although progressive management may do much to encourage consultation, the latter is only a weak resource for institutionalized criticism. It is probably most effective when it takes the form of pressure on policy from segments of the enterprise that have their own interests and perspectives, such as a line department or staff agency. Moreover, consultation does not normally encompass the rank and file industrial worker. For most employees, there is no adequate opportunity *to test the rules themselves* in the course of presenting their own grievances. One nonunion company made this explicit when, in describing its grievance procedure, the following reservation was stated: "The propriety, need, or reason for any company rule or policy shall not be the subject or basis of the grievance."[49]

---

[48] Phelps, *op. cit.*, 413.
[49] Bambrick and Speed, *op. cit.*, 16. This company was one of only two of the fifty-seven nonunion firms studied, all having some form of grievance procedure, to include arbitra-

These limitations are not adventitious. They inhere in any enterprise, public or private, that has a mission to perform beyond the administration of justice itself or the fulfillment of democratic ideals. Even when the mission of the organization is distinctively legal, unilateral decision-making and an unresponsive apparatus may emerge when resources are scarce or when there is a specialized concern, such as the control of crime. Therefore we must conclude that bureaucratization is only partially effective as a source of self-restraint.

If we give two cheers for bureaucracy, recognizing its penchant for rule-governed decision, we must add the caution that bureaucratization cannot be *relied on* to sustain legality. Our argument is not that bureaucracy itself produces a high form of legal order. It is rather that the strain toward legality, being "natural" to bureaucracy, contributes to an evolution that requires impetus, and gathers support, from other sources.

In this discussion we have made a bland transition from Weber's model of bureaucracy to the style and aspiration of progressive management. Our purpose has been to stress the *continuity* of Weberian theory and modern managerial practice. This does not mean, however, that the two approaches are identical.

The bureaucratic institution Weber had in mind has important limitations from the standpoint of modern management. These limitations become apparent when we take another look at the idea of a "legal-rational" system. The very joinder of these terms suggests that we are dealing with rationality *of a particular kind*. Administrative authority is legal and rational if it is legitimate, if it is exercised in the light of objective purposes, if spheres of competence are defined, if decisions are made in the light of impersonal rules, if office and incumbent are separable. So much we have already stated.

But such a system can exist without fully conforming to all the canons of rational administration. Legality and rationality are to some extent conflicting ideals. Legality is at least in part a stabilizing principle. Under its aegis rights are vested and flexible management is limited. Seniority and other tenure rights are quite compatible with a bureaucratic-legal model of administration. But they introduce rigidities that compromise rationality

---

tion as the final step. The reluctance to accept arbitration in the nonunion context may reflect the fear that grievance arbitration cannot be effectively insulated from critical assessment of rules and policies. The explicit statement cited in the text may be meant for the arbitrator.

when, for example, new conditions call into question the urgency of granting such rights to induce sustained participation.

For Weber the law-minded bureaucrat is an apostle of modernity. He strikes down the intrusive irrationalities of nepotism, social status, and personal exploitation of official position. In time, however, he introduces his own constraints and heavy costs, as Weber also understood. The bureaucrat came upon the scene to enlarge the possibilities of free and rational manipulation of resources, including human resources. Yet his very commitment to legality must fetter managerial decision.

Vested rights and policy commitments are *expected* costs of rational-legal bureaucracy. In addition, such a system must bear its share of the distinctive pathologies of a legal order. Chief among these, for administrative settings, is the tendency of rule-oriented decision to become a substitute for practical problem-solving. Better understood, but not more important, is the excessive protection of defined statuses and jurisdictional spheres.

A number of writers have sought to qualify Weber's model in the light of a more general principle of rationality. Thus Parsons has noted that Weber did not adequately distinguish legal competence and technical competence.[50] Legal competence is a defined sphere of authority; technical competence is a matter of skill and expertise. As against earlier systems, Weber saw in bureaucracy the possibility of uniting authority and expertise, but he did not study the antinomies of legal and technical competence, nor did he consider the probable need for new forms of organization to give the expert greater weight in the determination of policy.

There is, indeed, a continuing tension between two conceptions of administration. One view, which we may call "engineering," emphasizes the fully rational deployment of manipulable human resources. Ideally, permanent delegations are avoided, and individual or group rights are a burden on the system. The alternative "bureaucratic" model sees the organization as made up of defined spheres of competence. Systematic delegation is inherent in the system, and the adjudication of claims of right is readily accepted as a normal aspect of administration.

Obviously, modern management operates on both of these principles. Yet we do not have an administrative theory that unifies the two conceptions, nor are we sure how much of each will endure as we move to new

---

[50] Talcott Parsons, "Introduction," in Weber, *op. cit.*, 58–60. Other critical materials in the same vein are discussed in W. Richard Scott, "Theory of Organizations," in R. E. L. Faris (ed.), *Handbook of Modern Sociology* (Chicago: Rand McNally & Company, 1964), 490–505.

levels of technology. There is reason to expect a new synthesis, with some modification of both the engineering and bureaucratic models.[51]

We may well doubt that the large enterprise, business or government, is fated to take on all of the classic features of bureaucracy. The effective organization is more fully purposive, more flexible, more susceptible to leadership, more congenial to initiative at all levels. The capacity to create *ad hoc* administrative entities—the interdepartmental team or task force— becomes a sign of managerial superiority. So also is the will and the wit to master a complex hierarchy and avoid the role of passive adjudicator among contending bureaucratic units.

Despite this quest for flexibility, it is reasonable to expect that management will continue to evolve as a law-making, organization-creating, standard-setting agency. These modes of action are positive managerial resources. By creating realms of freedom and commitment they make their own contribution to dynamic administration. Although bureaucracy tends to vest group rights and undermine leadership, it is also true that the egoism of sub-units is an important source of energy and initiative.

While a system of rules may lay a stifling hand upon organizational life, rules and established procedures liberate management from the tyranny of *ad hoc* response; and they enhance the environment of initiative by providing for security and self-respect.

Today we can observe a dialectical transition from the *ad hoc*, leader-dominated organization of pre-bureaucratic times to a new era of rational improvisation. Thus understood, bureaucracy becomes a historical "antithesis," a transitional polarity preparing the way for a higher stage of rationality and control. If this Hegelian conceit is apt, bureaucracy will not be completely eliminated. It will leave an indelible mark on the post-bureaucratic age. That mark will be a principle of self-restraint, especially in the use of human resources.

Human Relations and the Rule of Law

The movement for scientific management had two main branches.[52] One branch sought the rational reconstruction of forms and procedures. This would be accomplished by eliminating *ad hoc*, leader-centered deci-

---

[51] For a discussion of bureaucratic versus "technology management" forms of organization, see Howard Vollmer, *Adaptations of Scientists and Organizations* (Palo Alto, Calif.: Pacific Books, in press), Chap. 3; Warren Bennis, *Changing Organizations* (New York: McGraw-Hill, Inc., 1966).

[52] See L. Urwick and E. F. L. Brech, *The Making of Scientific Management* (3 vols; London: Management Publications Trust, 1949).

sion and turning to "organization engineering," symbolized in the vocabulary of "system," "staff-line relations," "coordination," and "decentralization." The other branch, more provocative and controversial, called for greater attention to human resources.

In one sense, to think of a man as a "human resource" is to affront his personality. For such a view suggests that he is potentially a fungible and even expendable unit of a technical system. The image is evoked of a "human engineer" bent on maximizing contributions to the system. This could be a chilling prospect, and some early efforts to assess and control the work situation, in excruciating detail, gave the scientific management movement a very bad name. But the larger significance of scientific management is that it opened the door to objective inquiry. The actual effects of conventional personnel practice were to be studied, *and the findings of such study were to be given an authoritative place in managerial decision-making.*

In the "mental revolution" sought by Frederick W. Taylor, the authority of knowledge was to be paramount. Both labor and management, he said, "must recognize as essential the substitution of exact scientific investigation and knowledge for the old individual judgment or opinion, either of the workman or the boss, in all matters relating to the work done in the establishment."[53] This understanding would spell the end of arbitrary decision-making:

> I have tried to point out that the old-fashioned dictator does not exist under scientific management. The man at the head of the business under scientific management is governed by rules and laws which have been developed through hundreds of experiments just as much as the workman is, and the standards which have been developed are equitable; it is an equitable code of laws that has been developed under scientific management, and those questions which are under other systems subject to arbitrary judgment and are therefore open to disagreement have under scientific management been the subject of the most minute and careful study in which both the workman and the management have taken part, and they have been settled to the satisfaction of both sides.[54]

Rational consensus, it was hoped, would resolve conflicts and create a new era of productivity and fairness.

The attack on arbitrary decision-making, and the appeal to science, stimulated theoretical reflection and empirical research on human relations. A modest intellectual "breakthrough" occurred when management experts

---

[53] Frederick W. Taylor, *Scientific Management*, Testimony Before the Special House Committee (New York: Harper & Row, 1947), 31.
[54] *Ibid.*, 189.

began to realize that the achievement of full participation required earnest attention and sensitive understanding. It could not be taken for granted as an incident of the labor contract. Nor would it yield to simple formulas of economic incentive or punitive threat.

The first premise of "human engineering for organization needs" is that most organizations operate at low levels compared to what they might do if their members were more adequately mobilized and disciplined. Organization potential, in other words, is largely a function of the human contribution. If men are adequately motivated, and if their energies are effectively channeled, they will give more and better service. And this applies to all levels of most enterprises.

The need for a heavy emphasis on efficient use of human resources varies with the nature of the task, the state of technology, and the scarcity of labor. Under modern conditions this emphasis, although by no means uniform, tends to increase. Problems of individual responsibility and commitment pervade the enterprise:

> Under the conditions of factory production . . . workers must be willing to do the work assigned with a degree of steady intensity. They must have a positive interest in accuracy and exercise reasonable care in the treatment of tools and machinery. And they must be willing to comply with general rules as well as with specific orders in a manner which strikes some reasonable balance between the extremes of blind obedience and capricious unpredictability. . . . These qualities of work must be coordinated with the production schedule, and that coordination depends to some extent on the good judgment of each worker in his every act of complying with rules and orders.[55]

No sustained cooperative activity can do without "good judgment," but the need for it increases as responsibility for costly equipment and coordinated effort is widely shared. Thus the "human contribution" is something more than energy expended. It is above all the acceptance of personal responsibility.

Of course, human commitment is not for sale at bargain prices. High-quality management and specialized staff personnel are expensive items. Since the human engineer looks to increasing the "inputs" of *particular* individuals, the costs of doing so must be weighed against the possibility of maintaining a larger but less stable and less efficient workforce. Therefore not every firm has found human engineering equally attractive, or equally suited to every stage in the development of an enterprise. Where

---

[55] Bendix, *op. cit.*, 204.

on-the-job training is important, however, and labor turnover is costly, the tendency is to strive for each individual's maximum contribution.

The emphasis on contributions invites a new view of the worker, one based on understanding of how he behaves in natural settings and guided by the quest for a positive, though realistic, view of his potential. Bendix has traced the changing image of the worker in the course of industrialization.[56] In eighteenth- and early nineteenth-century England workers were viewed as dependent rather than self-reliant, inherently irresponsible, in need of a firm governing hand. In the nineteenth century, and in the first decades of the twentieth, the morality of individualism, self-reliance, ambition, effort, and the "survival of the fittest" was extended from the middle-class entrepreneurs to the entire industrial community. With the coming of scientific management, "the worth of the workingman was no longer self-evident from his success in the struggle for survival, or even from his compliance with the wishes of his employer. It was determined, instead, by tests which ascertained his present and potential abilities, in order to place him where he would do the 'highest class of work' of which he was capable."[57]

Thus the ideology of scientific management rejected preconceptions. But it necessarily left open the questions: What are the bases of commitment to work and the job? What is the nature of motivation and what are its sources? What model of man will best serve the aims of rational enterprise? As such, scientific management carried no special theory of human nature. It would be compatible with foolishness or wisdom, depending on the sophistication of social inquiry and the genuine receptivity of management to fresh understanding.

The first enthusiasm of scientific management was for the study of time and motion. In these efforts the worker was perceived as a passive instrument, a mechanical adjunct of the machine he tended. The problem was to increase the efficiency of the human organism "by specifying a detailed program of behavior . . . that would transform a general-purpose mechanism, such as a person, into a more efficient special-purpose mechanism."[58] To this end human activity was analyzed into simple components whose characteristics could be studied in detail. The limits of physiological capacity were probed.

Once attention was focused on the organism, it was but a step to serious

---

[56] *Ibid.*
[57] *Ibid.*, 279.
[58] James G. March and Herbert A. Simon, *Organizations* (New York: John Wiley & Sons, Inc., 1958), 13.

concern for the work environment. If fatigue is important, and rest periods of value, then noise, lighting, and other environmental conditions must also be considered. And if the physical environment matters, what of the social environment? The Hawthorne studies, carried on between 1927 and 1932, served dramatic and compelling notice that the social aspects of factory life could not be ignored.[59]

This transition had a marked effect on how the worker was perceived. The man-as-machine conception faded as a new image emerged. The worker came to be recognized as a responsive being whose style of participation was greatly influenced by what he brought to the job and what that job could do for him. In due course it was also learned that human response is something more than mechanical reaction to determinate stimuli. The responding organism is selective, self-referring, and moved by psychic needs that are progressively elaborated as more primitive satisfactions are achieved.

Scientific human relations looks to the work environment as the strategic variable; it seeks policies, procedures, and relationships that will encourage self-discipline and willing conformity; it accepts and builds upon the group structure of the enterprise; and its style of supervision is "employee-centered," with emphasis on positive incentives rather than negative sanctions. The administrative ideal is self-generating commitment and self-executing policy. The basic premise is: Men do best when they are persuaded and supported, not when they are driven and constrained.[60]

We do not know how much real consensus there is on this managerial perspective. Even if there were wide assent to general principles, beyond lip-service, there would still be a serious question about their actual influence on industrial life. The practice of human relations is most visible in the proliferation of programs for (1) training of supervisors in employee-centered administration; (2) job placement that takes account of the individual's special needs and capabilities; (3) counseling and other assistance to employees in solving their personal and career problems; (4) employee induction and training; (5) follow-up interviews of new employees; (6) systematic concern for employee advancement; (7) development of better means of communication and consultation within the firm, including

[59] See F. J. Roethlisberger and W. J. Dickson, *Management and the Worker* (Cambridge, Mass.: Harvard University Press, 1939); Henry A. Landsberger, *Hawthorne Revisited* (Ithaca, N.Y.: Cornell University Press, 1958).
[60] See Rensis Likert, *New Patterns of Management* (New York: McGraw-Hill, Inc., 1961); Douglas McGregor, *The Human Side of Management* (New York: McGraw-Hill, Inc., 1957).

group decision-making; and (8) systematic measurement of employee morale.

There is evidence that at least some of these practices are increasingly prevalent. The Spriegel and Dale study showed "foremanship training" programs had spread from 34 per cent of firms studied in 1930 to 72 per cent of those studied in 1953.[61] A later survey by Spriegel and Mumma asked more specifically about the training of supervisors in human relations. It was found that 64 per cent of a national sample of companies "thought to be progressive in their personnel practices" had formal programs of training in human relations.[62] A 1950 study found that 71 per cent of respondent firms reported having some kind of training program in "human relations" for foremen, and 49 per cent reported training in "participation and conference leadership. Over 90 per cent indicated that some kind of training in human relations was needed, and 82 per cent said that training in participation and conference leadership was needed for foremen and first-level supervisors.[63] In 1960 the National Industrial Conference Board reported that, "although the growth of this activity has been relatively slow, more companies are making attitude surveys today than ever before."[64] Much the same may be said for other techniques of "progressive" personnel management.

In a larger sense, however, the specific techniques are less important than the new ideas that are reconstructing the premises of management. These are to be found in theoretical works on human relations, and in statements of management philosophy. Among these themes, three are of special importance:

1. **Respect for the person.**   A basic conclusion of human-relations studies is formulated by Likert as follows: "The leadership and other processes of the organization must be such as to ensure a maximum probability that in all interactions and all relationships with the organization each member will, in the light of his background, values, and expectations, view the experience as supportive and one which builds and maintains his

---

[61] Spriegel and Dale, *op. cit.,* 39.
[62] W. R. Spriegel and E. W. Mumma, *Training Supervisors in Human Relations* (Austin: Bureau of Business Research, University of Texas, 1961), 16.
[63] Harold P. Zelko, "Speech and Conference Leadership Training in American Industry," *Personnel,* 27 (September, 1950), 124–125.
[64] Stephen Habbe, "Trends in Making Employee Attitude Surveys," *Management Record,* 22 (February, 1960), 16. For later data, see National Industrial Conference Board, *Personnel Practices in Factory and Office,* Studies in Personnel Policy No. 194 (New York, 1964), 55 (manufacturing), Studies in Personnel Policy No. 197 (New York, 1965), 19, 57, 94, 131, 167 (nonmanufacturing); Stephen Habbe, "Attitude Surveys and Follow-Through Practices," *Management Record,* 22 (March, 1960), 10–16.

sense of personal worth and importance."[65] This he calls "the principle of supportive relationships."

Supportive administration is *respectful*. It is founded in the belief that men respond best when they are treated as persons who need self-esteem and can only have it when they are treated with dignity and concern. This simple truth has required rediscovery because it is so readily honored in the breach when the need for discipline seems paramount and when immediate pressures of time and economy invite supervisory short-cuts. Modern personnel research has reaffirmed the underlying principle and has sought the special administrative methods to give it life in the industrial setting.

2. **The "poverty of power."** This phrase of Charles E. Merriam's well expresses another of the conclusions of human-relations research. Merriam wrote of the "wide gap between the apparent omnipotence of authority and the actual operation of power, between the iron fist of force and its incidence upon human flesh and feeling."[66] Authority is only as effective as the mechanisms that sustain it. Among the more poignant discoveries of management is how severely limited are the resources of authority and how swiftly they may be eroded. Many managers will ruefully agree that "there is nothing more surprising to the holders of power, or perhaps to its subjects, than the frailty of their commands in certain types of crises."[67] That this can also be true of everyday life is seen in the malaise, manifested in grumbling and passive resistance, whose "special home," Merriam recognized, is "industrial rather than political relations."[68]

3. **The indivisibility of consent and control.** Human-relations theory conceives the firm as a "cooperative system."[69] Beyond a bare minimum, no one's participation is taken for granted. And a decisive phase of cooperation is the acceptance of authoritative communications. In business control must rest on consent, if only because the costs of coercive surveillance are prohibitive. Consent is especially needed where positive contribution, not mere passive conformity, is sought. The winning of consent does not require democratic decision, but it is furthered by respectful and considerate treatment, including some forms of communication and consultation.

In the larger context of social and political theory, these insights are scarcely new. *What is new is the recognition of their relevance to special-*

---

[65] Likert, *op. cit.*, 103.
[66] Charles E. Merriam, *Political Power* (1934), reprinted in H. D. Lasswell, C. E. Merriam, and T. V. Smith, *A Study of Power* (New York: Free Press, 1950), 156.
[67] *Ibid.*
[68] *Ibid.*, 163.
[69] The classic statement is C. I. Barnard's *The Functions of the Executive* (Cambridge, Mass.: Harvard University Press, 1938).

purpose organizations, especially organizations that have long been considered inescapably authoritarian in spirit and practice. This recognition stems partly from new knowledge about the conditions of effective human performance. It also reflects the fact that industrial management is itself implicated in a cultural setting and responds to broadened expectations for humane and dignified administration.[70]

In any administrative setting, the most important contribution of a human-relations perspective is enlarged awareness of human motivation and response. Employee, patient, client, inmate, soldier, student—each is seen as a whole person in inevitable (though highly variable) conflict with the requirements of administrative discipline. That awareness brings with it a change in the foundations of authority.[71]

Managerial absolutism has no place in an organization attuned to human needs. The progressive, human-relations-minded manager does not necessarily yield his authority, but he does control his authoritarian impulses. He avoids the degradation of subordinates and instead contributes to their self-respect. In attempting to maximize the acceptance of his authority, he rejects reliance on blunt expressions of arbitrary will. He willingly explains the premises of decision and seeks consent through varied measures of persuasion and influence.

Thus a concern for how people feel and respond adds its special weight to the critique of *unlimited* managerial authority implicit in scientific management and administrative rationality. One manifestation of this combined effect is the acceptance of "fairness" as a criterion of decision. Fairness as a managerial virtue has long appeared in lists of the personal qualities of successful business executives.[72] Frederick Taylor thought of fairness as a necessary condition for winning the assent of workers to scientific management.[73] But if fairness is to be more than a glittering generality it must be institutionalized. One phase of that process is the acceptance of specific commitments by those who help make the rules by which industrial life is governed.

---

[70] See James C. Worthy, "Management's Approach to 'Human Relations,'" in C. M. Arensberg *et al., Research in Industrial Human Relations* (New York: Harper & Row, 1957), 17 ff.; see also Robert L. Heilbroner, "Reflections on a Changing Business Ideology," in E. F. Cheit (ed.), *The Business Establishment* (New York: John Wiley & Sons, Inc., 1964), 13 ff.

[71] See Morris Janowitz, *The Professional Soldier* (New York: Free Press, 1960), Chaps. 1–4.

[72] See Bendix, *op. cit.*, 301.

[73] Taylor, *op. cit.*, 145 ff. Lawrence Stessin has suggested that "it was scientific management and not the labor unions which created the first barrier to the common-law right of the employer to fire for any or no cause." (*Employee Discipline* [Washington, D.C.: BNA, Inc., 1960], 6).

To gain a closer understanding of fairness in the perspectives of contemporary managers, especially those who have a professional commitment to good personnel relations, we interviewed the personnel directors of forty-four San Francisco Bay Area firms. The interviews were conducted in 1958 and centered on disciplinary practices. We presented these executives with seven hypothetical situations in each of which an employee is disciplined for an alleged offense. Two questions were then put to each respondent:

(1) Do you feel that management was within its rights or prerogatives in taking the action indicated?
(2) Do you feel that there would be any grounds for the employee to complain? If so, on what grounds?

Each of the hypothetical situations was based on cases that appear in grievance arbitration. They were in part designed to assess the correspondence between the orientations of personnel managers and the principles emerging in grievance arbitration.

To facilitate comparison, the present discussion treats four topics to be considered again in Chapter 4, where arbitration is discussed, and in Chapter 5, where employee attitudes are considered: (1) fairness as a general ideal in personnel administration, (2) the scope of managerial control over employees, (3) recognition of job security as limiting the power of management, and (4) procedural limitations on disciplinary action.

A word of caution may be in order before discussing the responses. The sample is small and restricted to the San Francisco Bay Area. The firms were not selected randomly, but were chosen to represent a wide variety of industries, for example, manufacturing, shipping, retail, financial. These findings cannot support any firm generalizations about the prevalence of attitudes among personnel directors. They are reported here for the glimpse they give of an emergent ethic.

Fairness as a general idea. Our first hypothetical case showed management taking decidedly arbitrary action in discharging an employee. Here we sought to evoke a general response rather than to elicit opinions on specific aspects of fair treatment. The hypothetical case was presented as follows:[74]

---

[74] The cases were slightly altered in interviews with personnel directors in "white-collar" industries, to allow for variations in occupation and setting. To avoid repetition we shall report the situations as prepared for manufacturing firms.

One afternoon after his work shift was completed, Sam Brown was given notice by his foreman that he was fired for not doing his job the way it should be done. Sam got mad about what the foreman did and went to see the superintendent in charge of the whole shop. Sam said to the superintendent, "Everybody knows I always do my job and I do it right—what right have you guys suddenly to say that I'm not doing the work now the way it should be done? The superintendent then answered Sam by saying, "I'm going to stand behind what my foreman did, because it has always been management's right to determine whether workers are performing their jobs properly, and furthermore, you know our union contract states that management has the right to discharge workers for "inefficiency." But Sam said, "Well, I agree that the contract says management can fire for 'inefficiency,' but the very fact that we have a union contract means that we are supposed to be treated fairly, and this doesn't seem like fair treatment to me."

Only eight of the forty-four respondents felt that management was "within its rights" in this situation, and even among the eight there was considerable criticism of management's action. The supervisors were faulted mainly for failing to warn the employee and thus afford him an opportunity to meet the company's requirements. Others emphasized that the company was wrong in not explaining the reasons for the discharge. Only four of the personnel directors felt that management should have been required to prove its case, however.

The following comments are indicative of the majority opinion:

This is an example of arbitrary treatment. I would want to know of the foreman, did you warn the man previously and did you make a record of the warning? Very often foremen try to get rid of men without putting in the personnel records a notice of previous warning, as they should. (*Railroad transportation*)

We would consider this action unjust. The man was never given any notice of the standards that were expected of him. Furthermore, the supervisor should not have discharged the man without an approval from the Personnel Office. If this happened, the employee would have grounds for complaint. (*Department store*)

Most of the respondents, including six out of seven representatives of nonunion companies, stressed the need for "corrective" discipline. This policy presumes that (a) easy resort to discharge as a way of handling infractions is bad for both the employee and the company, and (b) there is a gain in morale when discipline is measured and humane rather than arbitrary and punitive.

There was a striking response to the statement in the hypothetical case that "the very fact that we have a union contract means that we are supposed to be treated fairly, and this doesn't seem like fair treatment to me." Because of the altered form used for white-collar industries, this statement was presented to only thirty-three subjects. Of the twenty who commented on this aspect of the case, sixteen interpreted it as suggesting that fairness was based exclusively on the collective contract. These respondents expressed themselves strongly that fair treatment does not rest on the contract but is rather an obligation of management to its employees. For example, two personnel executives commented:

> It is true that a contract implies fair treatment. On the other hand, it is *inherent* that employees should be treated fairly, whether there is a collective contract or not. (*Shipyard*)

> A union contract is not necessary for fair treatment. We tell our people all the time that they should try to do the right thing, and not merely adhere to what the agreement requires them to do. The right thing to be done is not controlled primarily by the agreement, because what is "fair" by contract may be changed every time a new agreement is reached. (*Can manufacturing*)

Similar views are expressed in the following statements, which were volunteered in another portion of the interview:

> Because of the type of country we live in, where the individual is more important than any company, a man carries this idea about his rights into his work—this idea of his "dignity." Employees are particularly concerned with their rights to job security, fair treatment, and being respected by management and their fellow workers. (*Chemical and paper products*)

> There are actual rights and there are implied rights. Actual rights are overtly expressed in company policies and practices. Implied rights are implicit in the expectations of the mutual parties of a relationship—like the employment relationship. Usually, when employees talk about their rights, they are not referring to contract provisions. Employees use the term in a broader sense. For example, if an employee feels his supervisor has treated him ill, he speaks of his rights as an individual with human dignity. For instance, an employee who is publicly reprimanded in front of other employees is likely to feel that his rights as a human being with dignity have been violated by the supervisor. (*Food processing and packing*)

> As I see it, there are two kinds of rights: human rights and rights of contract. In respect to human rights, we might think of the preamble to the Declaration of Independence, mentioning rights to "life, liberty, and the pursuit of happiness." In the employment relationship, employees also have such rights as human beings, like rights to fair treatment and the right to be recognized as an integral part of a productive enterprise. (*Automobile assembly*)

These interviews indicate strongly that many personnel directors are highly sensitive to the need to justify decisions as essentially fair. And fairness is predicated on a view of the employee as a person invested with the right to be treated with dignity and restraint. Although fairness is conceived as a human-relations concept rather than a legal one, and does not necessarily carry with it a determinate set of restraints on management, it is clear that at least some commitment to procedural regularity is contemplated.

Scope of managerial control.   If the employee has a right to a private sphere of life, beyond the purview of management's control, his sense of personal worth and security may be enhanced. The acceptance of self-restraint, with respect to the scope of control, was explored by asking for responses to the following situation:

> Joe went out with a bunch of boys on Saturday night. Unfortunately Joe had a little too much to drink and he got into a brawl at a tavern. The police came and arrested Joe along with some of the others, and Joe spent the night at the city jail. Also, at the time of the fight at the tavern, Joe's foreman happened to be walking by, so he saw Joe being hauled off in the police wagon. When Joe reported for work on Monday morning, the foreman told him that he was giving Joe a five-day suspension without pay, because Joe had acted on Saturday night in a manner "unbecoming an employee of our company." The foreman said, "It is very important for our company to have a good name in town, and we can't have a good name if our employees get into trouble like you did." Joe, however, felt the five-day suspension was unfair. Joe said, "What I do on my own after working hours is my affair—it's none of the company's business."

A majority of our sample (61 per cent [27]) felt that management has no control over the off-duty behavior of the employee unless such behavior *directly* affects the firm adversely. As one personnel director put it:

> In a case like this the employee would have a grievance as long as his conduct outside the plant did not affect his job inside. Here we had a case of a man who cut his wife with a knife in an argument and was sent to jail. We would have re-employed him after he got out, even though he had only been here a short time. However, we did not re-employ him because we did not have an opening then. But we were not concerned with what he did at home. (*Electrical manufacturing*)

An additional twelve respondents (27 per cent) endorsed the idea that there is a legitimate limitation on managerial interest in off-duty conduct but did not believe that the company's interest was limited to activity that directly and *demonstrably* affected it adversely. It was considered enough that the off-duty conduct *might* harm the firm. This approach allows a great deal more discretion in disciplining employees for off-duty "misconduct."

Only four of the respondents felt that management has an almost unlimited concern for what employees do off the job. "Employees have to be good citizens as well as good employees," said the personnel director for an oil refinery. This would leave to management a great deal of latitude in deciding whether the employee has been a "good citizen."

Among the twenty-seven who held the majority position, seven felt that the firm's scope of legitimate concern was much broader for managerial personnel than for nonsupervisory employees. All seven pointed out that their responses would have been different if the person involved had been a member of management.

Employees of banks, offices, and retail stores are often felt to have greater responsibilities toward the firm than their counterparts in factories. Our interviews suggest that personnel managers consider white-collar employees more responsible for maintaining the good reputation of the firm and therefore legitimately required to refrain from conduct that may endanger public confidence in the firm. Of the ten firms employing mainly white-collar workers, the personnel directors of only two endorsed without qualification the idea that alleged misconduct off the job must be directly related to job performance. The other eight felt that the misconduct was punishable if it were shown that it might hurt the firm's reputation. This attitude was expressed as follows:

> If the employee were working as a laborer in a construction job, say, without public contact, and he wasn't fouling up his work detail, the company would be harsh if it took this action. On the other hand, if he were in a position of some kind of public trust, as in a bank, then management would have some reason to discipline him. (*Commercial bank*)

We conclude that there is a clear preference among these respondents for limiting management's jurisdiction over the lives of employees, and that where this jurisdiction is extended it must be justified. Although some would in effect place the burden of proof on the employee, most would require the company to show specific damage to its interests.

Job security and occupational identity. As a matter of personnel policy, apart from the requirements of contract, does an employee acquire any special claim to job security through the years of service he has given to the company or through the training he has undergone? These issues go to the sense of personal worth, for that worth is recognized if "membership" is in some sense an accrued right and if "job identity" is honored.

The following hypothetical case deals with the effect of seniority on the mitigation of discipline:

> George had worked for Smith Company for twenty years and had a record as a good employee. However, one day George got into an argument with another employee named Phil who had only been at the plant for a year and a half. The argument got more and more heated, and finally George and Phil stepped outside and began to fight with each other. Just after the fight started, however, their foreman came by and broke it up. Then the foreman asked, "Who started the fight?" Neither George nor Phil would answer the question—each man said he guessed they had both started the fight at the same time. Then the foreman recommended that they both be discharged. He said, "You both know that the penalty for fighting on company property is automatic discharge, and since neither one of you will say who started the fight, I am going to have both of you discharged." Phil didn't complain about the discharge action, but George said, "You mean you would fire me after the twenty years of good service I put in here at the Smith Company?" The foreman said, "In something like this, it doesn't make any difference how many years you have been here." But George still felt that it was unfair to discharge him for this action, even though he felt it would be fair if he had to take a lesser form of discipline, since he admitted that he was as guilty as Phil was.

Opinion on the correct course of action was almost evenly divided. Nineteen respondents (44 per cent) felt that the employee should have been given some special consideration; an equal number said that management handled the case properly. Six were unsure of the extent to which they should allow a man's seniority to influence the decision on discipline.

Typical comments by personnel directors who favored considering seniority a mitigating factor were:

> In this case management was within its rights. However, if this were the first time this happened, I would be inclined to give less severe discipline. The employee would certainly have grounds to complain in view of his long service. (*Public utility*)

> This is a tough situation. If it involved two short-time people, it would probably be better to get rid of them both. If this were a twenty-year man, then I just wouldn't see the fight. I mean that! I would say to the other men around the plant, "Say, I heard a rumor that there was a fight out here the other day between George and Phil. Did you see it?" Then after everybody said, "No, I didn't see it," I would forget about it and George would probably appreciate what I had done. On the other hand, if it developed so that I had to administer discipline, I would let the younger man go and I would try to keep George after a severe warning, saying, "You know I could fire you for this" and then perhaps give him a week's suspension. If a twenty-year man were discharged for an offense like this, he

would certainly have cause to complain, since too many years of his life and livelihood would be tied up in the years of service he had given the company. (*Petroleum products*)

Five of these respondents volunteered that to avoid discrimination, they would have to impose a lesser penalty on "Phil." Another felt that in the case of fighting both employees should be discharged but for a less serious offense he would give the senior man special consideration.

Those who thought management acted properly in this case mentioned both the severity of the offense and the necessity to apply rules uniformly:

The foreman and the company were right in taking this action in regard to fighting, provided they consistently enforced this kind of rule in the past. Fighting is not excusable, unless a man is simply attacked and thus is forced to defend himself. The more years of service a man has, the more he should know not to get into fights at work. Fighting, drunkenness, insubordination, and dishonesty are all inexcusable offenses. (*Paper products*)

Management here was within its rights. It should make no difference in discipline who starts a fight—the employees should get their differences ironed out another way. Both men were equally wrong, whether they started the fight or not. Also it makes no difference how long a man has been on the job. We had one case of fighting on company property like this. One man had considerably longer service than the other, but both men got fired. The longer-service man wanted to put in a grievance, but the union agreed with us that management action was proper in this case. (*Electronics manufacturing*)

What is fair for one is fair for all. It is most important to avoid discrimination in discipline, regardless of length of service, so I would agree with the management action in this case. (*Food processing*)

Management was within its rights here. You can't have two standards of punishment—one for high seniority and one for low seniority employees. Discipline has to be applied across the board, or otherwise you are open to the charge of discrimination. (*Cement and aluminum plant*)

The disagreement among personnel managers noted here reflects a basic dilemma in the application of fair-play standards. It is unjust to discharge the newer employee and keep the older one when both have committed the same offense. It is also unjust to dismiss, without special consideration, a man who may have given the best years of his life to the firm and has earned the right to be treated as a permanent member of the enterprise. Our case posed the issue in acute form. If the situation had not involved an immediate issue of discrimination, the responses might well have been more favorable to the acceptance of seniority as a mitigating factor.

Another hypothetical case dealt with the skilled employee's claim to an occupational identity:

> Bob was a skilled precision die-maker. One day he was asked by a plant superintendent temporarily to take a less-skilled job on a production line at a slightly lower rate of pay, because there was at that time a lack of work in his usual occupation. However, Bob refused to take the less-skilled job and said he would rather take a temporary layoff without pay until there was work for him in his regular job. The superintendent argued that management must be able to assign workers where they are needed in order to get out production, and that if Bob refused to take this temporary assignment, he would be subject to discharge. Bob said in reply, "I was hired as a precision die-maker and that's what I intend to do." Suppose the company then went ahead and fired Bob.

Thirty-three of our respondents (75 per cent) felt that the right to job identity did not exist or that it existed only when supported by specific provisions of the collective contract. The following are typical comments:

> Some contracts specifically give an employee a choice of taking a layoff or accepting another job (at the employee's regular rate) under such conditions. If the contract is silent on this matter, then the employee should take the new assignment or he is guilty of insubordination. (*Paper products manufacturing*)

> Management is always within its rights to offer an employee other work, and no employee has a right to tell the company what he will or will not do. The company has the right to discharge a man if it goes this far. It is a basic right of management to assign work. We once fired a union president because he refused to do a certain work assignment. (*Petroleum products*)

There was, however, a significant minority (eleven) who thought management was wrong in this situation. One personnel executive said:

> If an employee is reassigned in an overlapping skill area, he has no legitimate ground for complaint, unless he was reassigned at a lower pay rate. Then he certainly would have grounds to complain. Thus a tool and die maker might be legitimately transferred to machinists' work, but if his reassignment to a production line would be a bald violation of his skill, then he would have a legitimate right to complain, unless he were given the option of a temporary layoff. (*Automobile assembly*)

While there is support for the protection of occupational identity, this support is much more likely to be recognized for highly skilled employees than for unskilled or semi-skilled workers; and it is significantly weakened when it runs up against conflicting commitments to (a) a policy of equal treatment for all employees and (b) the protection of managerial discretion in the division of labor.

On this issue, as on that of job security, there may be considerable sympathy for the values at stake *abstractly considered,* and a readiness to implement them when there are no conflicting pressures. But the new managerial doctrine has apparently not produced a clear consensus on seniority and job identity as vested rights to be weighed whenever decisions are made that affect the individual. The fact that issues of "vesting" are raised undoubtedly complicates the response. Such issues can be avoided when general standards of fairness applicable to all are in question, but when the demand is for recognition of vested rights, however justified on human-relations premises, the prospects of uncoerced managerial support are limited.

Procedural regularity. We have already indicated that fairness as a general ideal entails some acceptance of procedural limitations on administrative decision, and is therefore a source of self-restraint. We explored some aspects of procedural fairness by asking for responses to three hypothetical situations. One of these dealt with the appropriateness of discipline for an offense apparently beyond the control of the individual:

> The rules of Ajax Company state that an employee who is over one hour late to work without phoning in to notify his supervisor is subject to disciplinary action. All the employees clearly understood this rule. However, Jim, who worked at the Ajax Company, was two hours late one morning. Jim claimed that his car broke down and that he had to get out and fix it in a spot where there was no telephone nearby, so he was unable to call in. When he finally got to work, his supervisor recommended that Jim receive a written warning to be placed in his personnel file and told Jim that he should keep his car in better working order so that this didn't happen again, because it caused a considerable problem in running the office that morning. "If this happens again," the supervisor said, "I will have to recommend that you be given a one-day suspension without pay. It is essential that our employees be impressed with the importance of getting to work on time." Jim, on the other hand, felt that it was unfair for him to receive the written reprimand this time. Jim said, "I know I violated the company rule, but it wasn't my fault my car broke down where I couldn't get to a phone so I don't think the written reprimand is fair."

Nineteen of the respondents (43 per cent) approved the action taken by management; another twelve (27 per cent) qualified their approval considerably; and thirteen (30 per cent) strongly disapproved.

The reasons given for upholding management in this case were quite varied. There was considerable feeling that the rule should be upheld and that the employee's responsibility for getting to work on time should be underlined. On the other hand, the punishment imposed was perceived as mild and this led at least seven of the personnel directors to feel that the employee had little basis for complaint.

Among those who were more doubtful about management's course of action, four held that a verbal warning would have been sufficient; three that the discipline was unwise but justifiable in view of the company's rules; three that management should have taken into account the employee's past record or years of service; and two that management was technically within its rights but the action was an example of poor management since the rules were being applied inflexibly.

The majority of those disapproving stated explicitly that the employee should not be punished for something beyond his control. Repetition of the offense might cast doubt on the veracity of the employee's excuse, and might justify more alertness to the problem of chronic tardiness, but it was stressed that management should take account of mitigating circumstances and avoid mechanical application of rules.

These responses do not indicate any great sensitivity to the complexities of government by rules. Especially wanting is a ready understanding that the raising of a standard defense (in this case, an unforeseeable occurrence causing lateness) is not necessarily subversive of a system of rules.

Another procedural issue is the significance of "past practice" for the legitimacy of punishment. If a rule is "on the books," but has not been enforced, a question is raised regarding the propriety of sudden enforcement without additional notice, as in the following situation:

> Harry was smoking one day in an area where there were posted "No Smoking" signs. His foreman saw Harry violating the company rule and recommended that Harry be given a disciplinary layoff for five days. Harry complained that this rule had not been enforced for many years and that many other employees were in the habit of smoking in this area. Harry said, "I can't understand why I was picked out among all the others who have also violated this rule." The foreman said in reply, "We have been worried for some time now about the laxity of the observance of safety regulations in this plant, and we figured that it is about time that we began to enforce them. If we don't enforce safety regulations, somebody is liable to get hurt. So we had to make an example of you, Harry, so everybody would get on the ball." But Harry still didn't feel that it was fair to pick on him.

In responding to this hypothetical case, almost 80 per cent (thirty-five) of the personnel directors indicated their disapproval of management's action. For this group, the issue of notice was central. Only after all employees had been put on notice that violations would result in discipline would it be fair to give this man a layoff:

Management was at fault here in being lax itself. They should advise employees first about enforcing the rule. This business of giving adequate notice in advance of enforcing personnel regulations is a pretty cardinal procedure in personnel management everywhere now. (*Airline*)

Three of the respondents, while upholding management's right to discipline in this case, felt that the punishment was too severe. Inconsistent enforcement should have mitigated the penalty. Even among the five who · could be classified as essentially supporting management's action, there was little enthusiasm for the supervisor's judgment.

Apparently the idea of notice is well established as an ingredient of fairness, at least among these personnel managers. However, in the situation as presented, the principle of fair warning was easy to affirm. There was no urgent conflict of principles, or any practical threat offered by the offense. Thus, in contrast to some of the earlier hypothetical cases, this one tests only an abstract commitment to a single principle.

In the administration of criminal justice, procedural regularity means above all that steps are taken to be sure that the accused has in fact committed the offense of which he is charged. For minor offenses, the standard of proof is probably very low. In more serious situations, there is a reluctance to inflict punishment unless charges are substantially borne out by the facts available, preserving to the accused a right to be heard. This reluctance was reflected in responses to the following account:

> In a certain company, tools had been reported missing from benches in the shop for some time. Then one day, a plant worker by the name of Tom was stopped by a plant guard while Tom was going out the gate to lunch. The guard found a crescent wrench in the pocket of Tom's overalls. Then Tom was taken to the office of the plant superintendent. The superintendent said to Tom, "I am going to have you discharged from your job, because you know that it is against company rules to go out the gate with company tools in your pockets. We have had too many tools stolen or lost recently, and as I recall, there were some tools missing from your bench last month." Tom answered, "I have always tried to be careful with tools. Today I just forgot the wrench was in my pocket. It was only a mistake on my part." But the superintendent felt that Tom's answer was not good enough for him, so he insisted that Tom be discharged from his job as an untrustworthy employee. Tom felt that the superintendent was being unfair.

Less than 10 per cent (four) of those interviewed would have been willing, given the facts as presented, to discipline the employee for untrustworthiness. Even though the employee had broken a rule, over half (twenty-seven) contended that sufficient evidence had not been presented to warrant serious discipline. The following are typical comments on the importance of adequate proof of intent:

> This case indicates that a hasty decision was made. We would look at a man's past record first. Unless there was other evidence of stealing and unless intent to steal is proven—and this is hard to do—then management would not be within its rights in taking this action. For example, we would want to investigate whether the man made careful preparation to conceal the item, as evidence of intent. We have found in the past that we can't make discharges for stealing stick if we have not proven intent. We have changed our approach on this through experience with this kind of thing. (*Aircraft maintenance*)

> On all these cases we would really need more facts. This is always the case in disciplinary actions anywhere, incidentally. We would want to know this man's seniority, his previous record, if there were any statements made by the man to other employees that he intended to walk out the gate with tools, etc. We've had cases like this here. If we felt it was just an accident, we only warned the man not to let it happen again. (*Automobile assembly*)

> This case involves a question of fact. Did he intend to steal this item? This might be bolstered by more information on the other supplies missing. The bank, for example, is very careful in suggesting that someone has taken money. In the case above, however, they have not established that the employee was stealing. There is not enough information upon which to base such a serious accusation. Therefore, they had no right to take this action against the employee. (*Commercial bank*)

Thirteen other respondents struck a somewhat different note. They held that the employee was subject to discipline, not for being untrustworthy, or specifically for stealing, but simply for having broken a rule. This approach avoids the difficult issue of proving intent to keep the tool, yet it retains some basis for disciplinary action. This "mechanical" or, perhaps, "behavioral" approach to government by rules, which looks only to external conformity, is a theme discernible in many of the responses to the hypothetical cases. In part this may reflect a naive approach to "law and order," as if justice were blind to subjective states of mind; but it is also convenient as a way of sidestepping vexing and costly appraisals of human conduct.

Politics and Human Relations

Neither the values affirmed by personnel managers, nor the human-relations doctrine summarized earlier, constitute a fully developed system of industrial justice. But the "legal" potential in the human-relations perspective has not been given sufficient recognition. This is understandable, because at first blush and in its early stages that movement of thought and practice seemed notably indifferent to issues of power and justice.

The lack of a proper appreciation of power, and of appropriate responses to it, has been the main burden of the heavy criticism to which human relations in industry has been exposed. This general indictment is based on the following special findings:[75]

(1) Human relations perceives the worker as a deployable instrument rather than as an autonomous being who has needs and objectives of his own. As one critic put it, "the individual is not seen as a goal-setting or goal-achieving creature. Rather, he is considered an inert 'element' that does not act unless acted upon and to be manipulated by means of human relations 'skills.' "[76] The aim of human relations is to produce contented workers much as the dairy farm seeks contented cows. Thus "the social science of the factory researchers is not a science of man, but a cow-sociology."[77]

In fact, as we have argued, human-relations theory does not presume that the worker is inert or passive, without a dynamism of his own. The valid point of this criticism is that the individual's characteristics, however dynamic, are "facts" to be dealt with by whatever measures are effective and least costly to the end that *management's* goals may be fulfilled. *The individual is not encouraged to have a will of his own.* The inherent tensions between the goals of the individual and those of the organization are not accepted as continuing parameters of industrial life, to be built into the human engineer's model of what is a viable and desirable form of organization.

(2) The organizational context of human action is slighted, especially the manifest and latent power contained in that context. In the human-relations perspective "labor" and "management" are seen as categories of persons, at best as social roles, not as organized power blocs. Elton Mayo, the "father" of industrial human relations, was vigorous in refuting the "rabble hypothesis"—the idea that management confronted workers as atomized individuals rather than as members of viable social groupings. But his vision of the group was foreshortened, focused mainly on the

---

[75] Many of these criticisms are discussed and rebutted in Landsberger, *op. cit.*, Chaps. 3–4.
[76] W. A. Koivisto, "Value, Theory, and Fact in Industrial Sociology," *American Journal of Sociology*, 58 (May, 1953), 570.
[77] Daniel Bell, "Adjusting Men to Machines," *Commentary*, 3 (January, 1947), 88.

"informal" relations that lend psychic and social coherence to the factory floor.

One result was the short shrift given to trade unions. To many critics this was the most obvious and the principal failing. In part this criticism reflected the lack of attention to unions in *Management and the Worker* and other representative literature of the human-relations school. It seemed naive, and subservient to management's anti-union perspective, to ignore the role of unions in industrial life. "When unions are ignored they are more likely to be taken as symptoms of trouble than as possible means of solving worthy problems."[78]

More important, however, was the sensed psychological bias of the new engineers. Human relations was the invention and the domain of the applied social psychologist. His skills would lead him in some directions but not in others. Mainly he would be concerned with the psychic organism responding to immediate settings marked by frustration, opaqueness, status-anxiety, and the like. He would worry most about motivation and communication. He would not take too seriously the possibilities of larger institutional change, not because he opposed it, but because its study was outside his field of competence and sensitivity. Therefore his influence, however benign, would deflect attention from the main agenda —the reconstruction of authority, of decision-making, of industrial policy.

(3) Human relations celebrates harmony and denigrates conflict. Critics who welcomed the rise of trade unionism were also inclined to stress that the clash of competing interests could not and should not be avoided. Human relations seemed to offer a utopian and enfeebling ideal of worker-management collaboration, to be achieved by resolving tensions and sublimating aggressions. The alternative was to see labor-management relations as essentially and properly political.

These criticisms were not entirely fair, for certainly *Management and the Worker* did not shrink from the recognition of conflicting aims and unfulfilled aspirations. One of its main findings could be read as the location of incipient unionism in the social structure of the plant.[79] Never-

---

[78] C. Wright Mills, "The Contributions of Sociology to Studies of Industrial Relations," *Proceedings*, Industrial Relations Research Association (1948), I, 212.

[79] This was recognized in Clinton S. Golden and Harold J. Ruttenberg, *Dynamics of Industrial Democracy* (New York: Harper & Row, 1942), 182. Landsberger, *op. cit.*, 64, points out that "the authors committed a well-nigh incredible sin of omission by not recognizing in 1939 that the conditions which they had observed some eight years earlier were precisely the ones which accounted for the rise of formal unionism in the intervening years. Their own analysis would have been fully congruent with such a conclusion."

theless, the critics were basically correct. A political perspective did not inform the diagnosis or guide the therapy.

But what is a "political perspective?" The critics of human relations have tended to equate participation with conflict and politics with power. While this has provided a healthy counterpoint to the social philosophy of Elton Mayo, it does not offer an adequate interpretation of industrial evolution. That evolution is marked by a synthesis of the social, the political, and the legal.

If human relations is to be assimilated to a political and legal model, the following conditions must be met:

1. **Employees should be treated as competent participants in a civic order.** Although human relations has emphasized participation, the latter has had a psychic, interpersonal, and *private* cast. The important thing is to "clue the man in," to make him feel wanted and appreciated, to allay his fears, to offer him a vehicle of personal fulfillment. These efforts may be humane and gratifying. They may mitigate authoritarian administration. But they do not necessarily presume that the individual can make up his own mind to pursue his rightful ends through a public process.

One might treat a slave humanely, with due regard to good "human relations." His personal and emotional needs would be considered, if only as a price to be paid for reliable service. But this would still leave the slave a dependent "unperson," incapable of asserting his own will save privately and by indirection. The political perspective asks that this basic dependency and incompetence be transformed; it blends into a legal perspective as the transition is made to orderly process for the invocation of rights and the redress of grievances.

Properly understood, therefore, the quality of participation sought in a "political" model of industrial order is not conflict and struggle, as such, but the capacity for legitimate self-assertion. The underlying assumption is that such capacity is a necessary condition for the full attainment of dignity and self-respect. The latter cannot rest on favor or good will alone. It must in some way be warranted by the institutional order and available as the basis of a claim of right.

2. **As a condition of civic competence, employees need organizational support.** To be effective, civic participation must be founded in latent power. This in turn presumes that the members of the polity are not an atomized aggregate confronting a single center of power—in this case the command structure of the firm. Rather, the employee's participation in the enterprise as a whole is mediated by his membership in relatively

autonomous subgroups or parallel organizations. These may take many forms, including kinship, departmental affiliation, political associations, and trade-unions. The only essential criterion is the capacity of the group to act as an independent center of support and influence.

The human-relations movement has been sensitive to some aspects of the group structure of the enterprise and has partly understood the concept of mediated participation. But the emphasis has been apolitical. Where group conflict is recognized, it is more as a symptom of ineffective management, or as a "natural process" limiting rationality, than as an appropriate means of clarifying and resolving policy issues. In its perception of group structure, human relations has been most impressed by the spontaneous outcropping of teams, cliques, and status groupings. The technical system of the plant or office is seen as a framework within which shared experience takes place and group cohesion emerges. Sometimes this cohesion serves the aims of management, sometimes it undermines them. The fundamental process is seen as responsive behavior resulting in group formation. It is not viewed as the creation of a legitimate setting within which ordered controversy among conflicting interests may take place.

To be sure, the employee may find protection and support in the fellowship of his immediate co-workers, and this finding has been a keystone of human-relations theory. But a truly political model of industrial organization cannot rest content with such evidence of group support. For that would reduce politics to power, without regard to how power is created or expressed. If the plant is a quasi-polity, a vehicle of civic participation, then the forms of participation must be public and legitimate.

3. In the quest for harmony within the enterprise, the strategic process should be accommodative, not integrative. Elton Mayo asked, "How can mankind's capacity for spontaneous collaboration be restored?"[80] The perspective of social harmony seeks out the conditions of oneness, of integration. And the mechanisms of integration are basically psychological: the internalization of common values, norms, and disciplines; the overcoming of barriers to mutual understanding.

Now consensus is also an ingredient of the political model. But on this count the political realm differs from human-relations in two ways:

First, political consensus is something more than the like-mindedness that springs from interpersonal cohesion or solidarity. To speak of "consensus" in the primary group would be misleading, for the latter is char-

---

[80] Roethlisberger and Dickson, *op. cit.*, Preface.

acteristically a union of private persons seeking psychic fulfillment. Consensus in the political order is agreement on publicly acknowledged principles and ends. Therefore the political presumes a certain self-awareness, an evolution beyond the "mechanical solidarity" of undifferentiated society. Consensus becomes public, and thereby political, when private, person-centered solidarities are transcended.

Second, in political consensus contending interests are recognized, not submerged. Demands for unmitigated compliance, for eradication of all "special interests," or for psychic union with a charismatic figure, are alien to the political process. Politics is subverted when it is transformed into administration or when it is diffused into cultural or pseudo-cultural symbolism. True civic participation affirms the worth of constituent individuals and groups. It does not absorb and extinguish them.

Totalitarianism is sometimes considered the apotheosis of politics, and in a sense that is true, for in the total state there is no private sanctuary. But totalitarianism is also the principle of anti-politics. It seeks to reduce civic participation to administrative subordination, and it offers symbolic surrogates for political consciousness. When total integration is sought, politics loses its distinctive contribution. Coercion and manipulation, not persuasion and alliance, become the preferred instruments of social action.

The lesson is that accommodation—the mutual adjustment of groups that preserve their distinctive identities and interests—is the only road to harmony consistent with a political model of industrial organization. That model is neither a derogation of harmony nor an affirmation of conflict. It does not deny the significance of common values and shared experience for the creation of consensus. But it does say that personal and group integrity are the touchstones of health in a political community.

Thus understood, the political model enriches and supplements, it does not supplant, the perspective of human relations in industry. Political experience cannot be divorced from modes of perception, response, and relatedness. How men perceive and treat one another—above all, how they allocate and act out the value of respect, including self-respect—is vital to political reality. Politics reduced to naked contests of power is to that extent debased. Without a concern for human relations, including precisely the values that are stressed in industrial studies, political life loses its capacity to enhance the autonomy, competence, and dignity of the individual.

The human-relations and political perspectives find a sustaining synthesis in the emergence of a legal order. As we have seen, human relations has its own impulse to curb authority and safeguard respect. But the impulse is not a guarantee, and without a guarantee the employee remains dependent on the goodwill or self-interest of others. The alternative is not dissolution into warring camps. It is the creation of a constitutional framework within which (1) legitimated controversy may proceed and (2) what was a gift of grace may be transformed into a claim of right.

Chapter 4 | *Collective Bargaining and Legal Evolution*

THE PRECEDING CHAPTER ASSESSED WHAT MIGHT BE called the "legal worth" of rational administration. The impulse to create a regime of rules was located in bureaucratization as a social process and in the effort to optimize the use of human resources. But it was also argued that those forces are in themselves inadequate to bring about the "legalization" of industrial life. To them must be added a political dimension—the creation of new organizations, the struggle for recognition and power, the demand for new foundations of authority and new forms of participation.

In contemporary American legal literature there is a curious bifurcation between the law of employment and labor law. Labor law deals mainly with the legal status of trade unions, the techniques of economic pressure, the duty to bargain, the establishment of bargaining units, the nature and enforceability of collective agreements, arbitration, and union democracy. On the other hand, a standard work on *The Employment Relation and the Law*[1] covers protective legislation affecting employees, including equal opportunity in employment, workmen's compensation, unemployment compensation, minimum wage-and-hour standards, old-age security, and other welfare legislation. There is no integrated "law of employment," although such a body of law is taking shape, mainly within the crucible of collective bargaining, with important assistance from public welfare policy.

---

[1] Benjamin Aaron (ed.), *The Employment Relation and the Law* (Boston: Little, Brown and Company, 1957).

Although labor law is still chiefly the law of labor-management relations, inevitably and increasingly it goes beyond the clash and accommodation of institutions to treat of the emergent rights of persons. Institutions are properly means to human ends, and in the long run they will be thus perceived, given half a chance by history. In labor relations that historical opportunity has made itself felt, and we can discern an evolution from arbitrary power to self-help to accommodation to the beginnings of a rule of law.

In tracing that evolution, we have a special concern for the work of law in mediating social change. Here the focus is on legal creativity, on the special contribution legal forms can make in providing the conditions for constructive outcomes. The argument is not that law "reflects" social change, or that it "determines" social change. Rather, we see the law as a vehicle of evolution that is itself transformed as its distinctive work is done.

Toward the Prerogative Contract

Throughout its history, the Anglo-American law of employment has been a changing blend of three basic policies: (a) the protection and guidance of a distinctive social relation, that of employer and employee; (b) the exercise of police power to regulate the terms and conditions of employment in the public interest; and (c) freedom of contract. By taking a look backward, and considering how these elements and the relations among them have been transformed, we can attain a fuller understanding of modern labor law. For that law is itself a still-evolving variant of the historic blend. In tracing this development, our main concern is with the legal foundations of managerial authority, employee rights, and the relation of these to the public interest in a workable economy.

For six hundred years—from the fourteenth century to the end of the nineteenth—the law of employment, such as it was, relied on the legal imagery of "master and servant." Toward the end of that period, as industrialism came into full swing, these legal concepts weakened and became anachronistic. But for a very long time the ancient usage persisted, although increasingly subordinated to the idea of contract. This transition is worth a brief inspection, if only as a case history of the effort to maintain a distinctive social relation while assimilating it to an abstract legal form.

In the classic view, the law of master and servant is a branch of the law of persons. Writing in the middle of the eighteenth century, Blackstone spoke of master and servant as one of the three most important relations of private life, together with marriage and parenthood. Even the late nineteenth-century treatises include master and servant in the law of persons or, more narrowly, in the law of domestic relations.[2]

The law of master and servant was rooted in a society in which everyone was presumed to belong somewhere, and the great parameters of belonging were kinship, locality, religion, occupation, and social class. In all spheres of life, including spiritual communion, *subordination to legitimate authority* was thought to be a natural, inevitable, and even welcome accompaniment of moral grace and practical virtue.

The old law of master and servant looked to the household as a model and saw in its just governance the foundations of orderly society. The household model made sense in an overwhelmingly agricultural economy where hired labor, largely permanent, supplemented the work of family members and all were subject to the authority and tutelage of the father-manager. The model also fit the early pattern of work and training among skilled artisans. In this setting, the relation of master and servant was highly diffuse and paternalistic. Work was carried out in the house of the master or in a small shop nearby. The workman lived as a member of the household and often remained for life with the same master. It was against this background that the law of master and servant developed.

The position of the master or servant, though originating in contract, was conceived as a legal status. It was entirely consistent with the legal theory that at least some terms of the relation, such as its duration and the wages to be paid, be subject to bargaining and mutual assent. Blackstone had no difficulty in referring to a "contract" between the parties.[3] But custom and public policy, not the will of the parties, defined the implicit framework of mutual rights and obligations. In the routine case, most of the terms and conditions of employment were implied by law rather than set by mutual agreement. That implication spelled out the legal obligations naturally and properly assumed by anyone who entered into the master-servant relation. Above all, *it was not contemplated that the parties would design their own relationship.* As in the case of mar-

---

[2] For example, James Schouler, *A Treatise on the Law of Domestic Relations; Embracing Husband and Wife, Parent and Child, Guardian and Ward, Infancy, and Master and Servant* (Boston: Little, Brown and Company, 1870). For Blackstone, too, master and servant was one of the domestic relations, which comprised the private branch of the law of persons. See Book II in Sir William Blackstone, *Commentaries on the Laws of England*, W. C. Jones (ed.) (San Francisco: Bancroft-Whitney, 1915).

[3] *Op. cit.*, 587. In his notes Jones states: "The relation of master and servant is essentially one of *status*" (581).

riage, the relation might be entered voluntarily but its character was fixed by law.

Insofar as there was a contract, it involved personal service, not a mere sale of goods. Nor was personal service conceived of as specialized labor power. It was a general contribution to the needs of the enterprise, be it farm, household, or craftsman's shop. In some vague but important sense, it was assumed that the whole person was committed to the relation. And this was the real basis for thinking of it as a status relation and assimilating it to the law of persons.

These premises, blending contract and status, were reflected in specific legal rules and doctrines. This does not mean that there was an explicit application of clearly enunciated principles. Rather, in keeping with the character of the common law, the rules developed unevenly and empirically, in response to practical necessities and opportunities. The master-servant imagery symbolized a shared understanding and provided some touchstones that could be taken for granted. As so often in the law, the relation of principle and rule was tenuous, allowing for much discordance and ambiguity, as well as wide latitude for unguided change.

The following are the more important legal attributes of the master-servant relation, as they were operative in the seventeenth and eighteenth centuries:[4]

1. The master had general authority to discipline the servant. The status of master carried with it the right of command. The master controlled and supervised the work of the servant. This he did of right, under the color of lawful authority. He could issue orders on any matter touching the conduct of the enterprise and expect to be obeyed. The scope of authority was very broad and might properly encompass many aspects of the servant's private life, particularly in the case of apprentices and indentured servants.[5] The breadth of authority had several practical foundations, including the master's responsibility for tutelage; his liability for the misconduct of the servant; and his proprietary interest in the servant's

---

[4] For details on this period, we are much indebted to Richard B. Morris, *Government and Labor in Early America* (New York: Columbia University Press, 1946).

[5] Lamenting the breakdown of an older pattern, Daniel Defoe wrote: "The point of conscience, indeed, seems to be out of the question now between master and servant; and as few masters concern themselves with the souls, nay, scarce with the morals, of their servants, either to instruct them or inform them of their duty to God or man, much less to restrain them by force, or correct them, as was anciently practised; so, few servants concern themselves in a conscientious discharge of their duty to their masters; so that the great law of subordination is destroyed, and the relative duties on both sides are neglected . . . so that a master seems now to have nothing to do with his apprentice, any other than in what relates to his business." *The Complete English Tradesman*, I, 105–106. First published in 1726.

contribution, potential as well as actual. The master could "correct" his servant for neglect of duty, defiance of authority, or other misconduct.

With respect to the authority of the master, two points should be noted: (1) The master's right to command, and the servant's duty to obey, were incidents of status and not terms of an agreement. (2) The master's authority was limited, at least in contemplation of law. He could administer "moderate" correction.[6] His commands must be lawful. He was answerable to the local court for cruel and oppressive conduct.[7]

2. The relation was not terminable at will. For the "ideal" case, the law visualized a relatively enduring relation and a commitment on both sides to honor the contract until the term of service was ended. Out of this image emerged the presumption that "if the hiring be general without any particular time limited, the law construes it to be a hiring for a year; upon a principle of natural equity, that the servant shall serve, and the master maintain him, throughout all the revolutions of the respective seasons; as well when there is work to be done as when there is not; but the contract may be made for any larger or smaller term."[8] This applied mainly to domestic or menial servants, broadly understood to include all those who worked *intra moenia* (within the walls), a figurative expression for all who belonged to the establishment[9] and were not merely casual laborers or artisans contracting to perform specific services. In addition,

---

[6] Blackstone, *op. cit.*, 590. In Tapping Reeve's treatise, *The Law of Baron and Femme, of Parent and Child, Guardian and Ward, Master and Servant* (Burlington, Vt.; first ed. 1818), it is stated that "the master has a right to give moderate corporal correction to his servant, for disobedience to his lawful commands, negligence in his business, or for insolent behavior." A fn. added to the 1846 ed. reads: "The early authorities clearly sustain the principle of the text, that the master may moderately correct his servant for negligence or misbehavior. . . . But this power does not grow out of the contract of hiring, and its lawfulness has been denied by a writer of eminent authority, as not being consonant with the spirit and genius of contract. . . . In Pennsylvania, this right is expressly denied . . . and the better opinion now is that it cannot be extended beyond apprentices and menial servants under age" (374).

[7] Morris, *op. cit.*, 470 ff.

[8] Blackstone, *op. cit.*, 587.

[9] See Schouler, *op. cit.*, 600: "Were the writer then untrammelled by authority, his treatment of this topic, as one of the domestic relations, would be confined to what are denominated at common law menial servants, so called from being *intra moenia*, or rather to domestic servants, extending the definition to all such as are employed in and about a family in carrying on the household concerns, whether their occupations be within or without of doors, so long as they constitute part of the family." It appears that this nineteenth-century writer would have preferred to restrict the master-servant relation so as to exclude the farm hand, but in the earlier period domestic service and husbandry were considered together. Thus the above quotation from Blackstone is in a section headed "menial servants," but it clearly deals with the non-casual agricultural worker. Morris, *op. cit.*, 219, reports that "annual employment was customary in such occupations as domestic service and husbandry, but in others the custom of annual hiring does not appear to have gained a foothold."

of course, apprentices and indentured servants were committed for a term of years.

On the employer's side, the right of dismissal was limited by the requirement of notice, normally three months for "domestic" servants.[10] Dismissal without just cause before the end of the term of employment could be restrained by law.[11] These restrictions probably had less to do with justice than with protecting the community against additional burdens for the care of the poor.

The fourteenth-century Statutes of Labourers forbade the workman "to depart from the service before the end of the term agreed upon without reasonable cause of license"[12] and also established the rule against enticement of servants from one master to another. The law against unauthorized quitting was an effort to deal with the problem of extreme labor scarcity following the ravages of the Black Death. At the same time, this rule, together with the prohibition of enticement, affirmed the proprietary interest of the master in the servant, or at least in the service purchased by the contract of hiring.

Although the idea of a proprietary interest is compatible with the principle of contract, it seems to have had a special place in the early history of the employment relation. It has been suggested that under the Statutes of Labourers, as interpreted by the courts, the master had "something in

---

[10] The requirement of a quarter's notice was specified in the Statute of Artificers (1563) and affirmed by Blackstone, *op. cit.*, 587. Morris, *op. cit.*, 220, states that "the requirement that three months' notice be given before discharge was widely observed in the colonies, although, as with other labor customs, there was no uniform adherence." At some point (when?) it was established that, in the case of domestic servants, the legal period of notice should be one month. See H. G. Wood, *A Treatise on the Law of Master and Servant* (San Francisco: Bancroft-Whitney, 1886), 3.

[11] "So far as regards the classes of servants who fell within the scope of the English statutes of laborers and the various master and servant acts . . . it is apparent from the authorities that, in respect of some breaches of duties, the right of the master to rescind the contract, without the intervention of the justices, was only recognized within comparatively recent times. In 19 Hen. VI 30 cited in Brooke's Abridgement, it is stated without any qualification: 'It seems the master cannot discharge his servant within the time, etc., unless he agree to it.' To the same effect is a passage in Dalton's Country Justices, 1697 ed., p. 128, where it is added that by the statute of 5 Elizabeth, discharge must be 'for some reasonable cause to be allowed by one justice of the peace at least.'" C. B. Labatt, *Commentaries on the Law of Master and Servant* (8 vols.: Rochester, N.Y., 1913), I, 971.

[12] 23 Edward III c. 2 (18 June 1349). This was the Ordinance of Labourers, followed by a series of Statutes of Labourers beginning with 1351. The Ordinance was issued by the King in Council, "parliament being unable to meet on account of the pestilence." See Bertha H. Putnam, *The Enforcement of the Statutes of Labourers* (New York: Columbia University Studies in History, Economics and Public Law, 1908), 2. Usually, the Ordinance and the Statutes proper are referred to without distinction as the "Statutes of Labourers."

the nature of a real right to his employee's services"[13] and it was this property right that was protected against the trespass of other employers. By the late eighteenth century, however, the basis of the cause of action had shifted from trespass against a property right to interference with a contractual relation.[14]

Morris points out that "in the seventeenth century servants could as a rule be sold or assigned and were deemed the property of the master's estate. The strict laws relating to harboring or enticing them grew out of this property concept of the master-servant relationship."[15] Since freedom of assignment runs counter to the ideal image of a status relation, we may conclude that though the property concept gave a kind of substance to the master-servant relation it also helped to undercut it. In any case it strengthened the notion that the employment relation was not terminable at will.

3. Specific performance of the contract of service was available as a legal remedy. Under modern common-law doctrine, "a promise to render personal service or supervision will not be specifically enforced by an affirmative decree."[16] This policy "is based in part upon the difficulty of enforcement and of passing judgment upon the quality of performance, and in part upon the undesirability of compelling the continuance of personal association after disputes have arisen and confidence and loyalty are gone. In some cases the decree would seem like the enforcement of an involuntary servitude."[17] This point of view, however, did not prevail before the nineteenth century. On the basis of close inspection of judicial decisions in the American colonies, Morris concludes that "in the seventeenth and eighteenth centuries the personal-service contract was specifi-

---

[13] W. S. Holdsworth, *History of English Law* (London: Methuen, 1924), IV, 384.

[14] "In this way a cause of action, introduced into the common law by the fourteenth century legislation which had created a special status for the servant or workman in relation to his employer, gradually came to be considered, as the contractual aspect of that relation assumed greater prominence, first as a peculiar incident annexed to the contract of service, and then as an incident annexed to all contracts." *Ibid.*

[15] Morris, *op. cit.*, 518f.

[16] American Law Institute, *Restatement of the Law of Contracts* (St. Paul: American Law Institute Publishers, 1932), 702. "Among the contracts that are included are all contracts of employment *creating the intimate relation of master and servant*; the latter's performance is personal service and that of the former frequently involves personal supervision" (703, emphasis supplied). Thus not all contracts of employment are covered by the rule and recent legislation affecting reinstatement of employees suggests that the rule must, indeed, be narrowed. Sec. 10(c) of the National Labor Relations Act (1935) provided for reinstatement of employees subject to discrimination as union members. See *Phelps Dodge v. NLRB*, 313 U.S. 177 (1941).

[17] *Restatement of the Law of Contracts*, 703.

cally enforced as a property right."[18] In a legal system deeply committed to the detailed regulation of both moral and commercial life, specific enforcement of personal-service contracts was no anomaly. More important, the master-servant relation was not thought of as an ordinary contract for whose breach damages would suffice. Too much was at stake in the relation, not only for the parties but for the community itself.

4. **The master had a responsibility to care for the servant.** So far as the law was concerned, the status of master carried with it a responsibility for the general welfare of the servant. This obligation was not very clearly defined, and Blackstone does not mention it. Yet it was acknowledged in principle and undoubtedly reflected traditional arrangements. It was the master's duty to provide subsistence and lodging appropriate to the servant's station and duties; to teach the apprentice; to care for the sick; to offer moral guidance and supervision. "The master as a general rule could not discharge a servant for an incurable illness, and he was obligated to provide him with medical, surgical, and nursing treatment when injured in his employ. In some jurisdictions masters were penalized for turning away servants who had not completely recovered from illness."[19]

An 1870 treatise, discussing the mutual obligations of master and servant, offered the principle that "a moral obligation, resting upon every master whose connection with his servant is a very close one, the latter being manifestly on an inferior footing, is to exert a good influence, to regard the servant's mental and spiritual well-being."[20] And it is suggested that this obligation underlay the traditional "common-law right of the master to chastise his servant or apprentice moderately . . . [a right] denied as to ordinary servants in this country."[21] By this time, the master's duty to provide medical care is said no longer to exist, but an earlier contrary view is cited "and reference to the authorities will show that,

---

[18] Morris, *op. cit.*, 529; see also 221 ff. and 399 f. See also Labatt, *op. cit.*, I, 1018: "The older English reports contain some decisions which indicate that, in former times, rights arising from contracts of service and apprenticeship may not infrequently have been determined by courts of equity under circumstances which would not now be regarded as entitling the parties to relief."

[19] Morris, *op. cit.*, 18. See also 520: "It is doubtful whether servants in colonial times could have recovered damages from their masters for injuries occurring in the course of their employment where their fault or negligence could have been proven. On the other hand, masters were expected to provide medical assistance for bound servants who fell ill in the course of their employment. This was the closest approach in the colonial period to any concept now embodied in our workmen's compensation acts." The preceding quotation is not restricted in its reference to bound servants.

[20] Schouler, *op. cit.*, 616.

[21] *Ibid.*

as to domestic servants, courts are not indisposed to infer authority [to insist on the master's obligation] from the master's own conduct."[22]

The courts made themselves freely available for the supervision of the master-servant relation and they used what resources they had, including both criminal and civil sanctions. They were asked to help enforce employee discipline, recapture runaways, bar enticement, recover wages, alleviate cruelty, and uphold standards of care, especially for apprentices and other youthful servants.[23] The magistrate was mainly at the service of the master, and the employee was at considerable disadvantage when he asserted a claim or grievance. Nevertheless, there was recognition that the servant needed protection and that "the master was accountable to the authorities for the conditions of employment."[24]

It is evident even from this brief sketch that the law of master and servant did not apply to all employees with equal force or clarity. From an early period there was considerable ambiguity as to just who "fit" the relation. Blackstone distinguished four classes of servants: (a) slaves; (b) menial servants or domestics, understood in the broad sense mentioned above; (c) apprentices; (d) laborers "who are only hired by the day or week and do not live *intra moenia*, as part of the family"; and (e) "ministerial" servants, such as stewards, factors, and bailiffs. Even in Blackstone's discussion, the last two categories are only weakly encompassed within the master-servant relation. The ministerial servants are already thought of as servants *pro tempore* and will soon be considered mere agents, not subject to the detailed control of the master. As to laborers, Blackstone refers only to the statutes containing "many very good regulations" affecting compulsory labor and the determination of wages.[25]

The more intimate, the more enduring, the more textured the relation, the more readily did the master-servant imagery apply and the easier it was to elaborate common-law rules and doctrines. When practical considerations called for a close and lasting connection between master and servant, the magistrate could read the common conscience with ease. He could conjure up clear and morally uplifting notions of what constituted a sound ordering of the household economy. The free and transient wage earner, on the other hand, was not a "representative" figure in the social order. He had no sure place in the scheme of things and his way of life

---

[22] *Ibid.*, 617.
[23] Morris, *op. cit.*, provides many examples of local court action in the colonies. See esp. Chap. IX.
[24] *Ibid.*, 526.
[25] Blackstone, *op. cit.*, 588–589.

offered little basis for legal creativity, especially in a system geared to the protection of a few essential social relations.

The uneven relevance of master-servant doctrine had a limited importance before the Industrial Revolution. Until the nineteenth century the status-oriented spirit of master-servant law was supplemented and reinforced by the restrictive labor policy of the Statutes of Labourers.[26] These late-medieval regulations were extended under Elizabeth I as contributions to public order and to the advancement of mercantilism. The Tudor code, widely adopted in the American colonies,[27] provided for compulsory labor, with the corollary that the community should see to it that work was available for the idle. A system of poor relief was established based on local responsibility for persons who had legal "settlement," a provision that underlined the significance of long-term employment.[28] The code restrained arbitrary dismissal of workmen. And it was required that "reasonable" wages be accepted, these to be pegged to the price of necessaries and fixed by the justices of the peace. All this added up to an elaborate system of governmental regulation.

Thus the old law of employment, dominant until the "great transformation"[29] of the nineteenth century, implicated all participants in a web of rules. These rules were fundamentally *prescriptive*. They did not facilitate or liberate. They contemplated detailed regulation of the conditions of work, in accordance with long usage, rules of craft and guild, and explicit public policy. As Holdsworth put it:

> In truth, until political economists of the earlier half of the nineteenth century converted the legislature to the belief that freedom of contract was the cure for all social ills, no one ever imagined that wages and prices could be settled merely at the will and pleasure of the parties to each particular bargain; or that the contract between employer and workman could be regarded as precisely similar to any other contract.[30]

Necessity, not freedom, constraint, not choice, lent their sober aspect to the labor policy of that age.

A truly contractual theory of employment did not emerge until the

---

[26] See above, at fn. 10.

[27] The principles of the Tudor legislation, and their continuity with the Statutes of Labourers, are discussed in Holdsworth, *op. cit.*, IV, 379 ff. For the American colonial experience, see Morris, *op. cit.*, 1–21.

[28] See Blackstone, *op. cit.*, 589: "And, first, by hiring and service for a year, or apprenticeship under indentures, a person gains a settlement in that parish wherein he last served forty days."

[29] Karl Polanyi, *The Great Transformation* (Boston: Beacon Press, 1957), Part Two.

[30] Holdsworth, *op. cit.*, IV, 386.

concept of a free market gained ascendance in economic life. In the late eighteenth and early nineteenth centuries, the idea of contract heralded a new age in politics as well as trade. Contract was the solvent of and the surrogate for a political community rooted in traditional and unquestioned authority. It was the key to growth and freedom for an economy bound and fettered by privileged guilds, chartered corporations, and the heavy hand of state control. With contract as master image and touchstone of legitimacy, the old constraints on political freedom, freedom of movement, and freedom of trade could be removed.[31]

In the new dispensation, contract would be more than a way of accepting obligations. The emphasis shifted from obligation to freedom of choice. To stress that the employment relation was a contract was to emphasize (a) the limited nature of the commitment made by the parties to each other and (b) the high value to be placed on the freedom of individuals, whatever their station, to enter contractual relations and define for themselves the terms of the bargain. In a subtle but decisive way, contract lost its meaning as a legal device for establishing sustained relations to be governed by law. Contract became a device for entering *legally unsupervised* relations.

The waning of legal supervision of the master-servant relation is the most striking feature of the law of employment in the early nineteenth century. This eclipse of social control invoked some characteristic resources and gambits of the common law:

First, *the employment relation was identified as contractual in essence, and thus subject to the conceptual and interpretive apparatus of the developing law of contract.* The terms of the contract were to be sought in voluntary agreement, express or implied. The categories of legal analysis would be the same as those applied to any contract. The law would state the conditions under which a valid contract of employment was formed, establish appropriate presumptions and rules of interpretation, and outline the remedies available for breach of contract. But it would not seek substantive justice in the workplace.

Second, *rules and working conditions were incorporated into the employment contract as implied terms.* The employee is presumed to have given his assent to the rules, and this assent is the font of their legitimacy. To be sure, contract doctrine did permit some challenge of rules where the presumptions of knowledge and assent could be rebutted. But since most workers were relatively helpless, and the tradition of subordination

---

[31] See above, 52.

was long, little legal resistance could be offered. The lack of legal resistance is itself the source of an impoverished law.

Third, *the employment contract was given a special status in the law, founded in the distinctive right of one party to exercise authority over another.* This was a continuing element throughout the century, and the more explicitly contractual doctrine of the later period did not alter the emphasis. Reeve's early treatise (1818) says: "A master is one who, by law, has a right to personal authority over another; and such persons, over whom such authority may rightfully be exercised, is a servant."[32] And Labatt (1904): "Where one person is employed to do certain work for another who, under the express or implied terms of the agreement between them, is to have the right of exercising control over the performance of the work, to the extent of prescribing the manner in which it shall be executed, the employer is a master, and the person employed is his servant."[33] The exercise of control is the criterion of the nature of the contract.

In this important respect the modern law of employment drew heavily on the old law of master and servant. The main contribution of the old to the new was the traditional authority of the master to control the workman. As the law developed, the desideratum of control became a very handy device for distinguishing the employment relation from other legal relations, such as that of agent, bailee, or independent contractor. This was no mere academic exercise, for legal classification is a way of fixing the liabilities of the parties involved, both to each other and to third persons. Ironically, the exigencies of conceptual clarity may have had something to do with emphasizing the employer's unilateral authority. The main outcome was to continue, in the heyday of contract, the traditional law of subordination.

Fourth, *the presumption emerged that the employment contract was terminable at will and therefore free of the restraints that accompany a contract of definite duration.* We have already noted the eighteenth-century presumption that a general hiring would be construed as for a year, absent evidence of a more limited commitment. The economic and ideological changes of the Industrial Revolution overturned that presumption. On the Continent, the contractual theory of employment was embraced as a way of preventing any resurgence of slavery or indenture. In the Napoleonic Code employment for life or for excessively long periods was made void as against public policy and the rule was established that any

---

[32] Reeve, *op. cit.*, Sec. 339.
[33] Labatt, *op. cit.*, 9.

contract for undetermined length is terminable at will by either party on reasonable notice. This rule applied to partnership, agency, and tenancy, as well as to employment.

In this country, legal change was more gradual, in part because a great deal of freedom and variation in hiring practices already existed as a practical matter. Nevertheless, the treatises of the period show that a transition in legal doctrine took place. An 1851 work held that "where there is a general hiring, nothing being said as to its duration, and no stipulation as to payments being made, which may govern its interpretation, the contract is said to be for a year."[34] In Schouler's 1870 treatise the matter is hedged considerably:

> If the hiring be general, without any particular time limited, the old law construes it into a year's hiring. But the equity of this rule applied only to such employment as the change of seasons affected; as when the servant lived with the master or worked at agriculture. By custom, such contracts have become terminable in the case of domestic servants, upon a month's notice, or, what is an equivalent, payment of a month's wages. Laborers are hired frequently by the day, and to hire by the week is not unusual. Yet, as to hiring in general, the rule still is that if a master engaged without mentioning the time, it is a general hiring, and in point of law a hiring for a year. Custom modified this principle, and the date and frequency of periodical payments are material circumstances in each case.[35]

In 1877, however, Wood flatly reverses the traditional presumption. After paying his respects to the English rule, he says: "With us the rule is inflexible, that a general or indefinite hiring is *prima facie* a hiring at will, and if the servant seeks to make it out a yearly hiring, the burden is upon him to establish it by proof."[36] An alternative view, recognizing *no* presumption as to the duration of the hiring, apparently gained little support.[37]

---

[34] W. W. Storey, *A Treatise on the Law of Contracts* (Boston, 1851), 1041.
[35] Schouler, *op. cit.*, 606–607.
[36] H. G. Wood, *A Treatise on the Law of Master and Servant* (Albany, 1877), 272. "I am aware," says Wood, "of no instance in which, for many years, the [English] rule has been approved by any American court. It must be remembered that these questions, in England, generally arise, not between master and servant, but in settlement cases, where it is sought to charge a pauper upon a community by showing that he acquired a settlement there by having been hired to serve, and having actually served under a contract for a yearly hiring, one year." (*Ibid.*)
[37] Labatt, *op. cit.*, 519, recommended the "no presumption" rule, suggesting that the at-will presumption would do violence to at least some business realities: "Having regard to the ordinary course of affairs in the business world, the higher the position to which the contract relates, the more certainly may it be inferred that the employer and employed expect their relationship to continue for a considerable period. It seems questionable whether a doctrine resting on a presumption which ignores that expectation as

Thus "contract at will" became the legal paradigm of the employment relation. No doubt, this faithfully reflected the actual conditions of employment. By the middle of the nineteenth century, employment contracts were made for extremely short periods, especially in the case of unskilled workers. The idea of a contract "of definite duration" had little meaning for most industrial workers. Yet in nineteenth-century legal doctrine the assumption of a meaningful period of employment underlay whatever restraint there was on the arbitrary action of the employer. The treatises on master and servant do spell out legal grounds for dismissal of the servant. These include, "first, willful disobedience of a lawful order; second, gross moral misconduct; third, habitual negligence in business, or other serious detriment to the master's interests."[38] To specify these grounds is to provide a legal basis for challenging unjust dismissals. In theory, the employer's right to fire was subject to fairly stringent limitations, and the cases cited are very similar to those that arise today, in arbitration, on the issue of just cause for dismissal.[39] But this assumes that the contract is for a definite term. Given a definite term, the legal issue is: Did the employee so breach his contract as to warrant termination of the employment?

Under the contract at will, the issue of breach does not arise, for the contract is so fleeting, so lacking in legal substance, that it provides no secure ground for the claim of an aggrieved party to be made whole, either through money damages or specific performance. In the field of employment, the contract at will brings to culmination the union of contract and the market. The contract does not establish a relationship. From a legal point of view, the encounter is as casual as the sale of a newspaper on a city street. This outcome led Commons to say that "the labor contract is not a contract, it is a continuing renewal of a contract at every successive moment, implied simply from the fact that the laborer keeps at work and the employer accepts his product."[40]

The contract at will went hand in hand with absolute managerial discretion. If the contract is at will, no legal limits are set on the authority

---

an element indicative of intention can with propriety be treated as one of general application."

[38] Schouler, *op. cit.*, 612.

[39] See Walter C. Tiffany, *Handbook on the Law of Persons and Domestic Relations* (St. Paul: West Publishing Co., 1896), 467–473.

[40] John R. Commons, *Legal Foundations of Capitalism* (Madison: University of Wisconsin, 1959), 285. First published in 1924. For a recent argument that "the fundamentals of contract are basically alien to the entire [employment] relationship," see R. W. Rideout, "The Contract of Employment," 19 *Current Legal Problems* 111 (London, 1966).

of the employer, especially on the key issue of dismissal. The employer is free to hire and fire unrestrained by the legal requirement that he have just cause for rescinding a contract not yet expired.[41] Moreover, the contract at will is not a device for framing agreed-upon conditions to govern day-to-day activities. Since there is no definite duration, the terms of the contract are not binding for the future. The employer is free to modify them at any time, without notice.

The main economic significance of the contract at will was the contribution it made to easy layoff of employees in response to business fluctuations. But it also strengthened managerial authority. By the end of the nineteenth century the employment contract had become a very special sort of contract—in large part a legal device for guaranteeing to management the unilateral power to make rules and exercise discretion. For this reason we call it the *prerogative contract*.[42]

To think of the employment contract as a wage bargain, a purchase of labor, is a radical abridgment of the true legal and social situation. Just what does the employer purchase? A reasonable amount of labor? So much as the employee is willing to do? Enough to keep the machinery running at a rate the employer finds proper? In purchasing labor, does the employer buy the right to regulate the employee's working day as he sees fit? Does he purchase the right to ignore the proprieties of conduct, or must he treat the employee with decency and respect for his physical and psychological needs?

These questions are not settled by formulating the employment relation as an exchange of labor for wages. More important, the labor-market theory does not specify how any of these issues are to be decided. Are they to be settled by bargaining, by reference to past practice, by common conceptions of fairness? And, what is the legal meaning of the norm that the employer may set the rules of plant behavior? Is the employer the sole judge of whether his rules are arbitrary or exceed the scope of his authority? Ideally, even under contract doctrine, the employer might be granted the right to make rules, but he would not have the unrestricted right to decide whether the rules he has made are consistent with the contract. But the prerogative contract gives to the employer just such authority.

The free labor market of burgeoning capitalism was real enough, and contractual freedom did much to create it. It does not follow, however,

---

[41] See Lawrence E. Blades, "Employment at Will vs. Individual Freedom: On Limiting the Abusive Exercise of Employer Power," 67 *Columbia Law Review* 1404 (1967).
[42] This concept was suggested by Harvey Sacks.

that contract was an adequate foundation for governing the employment relation. The law could not and did not treat the conditions of employment as the outcome of free bargaining and mutual assent. Rather, the concept of contract was adapted to what had to be done to maintain the organizational strength of the business enterprise. The result was a marriage of old master-servant notions to an apparently uncompromising contractualism.

The contractual theory ostensibly gave full discretion to the parties in defining the nature and scope of authority. In fact, however, the law imported into the employment contract a set of implied terms reserving full authority of direction and control to the employer. Once the contract was defined as an *employment* contract, the master-servant model was brought into play. The natural and inevitable authority of the master could then be invoked, for that authority had already been established as the defining characteristic of the master-servant relation. In this way, the continuing master-servant imagery lent a legal foundation to managerial prerogative.

But the old master-servant model was only *partially* incorporated into the new law of employment. The traditional association of "master" and "authority" was welcomed, but in its modern dress authority was impersonalized, stripped of the sense of personal duty, commitment, and responsibility that once accompanied it, at least in theory. Although many employers felt such obligations, the new legal doctrine showed little interest in managerial benevolence. It presumed that each party would take care of his own interests and provide for them in a freely bargained agreement. The limited moral commitment of the employer justified any arrangement he could impose. The terms of the agreement, not the law of the employment contract, would have to be relied on for substantive justice in the plant.

The prerogative contract gave the employer an open-ended, sovereign power. But the capacity of contract imagery to legitimate that power was not complete. In the first place, a contract impliedly giving broad powers of decision to one party, and establishing the subordination of another, was hardly an ordinary contract. It was at best a Hobbesian social compact giving full discretion to the sovereign employer. This violated the spirit of nineteenth-century contractualism, which looked to voluntary agreements, based on bargaining over specific terms, as the substitute for prescriptive regulation by government.

Second, managerial authority was taken to be an incident of ownership, a matter of property right. Thus it did not depend on contractual agreement alone. This view probably had wide acceptance, but legally it was not clear that the employer's property right gave him the authority to govern employees as he saw fit. The Roman concept of *paterfamilias* was not assimilated to the law of employment, except by way of the master-servant model, as noted above. In the end, most stress was laid on the theory that ownership carried with it the right to freedom of contract, and any limitation of that freedom was a violation of the rights of property. This brought the argument back to consensual agreement as the foundation of managerial authority, an agreement tainted by the manifest inequality of the parties and by the reservation of all discretion to management unless specifically limited by a provision of the contract.

The contract of employment inevitably becomes a prerogative contract, a mode of submission, if provision is not made for *employee participation in the continuing process of rule-making and administration.* With control of that process reserved to the employer, contract can only fade to a shadow of its potential as an instrument of self-government. This lack of machinery for handling the continuity of membership and decision-making was the most radical defect of the individual employment contract. For the establishment of that machinery, a new era of collective bargaining was needed, one that would see still another reconstruction of the idea of contract.

The Constitutive Contract

During the first third of the twentieth century, the American working-man received little help from the law in his resistance to untrammeled managerial authority. At best legal change allowed enlarged freedom for collective action and laid a foundation for government support of collective bargaining, especially in the Railway Labor Act of 1926. The main thrust of change was the removal of legal *obstacles* to union organization and strike action. Even as late as 1932, the Norris-LaGuardia Act, written to free unions from crippling injunctions, reflected this laissez-faire orientation. The emerging policy was to allow maximum freedom of nonviolent economic conflict without the interference of government officials, including judges. In the struggle between capital and labor, the Neutral State was to take no sides.

The labor legislation of the New Deal brought a decisive new turn. Freedom of economic conflict remained very much in order, but now the government threw its support to the side of organized labor, at least long enough to bring it to a place of legitimacy and strength within the framework of American institutions. The Wagner (National Labor Relations) Act of 1935 greatly aided the unionization of industry. The new law (1) drastically limited the power of employers to oppose union membership drives in the plant by propaganda, intimidation, discrimination against union members, or by setting up company unions; (2) established machinery for selection by employees of "unions of their own choosing" and gave to the union so certified a legally protected exclusive right to represent a defined bargaining unit; (3) proclaimed collective bargaining the preferred road to industrial peace and made it an unfair labor practice for an employer to refuse to bargain collectively with employee representatives.[43] In effect this meant that the arena of conflict was to be narrowed to substantive issues. Recognition of unions, including dealing with them in good faith, was not to be a subject of economic warfare.

The elimination of battles over union recognition was no modest aim. Such struggles had taken on a life-and-death character and were often brutal and devastating. But the call for collective bargaining expressed an even larger vision. While preserving economic conflict, forces would be set in motion to mitigate and lessen it. With a minimum of legal intervention, with government only setting the rules of the game, free negotiation might summon a new era of accommodation, perhaps even of good will.

Revolutionary as it was in the field of labor, the New Deal did more to open doors to the future than bring about a settled framework of law and policy. The whole posture of the new legislation presumed that a broad evolution would take place affecting the business enterprise, the labor union, government policy, and legal doctrine. The spirit of the statute was open-ended and optimistic. It was also full of unanswered questions. The politics of the day were fairly clear-cut—the victorious alliance of labor and the Democratic party would bring the weight of government to the aid of union power in the shops—but the legal consequences were more complex and obscure, more halting in their elaboration. This was a necessary corollary of law-making that left so much for the future to decide.

In adopting the slogan, Let Collective Bargaining Become an Instrument of Industrial Peace, the Congress was boldly innovative and, at the same time, displayed its deep commitment to traditional ways of handling social problems. Gradualism, good hope, and faith in the benign effects

---

[43] On controversy over the intent of Congress regarding the employer's duty to bargain, see Phelps Ross, *The Government as a Source of Union Power* (Providence, R.I.: Brown University Press, 1965), Chaps. 3–4.

of self-help and self-interest were strongly affirmed. No quick solution to labor-management problems was offered. Nothing was guaranteed. No prescriptive order embodied in detailed regulations was established or even contemplated. The Congress did not begin with a definitive formulation of what the labor-management relation was or ought to be. It did not try to delimit, for example, the reach of managerial prerogative. The nature of a mature relation was something to be learned from experience.

From its inception the law of collective bargaining envisioned new forms of association. Although bargaining was emphasized, it was understood that this had to be something more than a casual encounter in the market-place. The union's legal status as bargaining representative, if nothing more, was evidence of that. Nevertheless, the evolution of labor law in the United States has been marked by *a continuing tension between traditional contract doctrine and an emerging law of association*. This strain was guaranteed by the complex reality itself, by the judicial effort to come to terms with a new social phenomenon while drawing upon the special resources of the common law, and by the inherent ambivalence of the national labor policy.

In the new law, contract retained its force as a dominant legal idea. This was only partly due to reliance on received legal concepts. That alone would undoubtedly have influenced the course of legal change, for law-making of all kinds is greatly facilitated when old ideas of established legitimacy can be applied, with whatever carpentering, to new situations. In fact, however, the imagery of contract served much broader needs. It was and is highly prized as an appropriate model for understanding labor-management relations and, more important, as carrying with it healthy political connotations.

The continued ascendance of contract was assured by the celebration of voluntarism and bargaining as foundations of labor policy. The law of collective bargaining was to be in spirit akin to traditional contract law in that its chief aim was to facilitate private transactions and arrangements. The parties were to remain autonomous and free. They were to settle for themselves the specific terms of their cooperation. Moreover, from the standpoint of the unions, the idea of contract offered a very convenient way of formalizing the recognition won and the concession extracted. The union was recognized when it became a party to a written agreement, and the terms of that agreement could stand as evidence of what the employer had granted. The rhetoric of the times paid little attention to the difference between a contract proper, meeting determinate legal criteria, and other forms of agreement. It was not clear, for example, that the parties to a "trade agreement" meant to be bound by the law of contracts and to accept its distinctive remedies and obligations. It sufficed that contract as a popular image could lend an aura of legality to the proceedings and, at the same time, give them a familiar and comprehensible cast.

In an important sense the Wagner Act sought to purify the contractual foundations of the employment relation by redressing "the inequality of bargaining power between employees who do not possess full freedom of association or actual liberty of contract, and employers who are organized in the corporate or other forms of ownership association. . . ."[44] This it would do by establishing a framework within which free negotiation could take place. This framework had three basic parts. First, in effect, a new branch of tort law—the unfair labor practice—was authorized. Second, a new substantive right for a special class of private associations was created —the right to be certified, under appropriate conditions, as an exclusive bargaining representative. Third, the right of freedom of association was protected and implemented.

It was hoped that these conditions—as such, like contract law itself, noncontractual—would facilitate private initiative for self-government. The New Deal legislators were wary of "freedom of contract" as a slogan used to attack welfare legislation and protect economic privilege. But the new law aimed to save freedom of contract, not to reject it. This would be accomplished by adapting a special law of contract-formation to the associational realities of industrial life.

The social function of the Wagner Act was to create the *conditions* for bargaining and formalized agreement. In 1941 the Supreme Court upheld the NLRB's ruling that an employer who reaches an understanding with a union as a result of negotiations may be required to sign a written contract. The NLRB's reasoning, cited by the court, shows the significance of contract for power and policy:

> This experience has shown that refusal to sign a written contract has been a not infrequent means of frustrating the bargaining process through the refusal to recognize the labor organization as a party to it and the refusal to provide an authentic record of its terms which could be exhibited to employees, as evidence of the good faith of the employer. . . . Contrasted with the unilateral statement by the employer of his labor policy, the signed agreement has been regarded as the effective instrument of stabilizing labor relations and preventing, through collective bargaining, strikes and industrial strife.[45]

---

[44] Sec. 1 ("Findings and Policy") of the National Labor Relations Act 49 Stat. L. (I) 449 (1935).
[45] *H. J. Heinz Co.* v. *NLRB*, 311 U.S. 514 (1941).

The *political* meaning of the written agreement is emphasized here, especially its significance for union recognition, for the integrity of collective bargaining, and for a public, explicit commitment by the employer to agreed-upon terms. The aim is not to produce a writing that would make the agreement legally binding. Rather, the written contract is to make its own contribution to industrial order, quite apart from its legal standing.

Indeed, the Wagner Act was not concerned with the legal status and enforceability of the collective agreement. Just what a collective agreement was, from a legal standpoint, was left open. Thus, although the idea of contract was very much in the foreground, the legal emphasis was shifted from contract law to the special area of unfair labor practice. With the Wagner Act law entered decisively and affirmatively into labor relations, but not by way of the administration of contracts. The NLRB enforced the duty to bargain, made representation effective, and enjoined discrimination against union members. This was a very large agenda, but it was mainly concerned with creating the machinery of effective collective bargaining, not with supervising or enforcing the resulting agreements.

Since the enactment of the Wagner Act, the significance of contract in labor law has greatly increased. The most important milestone is Section 301 of the Taft-Hartley Act of 1947, which provides that "suits for violation of contracts between an employer and a labor organization representing employees in an industry affecting commerce . . . may be brought in any district court of the United States."[46] By authorizing enforcement of collective agreements in the courts, this legislation implicitly recognized that a first stage of institution-building was past and that the legal status of the *outcome* of bargaining would have to be clarified. The earlier stage was mostly concerned with strikes launched to force nonunion employers to enter the world of collective bargaining. Taft-Hartley contemplated strife that might result from breaches of existing agreements. In fact, as things turned out, no simple application of contract law could meet that issue. A new stage of institution-building would be required, this time focusing on mechanisms of adjudication rather than of bargaining.[47]

Helped along by Section 301 and its fate in the courts, but also for the more general reasons to which we have alluded, the contract model has continued to dominate legal analysis of the labor-management relation. At the very least, contract is the idea to be wrestled with in the struggle for a more adequate interpretation. A striking example of the persistence of contract thinking is the Supreme Court's discovery, in the landmark

---

[46] Labor Management Relations Act, 61 Stat. 136 (June 23, 1947).
[47] See below, 154 ff.

Lincoln Mills case, decided in 1957, of an even-handed reciprocity between the union's no-strike commitment and management's promise to submit differences to arbitration. "Plainly the agreement to arbitrate grievance disputes is the quid pro quo for an agreement not to strike."[48] The Court went on to find that the Taft-Hartley Act meant to apply "the policy of our national labor laws" to the interpretation of labor-management contracts, and that this policy required, contrary to common law, that agreements to arbitrate future disputes should be enforceable by Court orders for specific performance. From the course of later decisions, notably the *Steelworkers* cases of 1960,[49] it is abundantly clear that the Court's real aim was to give maximum support to arbitration as a problem-solving and peace-keeping mechanism in industrial relations. Given that interpretation of national policy, the Court's conclusion did not have to rest on a finding of contractual reciprocity.[50] Yet the imagery seemed compelling and doubt-less added something to the felt legitimacy of a decision that struck many members of the legal community as an extravagant exercise in judicial creativity. Perhaps it seemed especially urgent because the Court was soon to grant to arbitrators a breadth of discretion that would be hard to justify in strictly contractual terms.[51]

In the 1962 case of *Teamsters Union* v. *Lucas Flour Co.*, the Court's ambivalence was poignantly revealed.[52] In this decision it was held that the agreement to arbitrate disputes carried with it an *implied* no-strike pledge. "To hold otherwise," said the Court, "would obviously do violence to accepted principles of traditional contract law."[53] To this Justice Black dissented, pleading that he "was unable to find any accepted principle of contract law—traditional or otherwise—that permits courts to change completely the nature of a contract by adding new promises that the parties themselves refused to make in order that the new court-made contract might better fit into whatever social, economic, or legal policies the courts

---

[48] *Textile Workers* v. *Lincoln Mills*, 353 U.S. 448 (1957).

[49] *United Steelworkers of America* v. *American Manufacturing Co.*, 363 U.S. 564; *United Steelworkers of America* v. *Warrior & Gulf Navigation Co.*, 363 U.S. 574; *United Steelworkers of America* v. *Enterprise Wheel & Car Corp.*, 363 U.S. 593.

[50] In his concurring opinion to *Steelworkers* v. *American Manufacturing*, Justice Brennan added the following comment: "The Court makes reference to an arbitration clause being the *quid pro quo* for a no-strike clause. I do not understand the Court to mean that the application of the principles announced today depends upon the presence of a no-strike clause in the agreement."

[51] See especially *Steelworkers* v. *Warrior & Gulf* and the dissent by Justice Whittaker. Also below, 158.

[52] See Harry H. Wellington, "Freedom of Contract and the Collective Bargaining Agreement," 14 *Labor Law Journal* 1016, 1030 (1963).

[53] *Local 174, Teamsters Union* v. *Lucas Flour Co.*, 369 U.S. 95, 105 (1962).

believe to be so important that they should have been taken out of the realm of voluntary contract by the legislative body and furthered by compulsory legislation."[54] This exchange is symptomatic of an underlying tension that has produced considerable soul-searching in the legal literature.[55] The Court must hold onto the idea of contract at the same time as it seeks to reconstruct the legal foundations of labor-management relations. These doctrinal troubles arise because contract is at once a very general idea, adaptable to many different contexts and is, at the same time, a legal category that carries a heavy weight of received doctrine and of traditional attitudes.

Although the application of a contractual model to labor-management agreements has been vexing from a legal standpoint, the experience is valuable as a case study of social and legal dynamics. To trace this episode in the history of law is to show the straining of legal concepts against social reality. Yet this is no simple institutional lag, for the reality itself has been in process of evolution. It is not that "the law is an idiot" or that legislators and jurists are unable to understand society and deal with it effectively. Rather, we see a complex interaction of authority and cognition. The historic legal problem has been to maintain legitimated ways of thinking while making those thoughtways more effective in guiding social change. The law shows a characteristic conservatism by holding onto what is received and by adopting a tentative, not-too-intrusive stance toward historical developments that are still obscure.

It is arguable that the very generality of the contract idea has been an important resource for legal adaptation. The capacity of contract to serve many different settings and transactions, as well as its emphasis on the autonomy of private spheres of action, facilitated the development of a living law. The latter could only suffer from the imposition of some more specific legal theory upon industrial life. Even the long period during which competing theories of the collective agreement were invoked by the courts may have served this end by offering a moratorium, a time of openness and ambiguity in the course of which private institution-building could go on.

We should also be mindful of the truth that legal concepts are not to be assessed by the extent to which they "fit" reality. Legal ideas involve cognitive judgments, but something more as well. They must be effective tools for bringing existing authoritative materials to bear on new situations.

---

[54] *Ibid.*, at 108.
[55] See Harry H. Wellington, *Labor and the Legal Process* (New Haven: Yale University Press, 1968), Chap. 3.

Therefore the utility of contract in labor law derives from the distinctively legal work it has done, regardless of whether it has served as a fully accurate cognitive model of labor-management agreements.

But the idea of contract *has* been troublesome, and it is instructive to examine the sources of strain and the direction of legal change. We shall do this by considering three features of received contract doctrine and the limitations of each when applied to the collective agreement. These paragraphs should be read in the light of the discussion in Chapter 2, pages 55–60.

1. **Voluntarism.**   Contract doctrine presumes that the parties are free to decide for themselves whether and on what terms to establish a relationship. In the labor-management setting, these premises run up against the pervasively *involuntary and compelled* character of employment decisions. For the individual worker in prosperous times freedom of choice is often real, but historically and politically the more dominant fact has been the dependence of the worker on limited employment opportunities. He is neither an effective participant in a bargaining relation nor does he have realistic freedom to choose between working and not working. One result of this dependency is that more and more aspects of the employment relation are determined by public policy rather than by private arrangement.

At the collective bargaining table the weakness of the individual worker can be redressed. The relative strength of the parties can be equalized. Voluntarism, it would seem, can come back into its own. In fact, however, an important element of compulsion remains. The collective agreement is not a contract of sale to be made or not made at the option of the parties. The union cannot simply pick up its marbles and go home. The Supreme Court adopted this view in 1960:

> When most parties enter into a contractual relationship they do so voluntarily, in the sense that there is no real compulsion to deal with one another, as opposed to dealing with other parties. This is not true of the labor agreement. The choice is generally not between entering or refusing to enter a relationship, for that in all probability preexists the negotiations.[56]

In a vital sense, union and employer *belong to the same organization* and they are under heavy pressure to reach an agreement. What occurs is the

---

[56] *Steelworkers* v. *Warrior & Gulf*, 363 U.S. 574, 580. In the 1964 case of *John Wiley & Sons, Inc.* v. *Livingston* (376 U.S. 543, 549) the Court pointed out that the collective bargaining agreement "is not in any real sense the simple product of a consensual relationship."

reconstruction of already existing employment relations. While union and management may be establishing something new as between themselves, the basic fact is the *re*-establishment of effective participation and authority.

This context of commitment radically qualifiés the voluntaristic character of collective bargaining, with important consequences for how the ensuing agreement is to be interpreted. As Archibald Cox has pointed out, "the practical compulsion to sign and preserve collective agreements [means] that interpretation must assume a more creative role than in most commercial property litigation."[57] This creativity rests on two assumptions. First, the parties agreed to cooperate in a going concern despite the fact that they may have avoided many issues and left a great deal for future decision. Second, the nature of the arrangement does not offer the practical option of a rupture of the relationship when issues arise that cannot be referred to terms already agreed upon. As a result, some mechanism must be available for dealing with controversies in the light of what the agreement *hoped* to accomplish.

A large degree of voluntarism remains in that the parties are encouraged by government policy to settle their own disputes, make their own bargains, and establish their own arrangements for living together. But if voluntarism is to be retained in the law of labor relations it must be detached from older connotations of "freedom of contract." It is one thing to say that voluntarism sustains private autonomy against prescriptive regulation by government; it is another to associate voluntarism with specific legal doctrines, such as those to be considered in the next paragraphs, that inhibit the development of industrial self-government.

2. Limited commitment.   The policy of the law is to search out specific, clearly delineated promises. In this way, the principle of "voluntarism in depth" (see page 55) becomes a principle of limited commitment. As we have noted earlier, the modern contract may properly be called the "contract of limited commitment."

Some aspects of the collective agreement are well suited to close specification. Wage rates, number of paid holidays, the probationary period, and many other provisions, are routinely settled at the bargaining table. That settlement is meant to be defined and limited, reflecting the current strength of the bargainers, founded in conflict and compromise, perhaps even establishing the terms of an exchange.[58] Apart from problems of en-

---

[57] Archibald Cox, "The Legal Nature of Collective Bargaining Agreements," 57 *Michigan Law Review* 1, 4 (1958).
[58] The practical significance of the exchange may be only that the employees will stay on the job or go back to work, without promise of future abstention.

forceability, no special issues are raised. So far as the *scope* of the agreement is concerned, as distinguished from its validity, contract law is adequate to the occasion.

The difficulty arises when *settlements occur that alter the nature of
the parties' relation to each other and to the enterprise.* Whether wage
rates are 5 per cent higher or lower leaves the employment relation pretty
much as it was. But when the union becomes a continuing participant in
enterprise decision-making; when the employer is required to reconstruct
his style of administration and his notion of his own prerogatives; when
new institutions are established for adjudication of in-plant disputes; when
rights are created that can readily be perceived as vested and therefore
independent of any agreement; when the conditions of enduring cooperation frame the real issues at stake—then the whole structure of the enterprise is implicated and the character of the settlement is distorted rather
than illuminated by contractual imagery.

The most important limitation of contractual language, as a basis for
interpreting the collective agreement, is what the language leaves out. Of
course any moderately complex commercial contract takes a great deal for
granted. The collective agreement is not unique in requiring interpretation
of vague words, authoritative reference to standard practice, and acceptance of evidence that by some course of conduct a party has waived or
agreed to alter a provision of the contract. These difficulties appear in commercial arbitration no less than in labor arbitration, and they require close
understanding of industrial practice. But they do not of themselves refute
the premise that a finding of consent is essential to the interpretation of
the contract.

Given a broad enough view of the "terms" of an agreement, and granting the propriety of discovering terms not explicitly stated, the idea of contract offers few difficulties. Such breadth, however, is not envisioned by
the contract model. The latter is resolutely democratic. There must be a
showing of *specific* consent, even if that consent is inferred from standard
practice or the party's own conduct.

The intellectual and policy leap occurs when the collective agreement
is taken as establishing a new form of organization. The interpreter then
brings to the agreement a theory of what is necessary and desirable if the
new organization is to be sustained and developed. The *theory* becomes
the guide to policy. Reference to consent moves to the background. Its
function is to initiate the system and form the social compact. It is not
itself the touchstone of legitimacy for specific rules and decisions.

When a *system* becomes the focus of responsibility, the principle of limited commitment loses force. "There are too many people, too many problems, too many unforeseeable contingencies to make the words of the contract the exclusive source of rights and duties."[59] But a world of contingency and complexity is with us always. A contract may slice out a part of that world and be designed precisely to escape responsibility for the unforeseen and the contingent. The argument over the collective agreement comes down to this: Is it such a slicing of the world? Or does it define a sphere of institutional responsibility? If the latter, then whatever happens must be dealt with, in the light of the needs of the system, and there can be no refuge in the limited liability of contract. Commitment to a going concern is diffuse, not specific; it is open-ended, not determinate.

Despite much discussion of "past practice" as an inescapable though troublesome criterion for interpreting the provisions of a collective contract,[60] it is very often asked, as in the preceding quotation, whether the *words* of the contract are "the exclusive source of rights and duties." The problem is not resolved, however, by looking from words to conduct. The fundamental question is, can there be appeal to a putative *order*? If so, what is the nature of that order and what principles does it offer for the guidance of decision?[61]

It is now quite clear that the principle of limited commitment has been strongly modified, though not eclipsed, in the evolving law of labor relations. This appears in the judicial conclusion that "the collective agreement covers the whole employment relationship,"[62] with its implications for a very extended view of what the parties intended would be submitted to arbitration; in a current tendency to recognize the survival of seniority rights[63] and grievance procedures[64] despite the expiration of an agreement;

[59] Archibald Cox, "Reflections Upon Labor Arbitration," 72 *Harvard Law Review* 1482, 1498 (1959).

[60] See Benjamin Aaron, "The Uses of the Past in Arbitration," in *Arbitration Today*, Proceedings of the Eighth Annual Meeting of the National Academy of Arbitrators (Washington, D.C.: BNA, Inc., 1955), 1–23; Neil W. Chamberlain, "Discussion," in *Management Rights and the Arbitration Process*, Proceedings of the Ninth Annual Meeting of the National Academy of Arbitrators (Washington, D.C.: BNA, Inc., 1956), 138 ff.

[61] Chamberlain, *ibid.*, argues that "even when the agreement has been signed and sealed, it does not encompass the whole of the relationship. . . . It sets out the explicit understanding of the parties, but there is usually more existing between them than is made explicit. The relationship as well as the agreement creates obligations." This suggests that the assessment of past practices should distinguish (and give special weight to) those that are important to the relationship.

[62] *John Wiley & Sons, Inc.* v. *Livingston*, 376 U.S. 543, 550 (1964).

[63] *Zdanok* v. *Glidden Co.*, 185 F. Supp. 441 (1960); *Oddie* v. *Ross Gear & Tool Co.*, 195 F. Supp. 826 (1961). See Benjamin Aaron, "Reflections on the Legal Nature and Enforceability of Seniority Rights," 75 *Harvard Law Review* 1532 (1962).

[64] "The grievance procedure, once established by the collective bargaining agreement,

and in the enforcement of arbitration awards that go far beyond the limited sphere of money damages. In the modern setting, for example, workers are routinely reinstated on a finding of wrongful discharge despite the policy of contract law against specific enforcement of contracts for personal service.[65]

In principle, contractual liability is limited liability. The range of remedies is restricted. The "cost" of a breach of contract should be coldly assessable in economic terms; it should not be punitive. This accords with the market orientation of modern contract law and with the latent image of a social system composed of discrete individuals entering revocable arrangements based on a temporary balancing of interests. If the aim of the law is to restore equilibrium and, at the same time, preserve maximum freedom of action, then the restriction of remedies, and especially the emphasis on money damages, makes sense. But where the problem is essentially administrative, and the task of law is to help fashion and uphold a system of decision-making, then remedial resources must be more flexible, more complex, more fully adapted to the needs of continuous cooperation.

3. Boundedness. The doctrine of privity (see above, page 59) has played an ambiguous role in the interpretation of collective agreements as contracts to which "the general principles of the law of contracts" are applicable. When the employer covenants with the union, in what sense are employees parties to the agreement? Is the union a principal, the employees third-party beneficiaries? If so, what of the employees' *obligations* under the agreement? Or is the union an agent for the employees? If the employees are parties, does this group include all who are "covered" by the agreement, such as future employees and nonunion members of a legally defined bargaining unit?

One way of handling these perplexities is to construct a two-level theory of the collective bargaining agreement.[66] First we conceive of two organizations, union and employer, exchanging promises. The employer gains from the union a governed workforce and a period of industrial peace, so far as this lies within the power of the union to assure. The union gains organizational and financial security, especially some form of union shop

---

was no longer dependent upon its existence, but only upon the continued relation of employer-employee."*Independent Union* v. *Proctor & Gamble*, 49 LRRM 2703 (1962).
[65] "The common traditions of liberalism and the maxims of contract law in the four countries [United States, Great Britain, France, Mexico] placed on the same plane the essential liberty of the employee not to be required to work involuntarily and that of the employer not to be required to continue a particular employee in his employ." Frederic Meyers, *Ownership of Jobs: A Comparative Study* (Institute of Industrial Relations, University of California, Los Angeles, 1964), 103 f. See also above, 127.
[66] See Cox, *op. cit.*, 19–20.

with dues payments "checked off" automatically from wages, as well as special provisions for shop stewards, use of company property, and the like. Both parties may gain from a provision for arbitration of disputes.[67]

Supplementing this union-management contract is the *individual* employment contract, one for each employee. On this theory, the individual contract remains the only true contract of employment. It alone calls for services to be performed and wages paid. The collective agreement and the individual contract are bridged by a legal presumption: The relevant provisions of the former are accepted *en bloc* as an implied term of the individual contract of employment. Any new employee is hired on the same terms, an approach harking back to a respectable tradition in contract law that "custom and usage" may be incorporated as implied conditions, assuming that the parties have made no explicitly different agreement.

This binary theory of the collective contract is heavily influenced by the principle of privity. It is not, however, a mere formalist exercise, a way of invoking traditional contract principles so as to maintain the integrity of the contract model in labor law. In upholding privity, the courts have sought to defend the "uniquely personal right" of the employee to act in his own interests. If the union is competent to sue for enforcement of the employer's promises to his employees under the collective agreement, then control of the cause of action will drift to the union and the employee's rights will be attenuated. No doubt this conclusion has more often reflected a general animus against unions than a tender regard for employee rights. Still, it is no idle fear, as experience in grievance arbitration has shown.[68]

In the celebrated *Westinghouse* case, the Supreme Court held that Section 301 of the Taft-Hartley Act, though it gave the union standing to sue as a "natural or corporate legal person," did not necessarily contemplate that the union could maintain an action based on the individual rights of employees as distinguished from a duty owed the union as such.[69] It has

---

[67] Recognition of the union's status as a party to the collective agreement was long resisted by the courts, in part reflecting the common-law difficulty of treating unincorporated associations as legal entities. See Charles O. Gregory, *Labor and the Law* (New York: W. W. Norton & Company, Inc., 1961), 446 ff. However, Section 301 of the Taft-Hartley Act (see above, 141) seems to have settled the matter, at least with respect to union's legal competence to sue for protection of its distinctively organizational interests.

[68] See Sanford J. Rosen, "The Individual Worker in Grievance Arbitration: Still Another Look at the Problem," 24 *Maryland Law Review* 233 (1964).

[69] 348 U.S. 437 (1955). In this 6–3 decision Justice Frankfurter, speaking for himself and two colleagues, took the view that under Sec. 301 the union gained only such rights as were allowed it under prevailing state law, and this, rather than the Supreme Court's own policy, would bar unions from maintaining actions to enforce individual rights under

also been held that individual employees or union members do not have a right to sue for breach of contract under Section 301, that is, in the federal courts, since the statute deals only with agreements between unions and employers, not with individual contracts of employment.[70]

These legal outcomes are hardly stable, but they have lent a sense of unreality even to quite recent judicial interpretations of the collective agreement.[71] The effort to protect voluntarism and personal rights by means of rules governing standing to sue tends, in this setting, to fragment a basically corporative relation. Leaders and members are artificially separated, and the union is barred from an important phase of the administration of the agreement—the enforcement of its provisions. Of course the union does participate actively in the grievance procedure, so that the practical result of rules grounded in privity is limited. But the law's effectiveness in the handling of social reality is not furthered.

The basic limitation of the contract model is this: *the contract, not the reality of institutional life, is the starting-point of reasoning and the source of obligation.* This serves the need for legitimacy. The contract provides an authoritative standpoint for making a claim of right or criticizing a course of conduct. But the idea of contract, as we have seen, runs up against the idea of association. Contract begins from different premises and offers tools of analysis that are irrelevant, unhelpful, and often downright inimical to the development of a jurisprudence of associations.

This is not to deny that in practice the law of contract has made many adaptations to the needs of associational life. Contractual terms have been interpreted broadly, the demands of mutuality and privity abated, the range of remedies enlarged, and the "policy of our national labor laws" looked to for judicial guidance. These developments, attenuating the received model, point to its inadequacies. But so long as the basic contractual imagery remains, the new developments have an *ad hoc* and acci-

---

the collective agreement. Two other justices, in a concurring opinion, denied that under Sec. 301 Congress "intended to authorize a union to enforce in a federal court the uniquely personal right of an employee. . . ." In the light of decisions taken by a realigned court in *Lincoln Mills* and the *Steelworkers* cases (see above, 142), it seems likely that the Supreme Court would now adopt the dissenting view of Justice Douglas in *Westinghouse* that "we make mountains out of molehills in not allowing the union to be the suing as well as the bargaining agency for members as respects matters involving the construction and enforcement of the collective bargaining agreement."

[70] *Capra* v. *Suro*, 236 Fed. (2d) 107 (1956).

[71] For a discussion of unrealistic applications of the doctrine of privity where there are multiple collective agreements with the same employer, see Edgar A. Jones, Jr., "Power and Prudence in the Arbitration of Labor Disputes," 11 *UCLA Law Review* 675, 733 ff. (1964).

dental quality. They do not provide rationales to guide the growth of the law. They do not offer new authoritative principles as starting-points of legal reasoning.

The quest for an alternative theory of the labor-management agreement has centered on two related ideas: (1) the *constitutive* character of the contract and (2) the *governmental* nature of the institutions created under the aegis of collective bargaining.

The notion of a "constitutive act" takes us back to Otto von Gierke's effort to establish the social and legal uniqueness of the private association. Gierke argued that the establishment of an association is something more than the sum of individual acts of consent and adherence. The constitutive act creates a new social organism whose juridical nature cannot be wholly derived from the intentions or expectations of the founders. In developing appropriate legal principles the jurist is not to look to the terms of a putative agreement. He is to study the nature of the association and therein find the law.[72]

Collective bargaining is constitutive in that it creates new and continuing institutions, new and irreversible commitments. This has been implicit in much comment on the puzzles and ambiguities of the collective agreement. Such an agreement, it is said, is only in part a determinate bargain struck. More important, it is an exchange of general vows, a pledge of continuing cooperation; it establishes an "autonomous rule of law and reason";[73] it is a treaty, a charter, an instrument of industrial self-government. These and similar epithets do not necessarily agree on the character of the institutional outcome; but they do reflect a widely held view that collective bargaining is constitutive of an organic social unity and that this, inevitably, will have to be handled by the law in its own terms.

The constitutive character of the collective agreement is manifested in (a) the creation, within the enterprise, of new forms of responsibility and new agencies of administration, notably the bargaining unit and the grievance machinery; (b) the transformation of the legal requirement to "bargain in good faith" into a *modus operandi* extending over the entire life of the agreement and suffusing the relationship in depth;[74] and (c) the

---

[72] Gierke's theory appears in his *Die Genossenschaftstheorie und die Deutsche Rechtsprechung* (Berlin, 1887), 114 ff. A critical but closely related standpoint is adopted in Leon Duguit, "Collective Acts as Distinguished from Contracts," 27 *Yale Law Journal* 753, 762 (1918).

[73] Harry Shulman, "Reason, Contract, and Law in Labor Relations," 68 *Harvard Law Review* 999 (1955). See also Gregory, *op. cit.*, Chap. XIV.

[74] Benjamin Werne, *Law and Practice of the Labor Contract* (Chicago: Callaghan and Company, 1957), 250.

de facto and legal modification of the doctrine of managerial "reserved rights."[75] These developments have not been adventitious. They have their source in a compelling institutional logic. And taken together they delineate what is really fundamental in the collective bargain: the fashioning of a new set of roles and relationships; commitment to the ensuing system of order; affirmation of a new principle of legitimacy.

Thus conceived, the constitutive contract in labor-management relations is a kind of "social contract." Its function is to create a political community. In keeping with the premises of social-contract doctrine, contract is looked to as a font of legitimacy, and as a way of conceiving the formation of a polity, but it is not imposed as a theory of the constitutional outcome. The idea of contract is important in upholding the principle of consent and pointing to broad reciprocal obligations of the governors and the governed. But room is left for autonomous theories of fidelity to law, just governance, and the affirmative responsibilities of statesmanship.

This line of thought is obviously congenial to the view that the collective agreement brings into being a system of government. And indeed, the governmental analogy was adopted by some at an early point in the discussion. In 1921 William M. Leiserson, then chairman of the Board of Arbitration of the men's clothing industry in New York, wrote of "trade agreements" as "industrial constitutions."[76] The absolute right of the employer to make and change the rules of work is contested by the union in the shop:

> Thus government by discussion enters into industry (as it did in the state) when the ruler can no longer arbitrarily force obedience to his laws, and must get the consent of those who are to obey the regulations.
> Then a parliament is set up, a talking place, if you please, in the form of periodical conferences or conventions of the employers and the wage-earners. The employers come to these meetings in their own right, as the lords of the industry, the wage-earners come by their representatives; so that a parliamentary form of government is organized with the employers acting as a sort of House of Lords and the union representatives as a House of Commons.[77]

In this perspective, "industrial disputes and strikes appear in a new aspect . . . not so much as interruptions of industry, but more as incidents in a

---

[75] See below, 178 ff.
[76] William M. Leiserson, "Constitutional Government in American Industries," *The American Economic Review*, 12 (March, 1922), 60. (Supplement: Papers and Proceedings of the Thirty-fourth Annual Meeting of the American Economic Association, December, 1921.)
[77] *Ibid.*

long struggle for representation of labor in the government of industrial enterprises.[78]

In 1940 a federal court adopted this view, saying that "the trade agreement thus becomes, as it were, the industrial constitution of the enterprise, setting forth the general principles upon which the relationship of employer and employee is to be conducted.[79] And finally, in the *Steelworkers* cases of 1960, referred to above (page 142), the Supreme Court lent its authority to the governmental analogy: "A collective bargaining agreement is an effort to erect a system of industrial self-government."[80]

For the courts, the idea of government has been relied on to escape the confines of a narrowly contractualist interpretation of the collective agreement. That the notion of government has been needed is evidence for the conclusion that the idea of contract could not by itself provide the doctrinal foundations for sustaining in law the new institutions of labor-management accommodation.

If the collective agreement is "an instrument of government as well as an instrument of exchange,"[81] what makes it so? The basic argument for this position is that *rule-making is an indispensable feature of the administration of the collective agreement.* Rules are not given but must be elaborated over time. Otherwise the agreement could not be effective as a way of regulating a large number of activities marked by unceasing change and heterogeneous interests.

The authority to make rules is inherent in the function of management. Hence the relevance of the "common law of the shop" to the governmental model:

> The collective bargaining agreement states the rights and duties of the parties. It is more than a contract; it is a generalized code to govern a myriad of cases which the draftsmen cannot wholly anticipate. . . . The collective agreement covers the whole employment relationship. It calls into being a new common law—the common law of a particular industry or of a particular plant.[82]

This "common law" is related to, but should not be confounded with, the

---

[78] *Ibid.*, 75. On p. 63 Leiserson says: "It is in the lack of a properly developed judicial department that the constitutional government established by trade union agreements shows its greatest weakness." After the Second World War this statement would need radical revision.

[79] *National Labor Relations Board v. Highland Park Manufacturing Co.,* 110 Fed. 2d 632, 638 (4th Cir. 1940).

[80] *Steelworkers v. Warrior & Gulf,* 363 U.S. 574.

[81] Archibald Cox, "The Legal Nature of Collective Bargaining Agreements," 57 *Michigan Law Review* 1, 22 (1958).

[82] *Steelworkers v. Warrior & Gulf,* 363 U.S. 574, 578–579.

"living law" of industry, that is, the observable patterns of decision-making and conduct. Common law results from authoritative determinations of which practices are to be upheld as binding, which changes are to be recognized as warranted. Though it may invoke what has been regularized in practice, it is necessarily selective. This is a procedure quite distinct from treating past practice as an implied term of an agreement or interpreting variant, acquiesced-in conduct as an implied revision. If the idea of a common law is to be taken seriously, legal creativity must be acknowledged, however much it may be contained by reference to a basic charter or to received premises of decision.

Chamberlain has suggested that "collective bargaining, at least in some areas, is now ripening into a *method of management* in the firm."[83] When unions win the right to participate in decisions affecting the conditions of employment, this does not change the managerial character of the decisions. The procedures of management have changed, but not the function itself. Collective bargaining, he points out, should be seen as a phase of the evolution of management. Whatever else this new method of management may entail, it includes a new approach to the formulation and administration of rules. The distinctive office of the union is to shift the focus of rule-making from the achievement of external business objectives to the validation of *internal* claims of right. Whenever this transformation takes place, rule-making takes on a legal aspect, in the sense that standards of fairness are systematically invoked as limitations on managerial authority. The cost of upholding those standards and validating legitimate expectations becomes a burden on the enterprise, partly as added expense in operating the system, partly in the form of limitations placed on freedom and flexibility of management.

It follows that if collective bargaining "creates" a system of government, it does so by helping to reconstruct the managerial process. Management becomes more conscious of rules, more conscious of rights, *and more capable of building that consciousness into the routines of institutional life*. The administration of "things" becomes the governance of men as this reconstruction proceeds.

Creative Arbitration

The constitutive, institution-forming character of collective bargaining is most fully revealed in the rapid growth and widespread acceptance of

---

[83] Neil W. Chamberlain, "Collective Bargaining and the Concept of Contract," 48 *Columbia Law Review* 829, 845 (1948).

grievance arbitration. There are about 125,000 labor-management agreements in the United States, and 94 per cent of these contain a provision for arbitration as the final step of a grievance procedure.[84] Grievance arbitration presumes the existence of a collective agreement. It is a machinery established by that instrument. Therefore grievance arbitration should be distinguished from arbitration relied on to settle deadlocked negotiations prior to the reaching of an agreement. The latter procedure is less common, usually resorted to *ad hoc,* and more likely to deal with wage rates or fringe benefits rather than individual grievances or administrative procedures. This discussion is exclusively concerned with grievance arbitration.

The rise of grievance arbitration, and the legal evolution to which it has contributed, lend much support to the governmental analogy. For in this institution we see a response to the need for lawfulness in the day-to-day administration of the large enterprise. The achievement and nurture of a rule of law is a governmental function par excellence, and grievance arbitration has contributed to that outcome in three fundamental ways.

First, arbitration has helped transform managerial authority by providing a forum for criticizing managerial decisions and holding them accountable to objective criteria. This means that the issue of legitimacy is pursued in depth. The propriety of a decision is not settled by reference to a general grant of authority. It is always open to question and may be addressed by resort to an institutionalized procedure. As we have noted above, this opportunity is one of the marks of a developed legal order.[85]

Second, by offering a machinery for case-by-case interpolation, arbitration has helped sustain the collective contract as a charter establishing a system of order rather than an aggregate of specific, bargained-out provisions.

The availability of arbitration can make sense of the negotiators' decision to write into the contract such general formulas as "employees shall not be discharged except for just cause."

> What this is to mean in practice is left to the grievance procedure and, if there is no agreement, ultimately to arbitration. Similar general phrases are found in other areas of the contract. Promotions will go to the senior employee, provided he is "reasonably" qualified to do the work; call-in pay will be given, except when work is unavailable because of an "emergency"; employees will be given their choice of vacation periods "whenever possible"—these and countless other phrases may have represented a meeting of minds at the time of negotiations, but are obviously too inexact to

---

[84] Bureau of Labor Statistics, *Major Collective Bargaining Agreements*: (1) *Grievance Procedures,* Bulletin 1425–1 (November, 1964), p. 2.
[85] See 30 f.

answer every practical problem that arises later. . . . Union contract interpretation is difficult enough when negotiators intended to express full
agreement. But it becomes more difficult when language was meant not to
express agreement, but—for pragmatic reasons—to conceal the absence
of agreement.[86]

The perils of this legislative open-endedness can be mitigated, and turned
to advantage, when it is agreed that disputed cases will be referred to an
independent tribunal. The tribunal is then something more than an
emergency resource. It becomes occasion and opportunity for reliance
on general language, not as a measure of desperation but as a self-
consciously established framework within which orderly adaptation can
take place.

Third, arbitration has tended to enlarge the meaning of the collective
agreement. The latter is increasingly viewed as a document endowed with
"constitutional" completeness. Characteristically the arbitrator cannot send
the parties back to the bargaining table on the ground that the agreement does not speak to the issue before him. Instead the logic of his role,
together with the urgencies of labor-management accommodation, press
for decision and summon creative interpretation.

This evolution has occurred in a basically autonomous way, as a system
of industrial *self*-government.

Although grievance arbitration received a considerable impetus from
the activities of the War Labor Board in World War II,[87] its postwar
entrenchment took place without supportive legislation and in a context
of considerable legal ambiguity. Perhaps the greatest influence of the law
stemmed from the involvement of lawyers in the work of arbitration,
both as arbitrators and as counsel. They inevitably brought with them
many of the attitudes and concepts of the Anglo-American legal tradition.
Still, the setting was a private one and litigation was not in the offing.

The autonomy of grievance arbitration was stressed in an influential
address by Dean Harry Shulman of Yale Law School, a leading figure
among labor arbitrators and for many years permanent umpire under the
agreement between the Ford Motor Company and the United Automobile

---

[86] Morris Stone, *Labor-Management Contracts at Work* (New York: Harper & Row, 1961), 4f.

[87] Gregory, *op. cit.*, 453, 477. However, "in 1941 the United States Conciliation Service found that 63 per cent of the 1,200 agreements in its files included arbitration as a final step in the grievance procedure, and in 1942 the National Industrial Conference Board noted arbitration in about three-fourths of the 163 contracts which it studied." R. W. Fleming, "The Labor Arbitration Process: 1943–1963," in *Labor Arbitration: Perspectives and Problems*, Proceedings of the Seventeenth Annual Meeting of the National Academy of Arbitrators (Washington, D.C.: BNA, Inc., 1964), 33f.

Workers. In that essay he described "the autonomous rule of law and reason which the collective labor agreement establishes," but went on to say:

> The arbitration is an integral part of the system of self-government. . . . It is a means of making collective bargaining work and thus preserving private enterprise in a free government. When it works fairly well, it does not need the sanction of the law of contracts or the law of arbitration. It is only when the system breaks down completely that the courts' aid in these respects is invoked. But the courts cannot, by occasional sporadic decision, restore the parties' continuing relationship; and their intervention in such cases may seriously affect the going systems of self-government. When their autonomous system breaks down, might not the parties better be left to the usual methods of adjustment of labor disputes rather than to court actions on the contract or on the arbitration award? I suggest that the law stay out—but, mind you, not the lawyers.[88]

While upholding the constitutive and governmental character of the collective agreement, Shulman stressed that that ordering would be most effective if it were fully self-administered.

Within a very short time the Supreme Court gave its own answer to the issue posed by Shulman. This response had two main parts. The first was revealed in 1957 in the case of *Textile Workers Union v. Lincoln Mills*,[89] to which we have already had occasion to refer, and two companion cases. With this decision, declaring that arbitration awards under labor-management contracts would be enforced by the federal courts under Section 301 of the Taft-Hartley Act, and that those courts should develop a federal common law "from the policy of our national labor laws,"[90] the authority of judicial intervention was established and its possibility loomed large. In the wake of the *Lincoln Mills* decision, anxiety was expressed that the courts would lay a rude hand on the delicate fabric of collective bargaining, interfering with the autonomy of arbitration and introducing their own legal preconceptions into the interpretation of collective agreements.[91] The main danger perceived was that the courts, especially in cases where "arbitrability" was at issue, that is, when they were required to decide whether or not a dispute was properly subject to arbitration under the agreement, would take too much on themselves. In so doing, it was feared, they would weaken the institution of arbitration by

---

[88] Shulman, "Reason, Contract, and Law in Labor Relations."
[89] See above, 142.
[90] *Textile Workers Union v. Lincoln Mills*, 353 U.S. 448, 457 (1957).
[91] See Benjamin Aaron, "On First Looking into the Lincoln Mills Decision," in *Arbitration and the Law*, Proceedings of the Twelfth Annual Meeting of the National Academy of Arbitrators (Washington, D.C.: BNA, Inc., 1959).

narrowing its jurisdiction, and they would usually be passing on the merits of the underlying grievance.[92]

The second peal of the bell allayed these fears and, at the same time, gave to arbitration a remarkable mandate. The *Steelworkers* cases of 1960[93] sharply restricted judicial intervention. On the premise that the national labor policy stated in the Taft-Hartley Act called for a consensual method of settlement[94] which could be "effectuated only if the means chosen by the parties for settlement of their differences under a collective bargaining agreement is given full play," it was concluded that courts "have no business weighing the merits of the grievance, considering whether there is equity in a particular claim, or determining whether there is particular language in the written instrument which will support the claim.[95] "An order to arbitrate the particular grievance should not be denied unless it may be said with positive assurance that the arbitration clause is not susceptible of an interpretation that covers the asserted dispute. Doubts should be resolved in favor of coverage."[96]

Thus, without giving up the ultimate power of interpreting labor-management contracts, the Supreme Court lent its support to a private mode of decision. As it did so, it reached out for a distinctive view of the collective contract and, as we have seen,[97] embraced the governmental analogy.

The imagery of law and governance was evoked to reinforce an autonomous system of adjudication, granting to the arbitrator authority to reason from general principles so that unforeseen problems might be "governed by an agreed-upon rule of law."[98]

> Courts and arbitration in the context of most commercial contracts are resorted to because there has been a breakdown in the working relation-

---

[92] One New York case along this line that created considerable consternation among arbitrators was *International Association of Machinists* v. *Cutler-Hammer, Inc.*, 271 App. Div. 917 (1947). The court refused the union's request that a dispute over payment of a bonus be required to go to arbitration, saying "If the meaning of the provision of the contract sought to be arbitrated is beyond dispute, there cannot be anything to arbitrate and the contract cannot be said to provide for arbitration." This means that the court rather than the arbitrator decides the meaning of the contract. The Cutler-Hammer doctrine was explicitly rejected by the U.S. Supreme Court in *United Steelworkers* v. *American Manufacturing Co.*, 363 U.S. 564, 566–567 (1960).

[93] Cited above, fn. 47.

[94] The court referred to Sec. 203(d): "Final adjustment by a method agreed upon by the parties is hereby declared to be the desirable method for settlement of grievance disputes arising over the application or interpretation of an existing collective-bargaining agreement."

[95] *Steelworkers* v. *American Manufacturing*, 363 U.S. 564, 566 (1960).

[96] *Steelworkers* v. *Warrior & Gulf*, 363 U.S. 574, 582–583 (1960).

[97] See above, 153.

[98] *Steelworkers* v. *Warrior & Gulf*, 363 U.S. 580 (1960).

ship of the parties; such resort is the unwanted exception. But the grievance machinery under a collective bargaining agreement is at the very heart of the system of industrial self-government. Arbitration is the means of solving the unforeseeable by molding a system of private law for all the problems which may arise and to provide for their solution in a way which will generally accord with the variant needs and desires of the parties. The processing of disputes through the grievance machinery is actually a vehicle by which meaning and content are given to the collective bargaining agreement.[99]

Clearly the prior development of grievance arbitration had created the social foundations for legal recognition. Its *de facto* institutional strength was a resource for the common law. In turning to it, the court elegantly reaffirmed the basic national policy established by the Wagner Act: Let voluntary arrangements be the source of viable law; use law to encourage, require, confirm, and strengthen institutions of private accommodation.[100]

In preferring the private arbitrator to the public judge, the Supreme Court was saying that disputed issues should not be subject to purely legal analysis, that is, assessed in the light of received concepts. Rather, a forum closer to the scene should adapt law and law-making to the industrial realities. For example, if "insubordination" is to be a basis for discharge, there should be assessment of what conduct actually is an insupportable affront to the employment relation. The case should not be decided by application of a general formula drawn from the law of master and servant.[101]

Although the mechanism of decision is to be private, the function performed is inescapably a public one. This is so in two senses. First, arbitration is to be an instrument of national policy. Second, the work of rule-making is to be carried out in contemplation of a microcosmic public order—the quasi-polity of the enterprise. These expectations could not but require a firmer definition of the arbitrator's role.

The dilemmas of that role have their source in the simultaneous pursuit of peace and justice. The avowed aim of the national labor policy is peace, not justice. But is it peace *through* justice? This would seem a reasonable conclusion, at least so far as grievance arbitration is concerned. But there has not been an explicit commitment to such a policy, and the

---

[99] *Ibid.*, 581.
[100] For a more negative view of the Supreme Court's reasoning and policy, by a federal judge, see Paul R. Hays, *Labor Arbitration: A Dissenting View* (New Haven: Yale University Press, 1966); for an arbitrator's response, see the review by Saul Wallen, 81 *Harvard Law Review* 507–512 (1967).
[101] See Jones, *op. cit.*, 675, 729–733.

nature of arbitration cannot be clearly derived from the legal theory up-holding it.

If industrial harmony is the objective, two conclusions may be drawn for the work of arbitration:

(1) The arbitrator may be expected and authorized to serve as a medi-ator-physician rather than as a judge; his primary objective is to continue the work of collective bargaining, helping the parties to settle grievances in the same spirit that they arrived at the collective agreement itself. "By this view the arbitrator has a roving commission to straighten things out, the immediate controversy marking the occasion for, but not the limits of, his intervention."[102]

(2) The standards of decision, including the procedures of hearing and assessment, are established autonomously by the parties themselves. If *they* agree on a way of deciding their own disputes, then no external requirements need be set. In the interest of peace the law will refrain from imposing a theory of arbitration and the special constraints that would go with it. We shall briefly assess both of these hypotheses.

1. Arbitration as adjudication.   Peace may be won by helpful problem-solving, including *ad hoc* changes in the arbitrator's role and the bargained sacrifice of some interests to others. In the event, the general welfare may be served. But if justice is uppermost, if it is the chosen vehicle of peace-making, it should be more than the benign outcome of pressure and counter-pressure, mediation and consultation. The doing of justice must be embodied in a procedure that has distinctive attributes of legitimacy and fairness.

In some provocative dicta, the Supreme Court has emphasized the ameliorative work of arbitration. We quote again from Justice William O. Douglas, who spoke for the court in *Warrior & Gulf*:

> The labor arbitrator is usually chosen because of the parties' confidence in his knowledge of the common law of the shop and their trust in his personal judgment to bring to bear considerations which are not expressed in the contract as criteria for judgment. The parties expect that his judg-ment of a particular grievance will reflect not only what the contract says but, insofar as the collective bargaining agreement permits, such factors as the effect upon productivity of a particular result, its consequences to the morale of the shop, his judgment whether tensions will be heightened or diminished. For the parties' objective in using the arbitration process is primarily to further their common goal of uninterrupted production under the agreement, to make the agreement serve their specialized needs. The

---

[102] Lon L. Fuller, "Collective Bargaining and the Arbitrator," 1963 *Wisconsin Law Review* 4 (1963).

ablest judge cannot be expected to bring the same experience and competence to bear upon the determination of a grievance, because he cannot be similarly informed.[103]

These and similar comments seem to undercut the theory of arbitration as an essentially adjudicative process in which "the law of the contract" is applied to specific disputes. On the other hand, that theory is not explicitly refuted, as it was by Dean Shulman, who once objected to speaking of the grievance procedure as the "judicial branch" of industrial government. This "beguiling metaphor," he said, diverts attention from the principal function of arbitration, which is "to advance the parties' cooperation in their joint enterprise."[104]

The key problem here, glossed over in the opinions, is whether a valid distinction can be drawn between (a) the "tailored" decision, in which the probable consequences of deciding the specific case one way or the other, or granting a certain remedy, are allowed to determine the outcome, and (b) interstitial rule-making. The former does indeed strain the judicial role, for equal protection of the law cannot be afforded where the merits of each case vary according to the needs of the social system. If a judge is one who, among other things, decides cases according to rules and principles applicable to all similar fact-situations, the integrity of what he is about is gravely undermined when prudence is his only yardstick.

In the passage just quoted Justice Douglas spoke of "the effect upon productivity of a particular result." If this refers to the legislative work of arbitration, if by result is meant the formulation of an operative rule, there is no offense to the judicial character of the proceeding—so long as we bear in mind the nature and scope of judicial law-making. Strain there may be, but it is not fundamentally different from that which afflicts the judge who must exercise creativity. It should be remembered that the arbitrator does not sit as an inferior tribunal within a larger hierarchy. He is the final arbiter. As such, he combines the fact-finding work of the trial judge and the more interpretive duties of the appellate court.

When the arbitrator helps develop the common law of the shop, for example in recognizing seniority as a valid ground for mitigating punishment, he does not sacrifice judicial integrity if he takes account of morale

---

[103] *Steelworkers v. Warrior & Gulf*, 363 U.S. 582 (1960). In 1964 the Court was heard to speak of arbitration as a "therapy" that could produce a "curative effect." *Carey v. Westinghouse Electric Corp.*, 375 U.S. 261, 272, 265 (1964).
[104] Harry Shulman, "The Role of Arbitration in the Collective Bargaining Process," in *Collective Bargaining and Arbitration* (Institute of Industrial Relations, University of California, 1949), 20.

and problems of personnel turnover. If the case at hand is an occasion for the elaboration of rules and principles, a result-oriented jurisprudence makes sense and is consistent with the judicial role. Of course, the newly established rule must be applied to similar cases with an even hand.

When it is said that arbitration is an extension of collective bargaining, this can mean that the arbitrator serves as a political broker helping the parties to come to detailed agreements within the framework of the basic contract. But it can also mean that the arbitrator is granted authority, as part of the collective bargain, to make interstitial rules subject to later revision by the parties. In that sense his role is comparable to the judge whose similar common-law authority is, save on constitutional questions, subject to revision by the legislature.

Thus the objective of industrial harmony is compatible with the judicial role if the process of "applying the law" is not too narrowly conceived. The word "law" refers to a broad range of authoritative materials, some quite general and inchoate, some very explicit. A judge may "apply the law" by fashioning detailed rules from general principles. When he does so he engages in a discretionary assessment of the setting to which the rules are to be applied. In exercising that discretion he properly takes account of institutional needs.

2. The limits of authority.   Where should the arbitrator look for authoritative guides to decision? What is the applicable law? For those who think of arbitration as adjudication, the answer is usually plain: "It lies in the contract itself."[105] The arbitrator who cleaves to the contract will sustain his own legitimacy, for he is the creature of that instrument and is usually enjoined not to alter its provisions. He will preserve the integrity of adjudication by setting a frame within which reasoning and argument can proceed. And he will uphold the autonomy of industrial government.

But does "the contract itself" determine the standards that govern how arbitration is to be conducted? The parties may be content with rough and ready decision-making, and some arbitrators have said that that is up to them.[106] On the other hand, there is a notable strain toward recog-

---

[105] Fuller, *op. cit.*, 29.

[106] Thus one arbitrator has said: "The fundamental question is what do the parties expect of the arbitration process? I believe that they have the right to get what they expect and that if what they expect does not conform to the niceties of 'due process,' it is not the arbitrator's function to alter their voluntary arrangement in the absence of any applicable law which demands otherwise." Quoted in W. Willard Wirtz, "Due Process of Arbitration," in Jean T. McKelvey (ed.), *The Arbitrator and the Parties*, Proceedngs of the Eleventh Annual Meeting of the National Academy of Arbitrators (Washington, D.C.: BNA, Inc., 1958), 4.

nition of more objective criteria, especially where individual rights are affected.[107] Arbitrators are not anxious to be bound by procedural rules developed in the courts, but in practice the premise is widely accepted that essential fairness cannot be bargained away.

When the contract creates a distinctive institution, such as grievance arbitration, it establishes the relevance of a new set of moral and legal standards. These standards are founded in the nature of the institution created, not in the agreement of the parties. In varying degrees, this applies to other agreed-upon activities, such as the provision of medical services, where the autonomy of professional standards is presumed. In the case of arbitration, there is an especially wide-ranging commitment, potentially affecting almost any aspect of the enterprise. And the more it is perceived as adjudication, the greater is the expectation that arbitration will reflect the ideals of Anglo-American jurisprudence.

Even without its mandate from the courts, arbitration would inevitably respond to community expectations and to the arbitrator's own sense of professional integrity. This tendency can only be strengthened by the Supreme Court's vote of confidence. An implied premise of the Court's deference to arbitration is that, by and large, these private decision-makers will not offend the sense of justice; and the quality of their decisions will not be inferior to those of a court. Indeed it was thought that arbitration decisions would be superior in quality because of a greater competence to assess the facts of industrial life. It was taken for granted that the arbitrator would be capable of conducting his office with due regard for the integrity of the procedure.

The parties' autonomy is limited, therefore, by public expectations regarding the administration of justice. Grievance arbitration promises peace through justice. To make good on that promise the system must reflect, with sufficient fidelity, the public consensus regarding procedural fairness and minimal substantive rights. This will require an adjudicative role for the arbitrator; nor can that role be bounded by exclusive reliance on the terms of the contract.

In the not too distant future, the public interest in industrial justice may well create a legal presumption that the establishment of grievance arbitration is tantamount to the writing of a preambular clause stating that one aim of the collective agreement is "to establish justice." Such

---

[107] See *ibid.*; also R. W. Fleming, "Due Process and Fair Procedure in Labor Arbitration," in Spencer D. Pollard (ed.), *Arbitration and Public Policy*, Proceedings of the Fourteenth Annual Meeting of the National Academy of Arbitrators (Washington, D.C.: BNA, Inc., 1961), 69–91.

a presumption will both authorize and require that the grievance procedure be governed by appropriate standards of due process. To a considerable extent, as we shall see, the practice of arbitration has already assumed this responsibility.

Creative arbitration as industrial law-making draws upon three basic resources: (1) The collective contract, whose interpretation is the starting-point of reasoning; (2) the received Anglo-American legal tradition, not as a body of specific rules but as a reservoir of principles and of funded knowledge; (3) the social reality of the enterprise. We can illustrate this creativity by presenting, with only very brief elaboration, a few principles that appear to have emerged in the recent history of grievance arbitration.[108]

1. The formation of the collective contract creates an inherent bar to arbitrary action by the employer. This principle presumes that the contract is something more than its specific provisions. It is incompatible with the view that the contract reserves all power to management save what is explicitly given up. In the arbitration cases the discussion of this problem has centered on whether there exists an inherent bar to arbitrary discharge, even when a "just cause" provision does not appear in the agreement. In 1952 the majority of the New York Supreme Court adopted a "strict constructionist" doctrine:

> Paragraph "fifteenth" of the collective bargaining agreement places no restriction on the inherent right of appellant to discharge an employee with or without cause. Nor can any such restriction be found in any other clause of the contract. In the absence of such inhibition an employer has an absolute right of discharge.[109]

On this view, shared by a number of arbitrators, there is no recourse for an employee who feels he has been dealt with unfairly unless the contract specifically restricts the employer's right to discharge. Even when faced with a contract stipulating that discharge may be only for "cause," some arbitrators have contended that "cause" means only that the employer has a reason for the action taken.

---

[108] Based upon a systematic review of arbitration awards, primarily as reported in Vols. 1–35 of *Labor Arbitration Reports* (Washington, D.C.: BNA, Inc., 1946–1960), hereinafter cited as "LA." For studies summarizing the trend of arbitration decisions, see Myron Gollub, *Discharge for Cause* (State of New York, Department of Labor, Special Bulletin No. 221, 1948); Orme W. Phelps, *Discipline and Discharge in the Unionized Firm* (Berkeley and Los Angeles: University of Calif. Press, 1959); Lawrence Stessin, *Employee Discipline* (Washington, D.C.: BNA, Inc., 1960); Eli Ginzberg *et al.*, *Democratic Values and the Rights of Management* (New York: Columbia University Press, 1963); R. W. Fleming, *The Labor Arbitration Process* (Urbana: University of Illinois Press, 1965).
[109] See 18 LA 595 (1952).

In a number of other cases, however, arbitrators have relied on a quite different approach. An often-cited decision by Saul Wallen of the Connecticut State Board of Mediation and Arbitration included the following statement:

> In our opinion the meaning of the contract, when viewed as a whole, is that a limitation on the Employer's right to discharge was created at the birth of the instrument. Both the necessity for maintaining the integrity of the contract's component parts and the very nature of collective agreements are the basis for this conclusion.[110]

This doctrine has received considerable support. Thus in 1954 one arbitrator concluded: "It is part of the 'common law' of industrial relations—one of the tacit assumptions underlying all collective agreements—that the employer shall not exercise arbitrarily his power to discipline workers."[111] In another case it was asserted that "a 'just cause' basis for consideration of disciplinary action is, absent a clear proviso to the contrary, implied in a modern collective bargaining agreement."[112] The rationale of the doctrine was stated in a 1961 case:

> It has been justifiably said [that] "protection against arbitrary discharge is possibly the most important single benefit which the worker secures from trade unionism." It does more than anything else to make him a free citizen in the plant. Without commenting at length on this statement, where the working agreement is silent on the matter of discipline the very nature of the working agreement, absent a clear proviso to the contrary, makes clear an implied understanding that the Company does not have the unilateral right to discipline or discharge an individual without such action being subject to challenge by the Union as to whether the Company's action was for just cause. It is clear, for example, that the seniority provision of the working agreement would, in the final analysis, have little meaning if employees could be discharged promiscuously by the Company. This is true for the reason that an individual that otherwise could be discharged without just cause and rehired the following day . . . would thereby lose all of his seniority and related rights and be sent back to the foot of the seniority roster. The same observation could be made in varying degrees as regards many other valuable rights earned by employees under the terms of the working agreement. While the Impartial Arbitrator has generally followed the concept that the Union has only those rights bargained for and specifically set out in the contract, for the reasons set forth above he believes that management intended to discharge only for cause and that the Union does have the right to grieve, to process the grievance, and to have the matter determined on its merits by arbitration.[113]

---

[110] 13 LA 747 (1949).
[111] 22 LA 761 (1954).
[112] 25 LA 295 (1955).
[113] Commerce Clearing House, 62–1 *Labor Arbitration Awards*, #8172 (1962).

Here the authority of the contract is upheld, but a canon of interpretation is used ("absent a clear proviso to the contrary") that incorporates a social theory of what collective bargaining is about, including the legitimate expectations it creates. In addition a principle of contract law is relied on to the effect that "you read into a contract those obligations that are essential to achieve its principal objectives."[114]

2. The principles of industrial justice should not be so applied as to undermine the legitimate objectives of the firm. Although management may not act arbitrarily, it may apply objective criteria of efficiency and effectiveness in the administration of the enterprise. Accordingly arbitrators recognize that employees have obligations as well as rights. Among the more important obligations of employees, apart from minimal work performance, are (a) regular presence at the place of employment, (b) proper respect for authority, (c) an appropriate level of competence, and (d) cooperation with other employees.

Unexcused absenteeism is usually held to be sufficient ground for discipline.[115] Where absenteeism is excessive, even because of ill health, the arbitrator may uphold the discharge, concluding that such irregularity of attendance destroys the employee's value to the firm.[116] But employers may be required to exercise restraint when a prolonged absence is for good cause.[117] Absence due to jail sentences has been held justifiable reason for discharge when the sentence is long, but not when the period in jail is short.[118] The employer may be required to stay his hand pending a decision in the courts, for if the man is acquitted it would be unjust to penalize him for having to defend his innocence.[119]

There is no justifiable insubordination, but it may be difficult to determine how serious the act was or whether it was indeed insubordinate. The propriety of punishment where the worker has physically assaulted a supervisor is considered obvious.[120] Not only refusal to carry out orders but prolonged debate over them may subject the employee to discipline.[121] However, the mere verbal expression of a disagreement will not ordinarily be justifiable ground for discipline.[122] Arbitrators uphold management in

---

[114] Fuller, *op. cit.*, 9. Fuller compares the Wallen arbitration decision cited above with the process of implication in contract law, concluding that "it seems odd indeed that the award should be regarded as involving any unusual standard of interpretation."
[115] See 21 LA 248 (1953); 23 LA 223 (1954); 27 LA 812 (1956).
[116] 11 LA 419 (1948).
[117] 24 LA 385 (1955).
[118] 12 LA 759 (1949); 24 LA 606 (1955); 25 LA 281 (1955).
[119] 21 LA 771 (1953); 23 LA 574 (1954); 35 LA 77 (1960).
[120] 24 LA 401 (1955).
[121] 23 LA 696 (1955); 24 LA 804 (1955).
[122] 17 LA 436 (1951).

requiring the employee to obey orders promptly, but this does not bar the employee from giving reasonable expression to his own views. Insubordination will be excused where carrying out the order would clearly be dangerous,[123] and the penalty imposed by management may be reduced by the arbitrator because of mitigating factors, but in general arbitration has given management a relatively free hand in dealing with insubordination.

An employee must not only attend, obey, and be willing to work. He must also be capable. If he is not, the arbitrator will usually uphold management in discharging him provided objective criteria are used in the assessment of competence and the action is not discriminatory.[124] Strictly speaking, discharge or demotion for incompetence is not a matter of discipline, but it does strike at job security. For this reason arbitrators, while sustaining the right of management to weed out incompetence, insist that alleged inability be demonstrable.[125]

Efficiency is largely dependent on a cooperative workforce. Assuming adequate proof and no mitigating factors, the punishment of brawling employees will be upheld.[126] Arbitrators are also sensitive to more subtle disturbances of the harmony of the workforce. One sustained the dismissal of a female employee who had a "negative" attitude which led other employees to refuse to work for her. He observed that "in the work situation, perhaps more than in most outside relationships, the individual must adjust relatively well to the group or tensions will be created that interfere with efficiency and productivity."[127] Events disruptive of a peaceful atmosphere, such as a fight between employees before work has begun[128] or preaching the gospel during lunch hour[129] have been accepted by arbitrators as justifying discharge.

It is evident that arbitrators are conscious of management's right to have a dependable, efficient, and cooperative workforce to be directed as the needs of production dictate. In claiming these rights management must show that they are related to the efficient operation of the business. They are not simple prerogatives of legal ownership or control.

3. Conduct off the job, not clearly detrimental to the proper function-

---

[123] 8 LA 826 (1948).
[124] 20 LA 480 (1953); 19 LA 709 (1953); 35 LA 794 (1960); 12 LA 527 (1949); 27 LA 209 (1956).
[125] See Stessin, *op. cit.*, 164–166; Phelps, *Discipline and Discharge*, 61–67; 34 LA 610 (1960).
[126] 35 LA 1 (1960).
[127] 26 LA 272 (1956).
[128] 21 LA 106 (1953).
[129] 18 LA 788 (1952).

ing of the enterprise, is outside the purview of management control.
Arbitrators have adopted the view that the modern employment relation
is limited in scope. It leaves to employees a private sphere of life of which
management may disapprove but in which it has no legitimate interest.
"It is generally considered by arbitrators that a man's conduct outside of
the plant and outside working hours is his own affair and is not subject
to paternalistic control of the employer."[130] "The private life of an individual while away from work should not ordinarily, standing alone, be
the basis of a discharge by the company for which he has worked and
rendered good service."[131]

This doctrine, while stating a presumption, does not ignore the needs
of the firm. Physical assaults on members of management, even though
occurring during off-duty hours, have been upheld as grounds for discipline because of the probable effect on authority within the firm.[132] Employees may hurt the competitive position of the company by making
public statements damaging to its product.[133] Similar reasoning is often
applied when employees work for their principal employer's competitor
provided the employer has established rules prohibiting such work.[134] Control over this aspect of off-duty behavior is presumably based on the
conflict of loyalty that might arise. Nevertheless, such rules usually must
be officially promulgated and the employee given reasonable time to conform before they become the basis for disciplinary action.[135]

An employee's outside activity may place his job in jeopardy if it casts
doubt on his trustworthiness as an employee. The suspension until his
acquittal of a truck driver arrested for drunk driving was held proper. The
arbitrator denied the grievant's request for back pay in view of the fact
that the company had not prejudged him guilty but had merely exercised proper managerial authority in refusing him access to trucks.[136] An
employee who worked in the "killing department" of a packing house
firm was discharged after his arrest for assaulting two women with a
knife.[137] However, the mere arrest of an employee for engaging in violent
activity including the shooting of another person is not in itself grounds

---

[130] 35 LA 77 (1960).
[131] 15 LA 42 (1950).
[132] 22 LA 501 (1954); 27 LA 557 (1956); see also 24 LA 494 (1954) where discharge
was upheld for violent verbal insubordination after working hours.
[133] 24 LA 674 (1955).
[134] 27 LA 540 (1956).
[135] 27 LA 401 (1956).
[136] 26 LA 570 (1956).
[137] 24 LA 603 (1953).

for discharge.[138] The question is not whether the alleged offense is heinous but whether it may demonstrate that the employee cannot be trusted to carry out his duties.

Employers who discharge employees for moral reasons alone have a difficult time sustaining their position before arbitrators. The firing of a female employee for illegitimate pregnancy was reversed on the ground that illegitimate pregnancy has no greater effect on production than legitimate pregnancy.[139] One arbitrator held that the company could discharge an employee convicted of sexual perversion *provided* discord developed among the employees after a reasonable trial period.[140] In another case the company discharged a man who had been arrested for shooting his wife on the grounds that his usefulness vis-à-vis customers had been destroyed by the incident. The arbitrator ordered him reinstated, saying that the company could not merely speculate on the incident's effect on customers but could only assess this effect after a trial period.[141]

The issue of political belief and activity has arisen mainly in connection with alleged Communist affiliation or refusal to testify before legislative investigating committees. In the *Cutter Laboratories* case, the arbitrator refused to uphold a discharge on the ground of Communism, but the California Supreme Court overruled him saying that the employee "as a Communist, was not at any time or in any of her activities truly serving the cause of an American labor union or the interests of an American laboring man; she was but doing the bidding and serving the cause of her foreign master who 'tolerates no deviation and no debate.' "[142]

This decision ignored the issue of job relevance, but arbitrators have been more inclined to insist upon it. According to one arbitrator, *The New York Times* was justified in discharging an employee who admitted that he had been a member of the Communist party because he worked in a sensitive position—the rewrite desk. "The *Times* management has the right to be certain that the men who read, edit, and headline the news will do the kind of job expected of them not alone by the *Times* itself but by the public which reads and supports the *Times*."[143] When the issue of "company reputation" is raised, the job relevance of unpopular politics may not be difficult to show. For the most part, however, the

---

[138] 35 LA 77 (1960); 29 LA 54 (1957).
[139] 12 LA 593 (1949).
[140] 18 LA 788 (1952).
[141] 29 LA 54 (1957).
[142] 23 LA 715 (1955).
[143] 26 LA 609 (1956); 27 LA 548 (1956).

discharge of security risks needs to be justified by a clear demonstration that continued employment would adversely affect the enterprise by endangering morale, materially damaging business reputation, or threatening the continuance of government contracts.[144]

4. Long tenure of service creates a legitimate claim to the mitigation of punitive rules.   Arbitrators see the employee's accrued seniority as an important moral and proprietary right. They require management to carry out the spirit as well as the letter of the contract's seniority provisions. The significance of this injunction becomes evident in cases where long-service employees have been discharged. Seniority is an important factor in the arbitrator's assessment of the justice of management's disciplinary action. In fact, Gollub has observed that "it is probably true that what is just cause for discharge varies roughly with seniority."[145]

Dean Shulman once expressed his views on the ethical restraints management must accept when dealing with senior employees: "This treatment of an employee with long seniority, though guilty of the offense stated, is entirely improper, and I cannot believe that it is sanctioned by the Company. Old employees are normally an employer's pride and are pointed to as proof of the fairness of labor policy. X's twenty-two years' service is an impressive record that should not have been treated so lightly."[146] The employee had been loafing and urging others to loaf and Shulman felt that this misconduct should have given some lesser form of discipline. Even so grave an offense as assaulting a supervisor may not justify the discharge of an employee with considerable tenure where his prior record indicates that he has been a good and peaceable worker.[147] Where the prior record is poor, the discharge may be upheld.[148]

Dismissal may be commuted to layoff, thereby protecting "the valuable seniority rights" the grievant had at stake.[149] Recognition of these rights may bar the use of demotion as a form of discipline. Incompetence may result in demotion or even discharge, but it is not grounds for discipline; conversely demotion is not a proper punishment precisely because of the denial of seniority rights. "[A]ccording to accepted arbitration authority, . . . management must not use demotion as a form of discipline for negligence unless the Agreement specifically so provides because to do so

---

[144] These criteria are stated in 35 LA 315 (1960); see also 24 LA 1 (1955); 22 LA 751 (1954).
[145] Myron Gollub, *op. cit.*, 40.
[146] *Opinions of the Umpire*, Ford Motor Co. and UAW-CIO, A–42 (1943).
[147] 11 LA 57 (1948).
[148] 22 LA 255 (1954).
[149] 24 LA 783 (1955).

would abridge the seniority of the employees granted by the contract."[150]

5. A skilled or professional employee may assert a claim to the protection of his occupational identity. Special job rights may be recognized as accruing, not only to long-service personnel, but also to employees who have developed a distinctive skill. Arbitrators are not wholly deaf to the appeals of relatively unskilled workers for the protection of their occupational identity, but these appeals usually arise out of threats to job security, such as may occur when there is a transfer out of a bargaining unit.[151] The claim of an unskilled worker to avoid transfer, without penalty, from one kind of work to another is likely to be denied.[152] But a skilled worker, it has been held, may choose between transfer and temporary layoff, thereby protecting his occupational identity.[153] Thus a sportswriter refused transfer to the rewrite desk of a daily newspaper and the arbitrator upheld his right to refuse, reasoning that the craft of sportswriting is sufficiently distinctive to make a transfer to other fields of journalism unsuitable.

There is little development of this principle, perhaps because it threatens an important area of administrative discretion without providing secure guidelines. Given the large number of occupational specialties, it is difficult to decide what is a proper transfer. Nevertheless it appears that arbitrators have recognized the right of a skilled employee to question the suitability of a transfer, allowing him the option of working elsewhere while retaining his seniority and other privileges as an employee.

6. Industrial discipline should be (a) reasonably related to the gravity of the offense, (b) corrective whenever feasible, and (c) take account of mitigating factors. Many arbitrators have adopted the position that they have the authority to modify management decisions in discipline cases. They readjust penalties instead of merely reversing or sustaining what management has done. Although there is some difference of opinion as to how far the arbitrator should go in second-guessing management, a survey of published arbitration awards showed that the penalty imposed by management was modified in 30 per cent of all disciplinary cases and in 36 per cent of all discharge cases.[154]

Penalties will be modified on a showing of bad faith, discrimination,

[150] 23 LA 252; see also 25 LA 736 (1955).
[151] 8 LA 720 (1947).
[152] 20 LA 690 (1953).
[153] *Opinion of the Umpire,* Ford Motor Co. and UAW-CIO, A–125 (1944), A–223 (1946).
[154] Phelps, *Discipline and Discharge,* 140.

or capriciousness in the exercise of discipline.[155] In making these changes, arbitrators weigh the seriousness of the offense, invoke a positive ideal of correction, and allow leeway for excuses and mitigations. By implication, they ask that management abide by similar standards.

In assessing the penalty, the arbitrator may take account of the company's previous attitudes toward the offense, as well as the industrial context in which it occurs. If others have received less severe penalties for similar acts, the arbitrator may rule that the company, as evidenced by its own conduct, does not consider the offense so grave as to warrant the harsher penalty.[156] One arbitrator commuted the discharge of a union steward to a disciplinary layoff because company rules did not make dismissal mandatory for his offense and no one had ever been fired for such activity before.[157] The employer may also suggest to the arbitrator that an offense did not really merit discharge if it postpones action against the employee in the interests of effective operation.[158]

The industrial context is also relevant. Abusive and vulgar language may not be as serious an offense in a shop as it might be in a bank.[159] A discharge for horseplay was held too severe where such activity was common practice among the employees.[160] Even sleeping on the job, in some settings, may not be so grave an offense as to warrant dismissal.[161]

The idea that discipline should be corrective takes "judicial notice" of a particular personnel policy, summarized by one arbitrator in the following way:

> Indeed, it has long been recognized that the essential purpose of industrial discipline is not so much to punish workers as it is to correct their faults and behavior and thus to make them better and more productive workers. This belief which is held by many persons in the personnel and related fields has led to the development of the principle of corrective discipline. It is a concept that calls for lighter penalties for first offenses and progressively harsher penalties for repeated offenses, culminating in discharge when all possibilities of correction have been exhausted.[162]

---

[155] 31 LA 920 (1959); 34 LA 390 (1960); 26 LA 395 (1956).
[156] 24 LA 103 (1955).
[157] 25 LA 124 (1955).
[158] 34 LA 14 (1959).
[159] 7 LA 780 (1947).
[160] 25 LA 723 (1955).
[161] 35 LA 615 (1960).
[162] 25 LA 733 (1955). See also Sanford Kadish, "The Criminal Law and Industrial Discipline as Sanctioning Systems: Some Comparative Observations," in Mark L. Kahn (ed.), *Labor Arbitration: Perspectives and Problems,* Proceedings of the Seventeenth Annual Meeting of the National Academy of Arbitrators (Washington, D.C.: BNA, Inc., 1964), 138 ff.

If a lesser penalty will bring about the desired improvement in the employee's behavior, the penalty may be modified.[163] One employee, discharged after a first warning, was reinstated on the ground that the company did not give him an opportunity to improve.[164] A distinction has been drawn between serious offenses, such as striking a supervisor, which might justify summary dismissal, and those less serious infractions of company rules, such as absence, tardiness, or carelessness, which should be dealt with by corrective sanctions.[165] This is comparable to the distinction in criminal law between crimes *mala in se* and those *mala prohibita.*[166]

The appropriateness of a penalty may depend upon the special circumstances of the offense and the special characteristics of the offender. As mentioned above, length of service may be a mitigating factor. The employee's prior record or his apparent motivation may be considered.[167] A close scrutiny of what occurred may bring to light facts that cast doubt on the justice of the penalty. Dismissal for fighting may be too severe when the company did not make a thorough investigation and the grievant had ample reason to be angry with the person who provoked him.[168] One arbitrator reduced the penalty of an employee charged with calling the personnel manager a liar after it was determined that the grievant had only asserted that the official was lying. The employee said this without raising his voice or acting belligerently, and it was revealed that the personnel manager had not been telling the whole truth.[169]

7. **The occurrence of events beyond the control of the individual is a proper defense to the application of a punitive rule.** This principle is consistent with the view that industrial discipline should be both just and corrective. To penalize an individual for events over which he has no control would violate the sense of justice and could not improve his conduct. Most supervisors probably accept this restraint as a matter of routine common sense, but arbitrators have been asked to rule on some marginal cases. Thus it has been held that an assault arising from mental illness should not be punished.[170] Failure to respond to a recall notice delivered to the wrong address has been excused.[171] An automatic penalty

[163] 25 LA 13 (1955).
[164] 25 LA 881 (1956).
[165] 24 LA 490 (1955).
[166] See Kadish, *op. cit.*, 129 f. for comments on this distinction as it bears on the question of notice.
[167] 24 LA 555 (1955).
[168] 27 LA 279 (1956).
[169] 26 LA 480 (1956).
[170] 26 LA 295 (1956).
[171] 23 LA 135 (1954).

for wage garnishment has been ruled unfair, on the ground that the laws of some states make it possible to garnishee wages without any fault on the part of the employee.[172] Confinement in jail is considered beyond the control of the individual if he is acquitted.[173] Thus "control" is related to "fault," not only where it connotes inability to control the self, as in insanity pleas, but where other official action is triggered by the individual's conduct. If he was not at fault, the official action causing absenteeism or other inconvenience for the employer is viewed as beyond the employee's control.

There are limits to the protection offered by this principle. Excessive absences do not have to be tolerated by the employer even when justified on the ground of illness.[174] Although "accident proneness" is presumably beyond the individual's control, this may be an acceptable ground for discharge as damaging to the company's safety record. In such cases the individual may be thought of as "unsuitable" rather than guilty, comparable to the employee whose level of competence is too low. If thus conceived, the company may have some obligation to offer a transfer to a more suitable job.

Another limitation, apart from the needs of plant efficiency, is the degree of conscious choice involved. In one case the discharge of a husband and wife with thirteen years' seniority was upheld when they overstayed their vacation. The man fell ill while they were enroute to California from their home in Missouri. This caused two days' delay, but the pair decided to continue the trip since they had gone more than halfway. They returned to work two days late. The arbitrator felt they had made a decision with full knowledge of company rules and should accept the consequences.[175] In another case an employee who had recently converted to the Seventh Day Adventist faith refused to work Saturdays and was discharged. The arbitrator upheld the decision, noting that the employer had no replacement system to facilitate religious observance. Therefore the employee had to choose between his religious commitment and the requirements of his job. It was implied that religious adherence is not beyond the control of the individual and therefore is not an extenuating circumstance.[176]

8. **A rule to which conformity is demanded should be general in scope, definite in meaning, equal in application, and in force before an alleged**

---

[172] 14 LA 787 (1950).
[173] 23 LA 574 (1954).
[174] 24 LA 401 (1955).
[175] 23 LA 542 (1954).
[176] 17 LA 280 (1951).

infraction occurs. These are familiar standards for a system of government by rules. If a rule is defective, a defense is raised against its application. This characteristically legal approach has been adopted by many arbitrators. For example, speaking of production standards, one arbitrator commented:

> Conceding that the company has a right to establish a reasonable production standard, the fact remains that no such standards have yet been established with sufficient clarity to justify the termination of the four aggrieved employees. It will not suffice to (say) new standards call for "all the work we can get." Some known limits must be fixed.[177]

A charge of incompetence must be supported by some definite criteria.[178] Ill-defined standards, for example, that the employee "lacks character," are rejected by arbitrators as allowing excessive discretion to management and providing inadequate guidance to the employee.[179]

The ideal of uniform treatment is a restraint on arbitrariness, not a requirement that what is technically the same offense should always get the same response. "The discharge of an employee is not discriminatory, of itself, solely because the Company had imposed a lesser disciplinary penalty in two prior cases at the request of the Union. Each case . . . must be judged on its own facts."[180] A closer scrutiny may lead to the application of a supplementary rule, for example, with respect to mitigating circumstances, or even lead to the conclusion that the offenses were different in kind.

Nevertheless, arbitrators have assumed responsibility for barring discriminatory or capricious application of rules. An employer may exercise discretion, especially in taking account of special circumstances, but he may not discriminate. Thus management may be upheld if it discharges all employees participating in a wildcat strike or if it imposes differential penalties where the facts show some of the strikers were more responsible than others.[181] But the company cannot arbitrarily decide to discipline some strikers and not others.[182] There must be some reasonable ground for the differential treatment.

The criterion of due notice has been widely accepted by arbitrators:

> For what I have called the industrial *mala prohibita* [not obviously wrongful] offenses, arbitrators have indulged no fiction comparable to that

---

[177] 12 LA 527 (1949).
[178] 26 LA 866 (1956).
[179] 27 LA 209 (1956); 35 LA 77 (1960).
[180] 35 LA 1 (1960).
[181] 33 LA 594 (1956).
[182] 24 LA 761 (1955); 24 LA 95 (1955).

of the criminal law that all are conclusively presumed to know the law. Indeed, they have almost reversed the presumption. In virtually all cases, arbitrators have required the employer to take such steps to communicate his rules as will tend to insure that none but the wilfully ignorant will fail to know them, for example, by posting in conspicuous places, by conferences with groups of employees, by personal distribution of copies of the rules, sometimes by express warnings to offenders that further violations will be punished.[183]

In addition to publicity, notice entails consistent enforcement. The rule should actually be in force before the alleged infraction occurred.[184] If management has tolerated rule-breaking, and then decides to enforce a rule, it may have to give notice of this intention before disciplining employees for violations.[185] Non-enforcement not only attenuates the authority of a rule but empties it of its notice-giving function. This normal outcome is accentuated in the business enterprise because, as Kadish points out, "the employer is both the law maker and the law enforcer . . . in failing to enforce his rule he acts, implicitly, in his legislative function to unmake the rule itself, and its subsequent enforcement upon an individual is rejected as a new rule, notice of which has not been given.[186]

9. Fair standards of accusation and proof should govern the prosecution of charges against employees. Arbitrators tend to require not only that the rules themselves meet reasonable standards of fairness but that the evidence supporting a charge of rule-violation be convincing. It should not rest on mere suspicion. "Discharge is the most serious penalty management can inflict. To be used justly, it must be used only when the facts reasonably establish its propriety. In the instant case we have nothing but suspicions, surmises, and fears of the future. Certainly we have no facts which will establish the justice of this discharge.[187]

When no substantial evidence exists to support a charge the arbitrator's job is easy. More vexing is the question of the sufficiency of the evidence. Some arbitrators have insisted that the company prove its case beyond a reasonable doubt, as required for a criminal conviction.[188] Others have suggested that the civil-suit standard of "preponderance of evidence" be applied.[189] Another spoke of "substantial and convincing proof."[190] As

---

[183] Kadish, *op. cit.*, 130.
[184] *Opinions of the Umpire*, Ford Motor Co. and UAW-CIO, A–117 (1944).
[185] 13 LA 747 (1949).
[186] Kadish, *op. cit.*, 130.
[187] 12 LA 386 (1949).
[188] 23 LA 534 (1954).
[189] 27 LA 137 (1956).
[190] 27 LA 629 (1956).

in the law generally, the degree of proof demanded by arbitrators is likely to vary according to the penalty imposed and the nature of the charge. Much is made of the severity of discharge as a penalty and arbitrators are inclined to insist that the evidence be more substantial than might be demanded, for example, where the penalty is a disciplinary layoff.

Although most arbitrators are loathe to require the theoretically strict standards of a criminal court, it has been maintained that in a theft case the quantum of proof exceed that required in a court of law because in the industrial setting the accused does not have the same legal protection.[191] More realistic is the view that discharge for dishonesty may involve more than the loss of a job. It threatens the employee's reputation and for that reason the degree of proof may have to be at least equivalent to that required in a criminal proceeding. "It seems reasonable and proper to conclude that alleged misconduct of a kind which raises the stigma of general social disapproval as well as plant discipline should be clearly and convincingly established by the evidence. Reasonable doubts raised by the proof should be resolved in favor of the accused."[192]

As the foregoing implies, the burden of proving charges against an employee will be placed on the employer,[193] but it will be up to the union to prove mitigating factors.[194] Thus the employee may have to prove that his absences were justified.[195] These procedural rules, and the substantive presumptions on which they are based, are not applied rigorously or in a spirit of legal nicety. They are practical necessities arising from the requirements of principled decision-making.

The right to know and face one's accuser has been protected. Where a management decision was based on anonymous telephone calls, the arbitrator responded with some warmth:

> . . . under our American System of Jurisprudence, where these two men could not be convicted of even such minor charges as spitting on the sidewalk or passing through a red light, without having the chance to face and cross examine the witnesses to these acts, confidential telephone calls are certainly less than sufficient evidence on which to base reprimands which might at a later date contribute to both their discharge and to their difficulty in getting future employment.[196]

This right is not unqualified, however. If efficient operation requires pro-

---

[191] 21 LA 832 (1954).
[192] 25 LA 906 (1955).
[193] 24 LA 66 (1955).
[194] See Gollub, *op. cit.*, 14 f.
[195] 21 LA 428 (1953); 27 LA 562 (1956).
[196] 25 LA 906 (1955).

fessional detectives and "checkers" the arbitrator may allow the accuser to remain unknown, provided it is evident that the investigator is in no way biased against the accused.[197] Clearly, however, the inability to cross-examine limits the resources available for testing that objectivity. The weaker standard is a concession to the apparent needs of the firm.

The list of principles just reviewed is by no means exhaustive. Our purpose has been to display creative arbitration as interstitial rule-making and to illustrate the variety of resources relied on in this process. It is abundantly clear that the arbitrator finds authoritative materials outside of the contract and that he frequently invokes the funded experience of the legal system. This is especially true of procedural justice, but procedure includes modes of reasoning as well as conduct and therefore inevitably affects the weighing of substantive issues. At the same time, the arbitrator adapts generic legal experience to the industrial setting.

From Prerogative to Policy

It has been said that English law "knows nothing or little of the factory or mine, office or workshop, as a community organized by legal principles. The legal constitution of that community, if one may use that term, is still that of an absolute monarchy to the rule of which its members have submitted by contract."[198] Although there are many indirect effects of English law on industrial justice, especially in importing the terms of a collective agreement into the individual contract of employment, the state has not directly intervened to require collective bargaining, to supervise labor practices, or to lend its authority to a private system of adjudication. In the United States, on the other hand, the law has acted in a positive way to encourage the creation of limited government in the workplace.

The quest for a "community organized by legal principles" has inevitably led to an assault on managerial prerogative. From a doctrinal point of view, conflict turns on the concept of managerial "reserved rights." That idea was formulated by a management spokesman as follows:

> When we speak of the term "management's rights" in this context, we are referring to the residue of management's preexisting functions which remains after the negotiation of a collective bargaining agreement. In the absence of such an agreement, management has absolute discretion in the

---

[197] 23 LA 363 (1954); 25 LA 740 (1955).
[198] O. Kahn-Freund, "Legal Framework," in Allan Flanders and H. A. Clegg (eds.), *The System of Industrial Relations in Great Britain* (Oxford: Basil Blackwell and Mott, Ltd., 1964), 49.

hiring, firing, and the organization and direction of the working forces, subject only to such limitations as may be imposed by law.[199]

The claim to a residual "absolute discretion" may be seen as an effort to preserve, in the age of collective bargaining, the fundamentals of the prerogative contract.

In our discussion above[200] we noted that the prerogative contract presumes the employer's preexistent rights; it is read in the light of those prior rights. That comment had reference to the individual employment contract conceived as a narrow wage bargain terminable at will. If the collective contract is taken to be a set of specific restrictions on otherwise unlimited managerial powers, it must share this prerogative character. Thus understood, the collective bargain does not attack the premises of industrial order.

We have seen that some arbitrators have upheld the principle that the formation of the collective contract raises an inherent bar to arbitrary action by the employer. This necessarily requires the arbitrator to treat the agreement as incorporating basic canons of fairness. What does this mean for the doctrine of reserved rights?

One answer would preserve management's freedom of decision on matters not explicitly covered by the agreement but would allow the arbitrator to review and challenge clear cases of abuse of power:

> Conceivably, in rare and unusual situations, local or departmental management might be guilty of such extreme abuse of managerial authority that its action could be reviewed in arbitration. This type of jurisdiction is inherent as had been recognized from the beginning of contractual relationship between this Company and this Union.[201]

This approach would strike down a managerial decision not to promote a man who refused a supervisor's homosexual advance. It might go so far as to insist that the company's decisions be made in good faith and without caprice.[202] But the *presumption* would be that management was acting reasonably and in the light of legitimate company interests.

A somewhat greater restriction of managerial prerogative is suggested by the following comment:

---

[199] James C. Phelps, "Management's Reserved Rights: An Industry View," in Jean T. McKelvey (ed.), *Management Rights and the Arbitration Process*, Proceedings of the Ninth Annual Meeting of the American Academy of Arbitrators (Washington, D.C.: BNA, Inc., 1956), 105.

[200] See 135 ff.

[201] Quoted in James C. Phelps, "Management's Reserved Rights," 110, from a Bethlehem Steel Co. arbitration decision. The arbitrator's viewpoint was challenged by the author as a threat to the rights reserved exclusively to management.

[202] See the comments by Sidney A. Wolff in McKelvey (ed.), *op. cit.*, 129 ff.

[It is] argued that, in the absence of any bar in the agreement, management might change the starting hour, let us say from 9 to 8 o'clock. There is presumably no limitation on this authority, since none is provided in the agreement. Suppose management, in its right, announces on Thursday at 4 that the change will take place that Friday, the next day. Would workers who showed up at 9 with the excuse that they had not been able to adjust their schedules so quickly subject themselves to discipline for tardiness? At least some arbitrators would rule No. But this would suggest that management's right is not absolute but is limited by some kind of rule of reason, regardless of what the agreement says or does not say about its power to change the starting hour.[203]

Here the company might be required to justify its decision, perhaps by reference to some emergency. The burden of proof would shift from the union to the company. Nevertheless, a fairly narrow view of what is arbitrary would remain.

A more radical revision of the doctrine of reserved rights was proposed by Arthur J. Goldberg, then General Counsel of the United Steelworkers of America and later Associate Justice of the United States Supreme Court.[204] The collective contract, he said, "does not represent labor's imposition on management's reserved rights; rather it represents the basis on which both parties agree to go forward."[205] Management does have its distinctive duties and corresponding authority, usually stated as the right to "manage" the business, including the right to supervise the workforce and to make decisions regarding hiring, layoff, and discharge. Properly understood, however, this managerial right is "exclusive" rather than "reserved." It does not stem from a primordial pre-union past. Rather, it is an accepted division of labor in the cooperative present.

On this view management's authority to direct the enterprise is countered by the union's own right to dissent from a company decision and file a grievance. Moreover, adjudication of the issue presumes no absolute discretion. It leaves open the possibility of giving due consideration to all legitimate interests. The interest in administrative effectiveness, for example, may have to yield, in some cases, to a more compelling interest of the worker or the union. Therefore management has to do more than avoid an extreme abuse of power. To be reasonable and non-arbitrary is to act with appropriate regard for the rights of employees, whether formalized or inchoate.

In *Warrior & Gulf* the issue of what was "strictly a function of man-

---

[203] Neil W. Chamberlain, in McKelvey (ed.), *op. cit.*, 144.
[204] See McKelvey (ed.), *op. cit.*, 118–129.
[205] *Ibid.*, 120.

agement" arose because the union was disputing the right of the company to "contract out" certain work with the result that some men were laid off and rehired by the contractee under inferior conditions. The union did not deny the company's right to contract out but protested "the Company's actions, of arbitrarily and unreasonably contracting out work to other concerns, that could and previously had been performed by Company employees."[206]

The tenor of the Court's opinion, with its emphasis on the creation of a system of industrial self-government and an "agreed-upon rule of law," ran against the idea of absolute discretion. However, the Court's decision did not reach the substantive issue because the claim of the union was that the dispute be submitted to arbitration. Since "contracting out" was not expressly excluded from arbitration by the collective contract, it was held that whether or not this was "strictly a function of management" should be left to the arbitrator to determine.

On the other hand, the Court said that the phrase "strictly a function of management" must be interpreted as referring only to that over which the contract gives management complete control and unfettered discretion.[207] This seems too easy an acceptance of the view that a management *function*, however exclusive, necessarily involves unfettered discretion. What is strictly a management function is one thing. The manner of its exercise is another.

The doctrinal issue is still unsettled. But three circumstances have combined to weaken the claim of management to untrammeled power. First is the moral and legal anomaly of insisting on a received legal right when the whole course of institutional change runs against that claim and tends to chip it away. History is its own justification only when it is unquestioned. Second is the commitment of modern management to rationality, as discussed in Chapter 3. Rational discourse is not alien to the managerial style. Therefore resistance to it, in the face of union pressure and public expectation, is difficult to maintain. Third and most important is management's interest in the continuity of operations. That interest, given the existence and recognition of the union, leads to ready acceptance of a system for the orderly processing of grievances. To establish such a system is to embrace an industrial jurisprudence. The latter, in turn, obeys an inner impulse to extend its reach.

The constitutive contract and grievance arbitration, its juridical offspring, have done much to "constitutionalize" managerial decision-making.

---

[206] *Steelworkers* v. *Warrior & Gulf*, 363 U.S. 574, 575 (1960).
[207] *Ibid.*, 584.

The outcome has not been industrial democracy, if by that is meant worker or union participation in the councils of management. The emphasis is on due process and on protections that limit managerial authority. As the Supreme Court said in *Warrior & Gulf*, "Collective bargaining agreements regulate or restrict the exercise of management functions; they do not oust management from the performance of them."[208] Management is made subject to rule. Its discretion is limited. But these restraints do not fundamentally change the locus of responsibility.

The experience and the institutions of collective bargaining have given life and texture to the decisive promise of the Wagner Act. The demand of that legislation for "bargaining in good faith" meant that management was to be in some degree accountable for its employee relations. It would have to respond to criticism, give reasons for its acts, justify its decisions.

Once it is accepted that reasons and justifications are to be offered, prerogative must give way to policy. The idea that management can do as it pleases simply because of historic privilege loses credibility and therefore weakens in authority. For such an idea cannot meet the test of dialogue. It is a conversation-stopper, inviting an early test of power and a retreat from reason.

---

[208] *Ibid.*, 583.

Chapter 5 | *Employee Perspectives on Industrial Justice*

IN CONSIDERING THE LIVING LAW OF EMPLOYMENT, most of our attention is necessarily given to the evolution of institutional forms, procedures, and policies. But we should also know something about the beliefs and preferences of the employees themselves. To be sure, institutional policies and practices reflect public opinion. The claims pressed by trade union leaders presumably bear a close relation to the expressed desires of their constituents. Still, the policies of both management and labor are inevitably conditioned by the requirements of running a large enterprise. There may be a considerable gap between what is emphasized and accepted by the molders of institutional policy and what is experienced as important among the rank and file. At the same time, if public opinion among employees crystallizes, taking some forms rather than others, it will in the long run decisively affect the evolutionary process with which we are concerned.

Thus we are interested in employee opinion for what light it can cast on the meaning of fairness and on the claims of right that are associated with the modern industrial organization. We realize that such opinion may be evanescent and difficult to assess with assurance. Certainly no single study, even with the most representative sample, can be any more than suggestive. Only cumulative evidence, from many different sources, will tell whether a stable set of attitudes and perceptions exists.

An experienced *in*justice undoubtedly precedes the more positive statement, even the feeling or sense, of what is just. But a sense of justice does evolve *as appeal is made from the felt hurt to the legitimate expectation.* At that point the hurt becomes a grievance.

Despite real suffering and deprivation, the particular kind of hurt to which we refer, the sensed injustice, is not an inevitable response. And even when the hurt is felt, the grievance is often abortive and no claim of right is made. For the sense of justice, though fortified by historical opportunity, is inevitably tempered and restrained by the fixed parameters of the social order. It is the nature of that order, above all its commitments and competencies, that determines what expectations will be legitimate and even, to a large extent, what hopes and aspirations will arise at all.

Thus what is sensed as just depends not only on the broad historical context but also on the specific social setting within which deprivation is experienced and aspiration is quickened. Legitimate expectations differ in the family, in the church, in the corner gang, in the factory, in the army—and within each of these as variations in the requirements of group survival and achievement, and differences in the meaning of the group for the person, are given their proper weight. Closely observed, justice is indeed a variable phenomenon. Its full meaning is always problematic, always subject to discovery.

To say that the sense of justice is variable does not commit us, however, to a radically relativist view. Universal attributes may persist and be discoverable despite variation in detail. Equal treatment, respect for personal dignity, and getting what one deserves may be basic ingredients of a sense of justice, but the mode and measure of their achievement hinge upon the realities of group life.

This chapter reviews some elements of the sense of justice in the employment relation, drawing largely upon the findings of a survey of employee attitudes conducted in 1961.[1] To some extent, the survey explored issues raised by grievance arbitration, as discussed above, pages 164–178.

We are not unmindful of the great difference between arbitration decisions and employee attitudes, expectations, and perspectives. The arbitrator brings to bear a received system of legal and quasi-legal doctrine; he is acting not for himself but for others; he perceives himself as operating

---

[1] This was a group-administered survey of 3,026 employees in eight organizations in the western United States. Findings are reported here only for 1,991 male respondents. The organizations surveyed included one federal government installation concerned with the maintenance and storage of military equipment; three larger manufacturing companies of over two thousand employees each, with union contracts covering hourly employees; two comparably large nonunionized firms, one in manufacturing and the other in insurance; and two smaller nonunionized firms of less than two thousand employees each,

within set and limited bounds; there is much, indeed, that is objective in the stance he takes and in the conclusion he reaches. Nevertheless, in applying the general terms of the agreement to specific cases the arbitrator cannot avoid becoming spokesman for an inchoate sense of the right, formulator of rules and precepts that purport to do justice within the industrial setting. If the arbitrator's sense of justice lacks innocence, if it is mediated by specialized experience, professional training, and the opinion of his peers, it is still a reflection of, and a contributor to, the common conscience.

Two Meanings of Fairness

Although there have been many studies of employee attitudes, especially in the assessment of job satisfaction and morale, little attention has been given to the meaning of fair treatment, and the experience of it. For example, one extensive review of research on job attitudes[2] found that previous studies had uncovered ten factors affecting employee attitudes: (1) intrinsic aspects of the job, (2) supervision, (3) working conditions, (4) wages, (5) opportunities for advancement, (6) security, (7) company and management, (8) social aspects of the job, (9) communication, and (10) benefits. While a number of these factors have an indirect bearing on fairness, the studies did not deal directly with this problem. Perhaps the lack of attention to the norms of fairness, and to the degree of managerial conformity to these norms, reflects the mainly psychological, rather than sociological, character of most studies of workers' attitudes.

In his review of work satisfaction studies, Blauner[3] has noted that differences in reported levels of satisfaction reflect not only objective conditions of work but also differences in how various types of employees are expected to feel about work. The blue-collar worker is not supposed to like

---

one a manufacturing company and the other an independent research organization. Representative samples of employees in each organization participated in the survey, and the organizations are thought to be reasonably typical of government installations, larger unionized companies, large nonunionized companies, and smaller (but not very small) nonunionized companies. The total sample provides variety along dimensions relevant to this study, but obviously is not representative of the entire American labor force. The findings on seniority were previously reported in Philip Selznick and Howard Vollmer, "Rule of Law in Industry: Seniority Rights," *Industrial Relations*, 1 (May, 1962), 97–116.

[2] Frederick Herzberg, Bernard Mausner, Richard Peterson, and Dora Capwell, *Job Attitudes: Review of Research and Opinion* (Pittsburgh: Psychological Service of Pittsburgh, 1957), Chap. III.

[3] Robert Blauner, "Work Satisfaction and Industrial Trends in Modern Society," in Walter Galenson and S. M. Lipset, *Labor and Trade Unionism: An Interdisciplinary Reader* (New York: John Wiley & Sons, Inc., 1960), 343.

his work and therefore is thought to require more discipline, such as "clocking in," and griping on his part is taken for granted. This suggests a need for caution in interpreting reported satisfaction as well as allegations of unfairness.

A few studies have indicated some occupational differences in the *importance* attached to fair treatment by management, but these studies have not taken into account possible occupational differences in the *meaning* of fair treatment.[4] One research group attempted to measure "distributive justice" (an index relating perceived reward to amount of "investment" in work) and its effect on employee job satisfaction, but with inconclusive results. Nevertheless, on the basis of clinical evidence it was suggested:

> [An] important source of employee complaint and dissatisfaction is a sense of being wronged, or being dealt with unjustly *in comparison with* other people. Words such as "right or wrong," "fair and unfair," "should and shouldn't," connote the violation of moral precepts that are very important to the person concerned. The weight of the statistical evidence in this study is far from the point where we would abandon the pursuit of uniformities lurking somewhere in the minds and behavior of men as they assess justice in the distribution of rewards.[5]

In the survey we conducted, the meaning of fairness was examined by asking the employees in our sample to check which of the following phrases seems best to describe the primary meaning of fair treatment: (1) getting the same treatment that other employees get—no favoritism; (2) having one's abilities recognized by management; (3) having management live up to its promises; or (4) some other meaning.

About 41 per cent of the male employees surveyed said that fair treatment means equal treatment; a similar proportion (43 per cent) indicated that it means mostly recognition of individual abilities. Another 14 per cent of the male respondents said that fair treatment refers primarily to "having management live up to its promises," and 2 per cent checked "some other meaning."

These gross findings become more meaningful if we relate them to *other* differences among the respondents. By identifying *which* employees choose one or another meaning of fairness we can get a better understanding of why these choices are made and what their significance may be. Moreover,

---

[4] Thus John P. Troxell, "Elements of Job Satisfaction," *Personnel*, 31 (1954), 199–205, reports that craftsmen and foremen, operatives and laborers are more likely than persons in other occupations to emphasize the importance of "having a fair and understanding boss."

[5] A. Zaleznik, C. R. Christensen, and F. J. Roethlisberger, *The Motivation, Productivity, and Satisfaction of Workers* (Boston: Harvard University School of Business Administration, Division of Research, 1958), 298.

we can test the validity of the measure we are using by examining its relation to other data in which, prima facie, we may have more confidence.

In this analysis we are concerned only with the two most-chosen alternatives—fairness as equal treatment and fairness as recognition of individual abilities. This difference sets the frame for a continuing tension in industrial management, extending, as we see, to the sense of justice itself.

Let us examine these meanings of fairness as they relate to (1) occupational differences, (2) education, (3) social-psychological characteristics, especially orientation toward work and job anxiety, and (4) differences in the organizational context as more or less bureaucratic.

Occupational differences. Table 1 tells this part of the story concisely. Unskilled manual workers are most likely to think of fair treatment as equal treatment for all, whereas professional, technical, and managerial personnel are more likely to interpret fair treatment as relating primarily to the recognition of individual abilities. The table shows a fairly clear gradient, indicating that in general the relative emphasis on these two concepts of fairness varies according to level of skill and of supervisory responsibility. The responses of the relatively small group of male clerical personnel, who are neither supervisory nor especially skilled, however, suggest that an additional line of influence is at work—a more pervasive cleavage of values and self-image dividing blue-collar and white-collar employees.

These are fairly crude data and we should not press interpretation too hard. Nevertheless, it is interesting to note from Table 1 that the proportions of foremen thinking of fairness as equal treatment or as recognition of individual abilities are the same. This does not mean that individual

TABLE 1   *Primary Meaning of Fair Treatment, by*
Occupational Category*

	Primary Meaning of Fair Treatment		
Occupational Category	*Equal Treatment for All*	*Recognition of Individual Abilities*	*Total Number*
Unskilled manual workers	56%	31%	(409)
Skilled manual workers	49	33	(597)
Foremen	44	44	(160)
Clerical personnel	37	50	(102)
Professional and technical personnel	23	58	(477)
Office supervisors and managers	26	58	(202)

*In this and the following tables in this chapter, data are shown only for *male* respondents. Also, in tables on the primary meaning of fair treatment, percentages do not total 100 per cent because of a small number of respondents who indicated that fair treatment has some other meaning to them. Non-responses on particular questions account for slight variations in numbers of respondents in different tables.

foremen are necessarily ambivalent. For all we know, they may be lining up strongly, though on opposite sides. Nevertheless, the lack of any preponderance of choice does reflect the marginal position of the foreman, poised midway between the shop and the office. The result, apart from tensions felt by individual foremen, is to create fairly balanced alternative pressures to identify with either the blue-collar or the white-collar world.

The occupational differences in conceptions of fairness probably have something to do with the impact of the individual on the nature of the job. In the shop, it is the job that is important. Individuals are interchangeable. In the offices, drafting rooms, and laboratories of modern industry, on the other hand, individual capabilities and characteristics become quite important. Men come and go in these salaried positions, but because of the importance of initiative, creativity, and specific technical skills, each new employee is likely to have considerable influence on his job and on the jobs of those around him. This conclusion is supported by data presented in Table 2. Unskilled and skilled manual workers tend strongly to believe that the duties of their jobs would be the same, regardless of who filled the job, while managerial, professional, and technical persons are more likely to emphasize the contribution of the individual.

Educational differences. It is clear from Table 3 that education is strikingly associated with our two alternative meanings of fairness. Better-educated employees are less likely to be worried about discriminatory treatment and more likely to be concerned that their special contributions and potentialities be recognized. Obviously, education is heavily involved in the occupational differences just discussed, but closer analysis of the data shows that the effect of education is independent of occupation. In other words, the better-educated employees on all levels are more likely to think of fairness as recognition of individual abilities. Since we expect

TABLE 2 *Attitudes Toward Individual Influence on Job Duties, by Occupational Category*

	Attitudes Toward Job Duties		
Occupational Category	*Job Duties Would Be the Same, Regardless of Who Filled the Job*	*Job Duties Would Change, Depending on Who Filled the Job*	*Total Number*
Unskilled manual workers	65%	32%	(406)
Skilled manual workers	66	33	(602)
Foremen	53	45	(160)
Clerical personnel	61	37	(102)
Professional and technical personnel	44	56	(480)
Office supervisors and managers	34	65	(202)

TABLE 3 *Primary Meaning of Fair Treatment, by Educational Level*

Highest Educational Level Attained	Primary Meaning of Fair Treatment		
	Equal Treatment for All	Recognition of Individual Abilities	Total Number
Did not complete 8th grade	66%	23%	(64)
Some high school	56	31	(507)
High school graduate	44	42	(523)
Some college	35	46	(528)
College graduate (4 years or more)	23	60	(332)

levels of education to continue to rise, this association is of special importance as a possible harbinger of future attitudes and values.

Social psychological characteristics. In planning the survey, we expected to find some connection between a man's orientations toward work and his job and his assessment of specific personnel policies. This is of considerable interest because it may help us to know whether the sense of justice reflects something inherent in the work situation or rather a set of dispositions that may be expected to change as the industrial setting is transformed.

Two measures of work orientation were devised, one getting at the employee's "self-involvement" in work, the other considering whether he was "achievement-oriented" or "security-oriented." Employees were classified as highly self-involved who said that to them work means more than getting paid, that they think of their work as part of a career, and that they enjoy talking about their work off the job. Those who reported that "trying to get ahead in a job" is more important to them than "having a steady job I can depend upon" were classified as primarily achievement-oriented in their work.

Table 4 shows that the percentages of employees who are involved in their work and achievement-oriented increases as we ascend the occupational scale. This confirms the findings of a number of earlier studies.[6] These marked occupational differences in orientations toward work and achievement undoubtedly reflect variations in the backgrounds as well as in the present work situations of the employees. Thus educational level has a marked effect on both of these orientations. The more education an employee has, the more likely is he to be committed to his work and oriented

[6] See Richard Centers, "Motivational Aspects of Occupational Stratification," *Journal of Social Psychology*, 28 (1948), 187–217; E. A. Friedmann and R. J. Havighurst, *The Meaning of Work and Retirement* (Chicago: University of Chicago Press, 1954), 173; J. P. Troxell, *op. cit.*, 199–205; E. L. Lyman, "Occupational Differences in the Value Attached to Work," *American Journal of Sociology*, 61 (1955), 138–144; Herzberg *et al.*, *op. cit.*, 53.

TABLE 4 *Orientation Toward Work, by Occupational Category*

Orientation Toward Work

Occupational Category	High Self-Involvement in Work*	Primarily Achievement-Oriented in Work†	Total Number
Unskilled manual workers	27%	48%	(406)
Skilled manual workers	47	49	(602)
Foremen	56	69	(160)
Clerical personnel	50	70	(102)
Professional and technical personnel	64	78	(460)
Office supervisors and managers	74	81	(202)

* Those employees who answered that work means "more than just getting paid," that they thought of their work as "part of a career," and that they "enjoy talking about their work off the job" were classified as having high self-involvement in work.
† Those who reported that "trying to get ahead in a job" is more important to them than "having a steady job I can depend upon" were classified as primarily achievement-oriented in their work.

toward achievement. Early socialization is also of undoubted importance.[7] On the other hand, concern for achievement may reflect present opportunities. According to our data, for example, younger workers are considerably more likely to emphasize achievement than are older workers. The latter, of course, have less mobility in the labor market and are more inclined to be concerned with job security.

Tables 5 and 6 permit us to consider simultaneously work orientation, occupational category, and meaning of fair treatment. As might be expected, Table 5 shows that those occupational categories with higher proportions of achievement-oriented persons (as we have seen in Table 4) also have higher proportions of persons who think of fair treatment primarily as recognition of individual abilities. The same can be said for high work-involvement, as indicated in Table 6. Both tables show, moreover, that work orientations are generally associated with concepts of fairness *within* each occupational category. Thus, regardless of the occupational category to which he belongs, an employee who apparently values achievement rather than security, and who is committed to his work or job, is more likely to think of fairness as recognition of individual abilities than as equal treatment for all.

Organizational context. It seemed to us plausible that the character of the work establishment would have an effect on the employees' sense

[7] In a study of high school sophomores in New Haven, Rosen found that middle-class youth tend to develop a stronger achievement motivation than working-class youth. See Bernard C. Rosen, "The Achievement Syndrome: A Psychocultural Dimension of Social Stratification," *American Sociological Review*, 21 (1956), 203–211. For a more general treatment, see David McClelland, *The Achieving Society* (Princeton: D. Van Nostrand Company, Inc., 1961).

TABLE 5 *Primary Meaning of Fair Treatment Among Security-oriented and Achievement-oriented Employees, by Occupational Category*

Occupational Category	Primary Meaning of Fair Treatment		
	Equal Treatment for All	*Recognition of Individual Abilities*	*Total Number*°
Unskilled manual workers			
Security-oriented	74%	27%	(185)
Achievement-oriented	54	46	(167)
Skilled manual workers			
Security-oriented	63	37	(234)
Achievement-oriented	56	44	(253)
Foremen			
Security-oriented	68	32	(44)
Achievement-oriented	42	58	(97)
Clerical personnel			
Security-oriented	52	48	(29)
Achievement-oriented	38	62	(60)
Professional and technical personnel			
Security-oriented	44	56	(84)
Achievement-oriented	29	71	(306)
Office supervisors and managers			
Security-oriented	31	69	(32)
Achievement-oriented	31	69	(138)

° In this table, percentages are calculated only for those who gave the two main responses on primary meaning of fair treatment.

of justice. This expectation is modestly supported in Table 7. Here the enterprises from which our sample was drawn are ranked by apparent degree of bureaucratization, with the government installation considered to be the most bureaucratized and small nonunionized companies to be the least bureaucratized.

Concomitant variations in the proportions of employees choosing one or another meaning of fair treatment are shown. Although the differences are not clear-cut in the two middle categories, it may be seen that *both* white-collar and blue-collar employees in the government installation are much more likely to associate fairness with equality of treatment; whereas in the small nonunionized companies the white-collar workers and even, though to a lesser extent, the blue-collar employees, are more likely to think of fair treatment as recognition of merit.

As more highly trained specialists enter industry under the aegis of new and more advanced technologies, and as bureaucratic systems adapt and become more flexible in job requirements, especially in assimilating individuals with special capabilities, a more achievement-based concept of jus-

TABLE 6   Primary Meaning of Fair Treatment Among Highly
Work-involved and Less Work-involved Employees,
by Occupational Category

| | Primary Meaning of Fair Treatment | | |
| | Equal Treatment for All | Recognition of Individual Abilities | Total Number* |
Occupational Category			
Unskilled manual workers			
Highly involved in work	57%	43%	(96)
Less involved in work	67	33	(258)
Skilled manual workers			
Highly involved in work	53	47	(228)
Less involved in work	66	35	(264)
Foremen			
Highly involved in work	45	55	(78)
Less involved in work	57	43	(63)
Clerical personnel			
Highly involved in work	34	66	(44)
Less involved in work	51	49	(45)
Professional and technical personnel			
Highly involved in work	30	70	(259)
Less involved in work	38	62	(132)
Office supervisors and managers			
Highly involved in work	26	74	(126)
Less involved in work	45	55	(44)

* In this table, percentages are calculated only for those who gave the two main responses on primary meaning of fair treatment.

TABLE 7   Primary Meaning of Fair Treatment, by Organizational Context

| | Clerical, Professional and Managerial Personnel | | | Manual Workers and Foremen | | |
Organizational Context	Equal Treatment for All	Recognition of Individual Abilities	Total Number	Equal Treatment for All	Recognition of Individual Abilities	Total Number
Government installation (1 installation)	57%	26%	(65)	64%	23%	(244)
Large unionized companies (3 companies)	27	59	(204)	51	35	(493)
Large nonunionized companies (2 companies)	25	57	(472)	43	45	(278)
Small nonunionized companies (2 companies)	13	67	(219)	18	38	(34)

tice should gain importance. Increased emphasis on recognition of individual abilities is likely to result, not only from the introduction of new professionals and technicians, but also from the upgrading and even "professionalization" of many occupational groups.

The data we have just reviewed suggest quite clearly that what a man takes as important to fairness has much to do with his social circumstances as well as with his personal fears and aspirations. The two conceptions of fairness emerge as directly related to occupational level, education, self-confidence, and commitment to achievement. As each of these rises, so does "recognition of individual abilities" as the criterion of fairness.

The conception of fairness as equal treatment reflects a desire for protection against potentially arbitrary action. Therefore the appeal to equality is more "legal" in connotation, more directly related to principles of due process and equal protection of the laws. Another way of putting this is to say that the concern for equality is a *status-based* meaning of fairness. Here the individual asks of authority that it take account of who he is, of his inherent rights as a member, or at least as a person, regardless of special merit or achievement. Equality looks to what men have in common, recognizing especially their right to be treated with the same consideration as anyone else who is similarly situated.

Fairness as recognition of individual ability seems to call for more individualized justice. Apparently, on this view, injustice occurs when men are treated as equal although in fact they are unequal, and this violates the principle that a just order gives to each his own. It could be argued that employees who respond in this way have but a weak commitment to principles of justice, that they see the plant or office as a setting for unbridled competitive struggle. On the other hand, a concern for individual merit does not necessarily entail a retreat to particularism, an abandonment of general principles for the assessment of individual cases. Rather, the assumption may be that *there are rules for assessing merit* and these can be applied objectively so as to safeguard the principle of equal opportunity. This interpretation seems to be borne out by the basic desire of almost all our respondents for a rule-ordered work setting.

The Commitment to Rules

How do employees feel about the desirability of limiting managerial discretion by creating a rule-governed system of decision-making? In our study opinions were sought on (1) the desirability of definite rules to prevent supervisors and other management officials from treating employees unfairly; (2) whether specific personnel actions, such as temporary layoffs, should be handled according to management judgment without using rules; (3) whether an employee caught in a hypothetical theft case with conflicting evidence should be given a hearing where evidence for and against him might be discussed, or should be discharged immediately without a hearing; and (4) whether an employee who is being disciplined should be given a hearing in all cases, only in cases involving the discharge penalty, or not in any case.

In response to these questions, 89 per cent of the 1,991 male employees included in the sample "strongly agreed" or "agreed" that there should be definite rules to prevent management officials from treating employees unfairly; 72 per cent thought layoffs should be conducted according to a set of rules; 42 per cent said the same for promotions and 51 per cent for overtime work assignments; 87 per cent said the employee in the hypothetical theft case should be given a hearing; and 70 per cent said a hearing should be provided for employees in all disciplinary actions, regardless of the potential severity of the penalty.

A closer examination of these findings, exploring the effect of organizational context, occupation, education, union membership, length of service, job anxiety, and orientation toward work showed only modest differences among the various categories of employees with respect to the *general* desirability of protective rules. A large majority gave ready assent to the proposition that personnel decisions should be governed by objective rules that limit managerial discretion.

As we become more specific, this consensus weakens. Considerably **fewer** employees, especially those of higher status, are willing to restrict management's judgment on the issue of layoff, for example. This is indicated in Table 8, where data are presented for *nonunion* employees. White-collar, professional, and supervisory personnel give fewer votes to rules as against management judgment on this issue, although there is virtually no disagreement on the desirability of hearings in disciplinary actions or on the abstract worth of rules to insure fairness.

The apparent inconsistency among the higher-status employees, reflected in their full support for protectives rules in the abstract and their lesser support for such rules on specific issues, can probably be explained on several grounds. For some, agreement with the general proposition—"there should be definite rules to keep supervisors and other management officials from treating workers unfairly"—must be discounted as a stereotyped or unthinking response, not to be taken seriously. More likely, the response is

TABLE 8 *Nonunionized Employees Who Favor Protective Rules,*
by Occupational Category

	Proportion Favoring:			
Occupational Category	*Protective Rules in General*	*Rules in Layoffs*	*Hearings in Disciplinary Actions*	*Total Number*
Unskilled manual workers	94%	76%	88%	(194)
Skilled manual workers	91	75	90	(232)
Foremen	90	80	90	(134)
Clerical personnel	91	58	92	(88)
Professional and technical personnel	83	56	88	(449)
Office supervisors and managers	81	66	92	(192)

a valid enough indicator of real feelings but those feelings are counter-balanced by other commitments when a more specific issue is weighed. Higher-status employees are more sensitive to the needs of management and may hesitate to limit discretion where efficiency may be compromised. Probably they would take the general proposition to mean that definite protective rules are indeed desirable when there is a proven necessity for them, and this necessity has been shown for some personnel matters, but otherwise management's judgment should govern.

It is worth recalling that many formalized personnel regulations, and especially those governing layoff procedures, are mainly designed to protect manual workers rather than technical and professional salaried employees. Moreover, the professional may be inclined to oppose formalized rules as part of a general opposition to "bureaucratic red tape" which limits his freedom as a professional. The office supervisor or manager is also wary of rules. It is interesting, therefore, that so many professional and managerial employees favor protective rules even on such an issue as layoffs, where the rules do not necessarily reflect their interests.

Blue-collar workers tend strongly to favor protective rules regardless of past or present union membership. This is shown in Table 9. While a

TABLE 9 *Manual Workers Who Favor Protective Rules in General,*
Rules in Layoffs, and Hearings in Disciplinary Actions,
by Union Membership Status

	Proportion Favoring:			
Union Membership Status	*Protective Rules in General*	*Rules in Layoffs*	*Hearings in Disciplinary Actions*	*Total Number*
Are now members of a union	94%	85%	83%	(582)
Have been members of a union	94	79	90	(247)
Have never been members of a union	90	70	88	(179)

somewhat larger percentage of union members favors rules on specific issues, a majority of all manual workers feels that "management judgment" should be subject to restraint. Clearly the wish for legality, for a setting in which decision by fiat is minimized, is more pervasive and more fundamental than unionization and collective bargaining. Indeed, the latter draws much of its strength from that underlying quest.

The "Regular Employee"

Earlier we interpreted the claim to equal treatment as a "status-based" concept of fairness. The significance of status in the employees' sense of justice is underlined when we consider certain substantive issues, especially the rights of regular as against probationary employees, seniority rights, limitations on the scope of managerial authority, and rights of occupational identity.

One way of giving recognition to the regular employee, apart from the more obvious benefits of presumptive tenure, is to require *a higher standard of due process* for the employee whose status as "regular" has been confirmed. The probationary employee, without equivalent status rights, has less claim to nicety of treatment. He must live for a while with a greater risk of arbitrary decision.

The employees in our survey were asked to indicate the extent of their agreement with the following statements: "It is all right to fire a new employee *during his probationary or trial work period* if his boss doesn't like his personality," and "It is all right to fire an employee *after he has been accepted as a regular employee* if his boss doesn't like his personality." Table 10 shows the results:

TABLE 10　*Employees Who Feel It Is Not Right to Discharge for "Personality Reasons" a Probationary Employee and a Regular Employee, by Occupational Category*

	Proportion Considering Discharge:		
Occupational Category	*Not Right for a Probationary Employee*	*Not Right for a Regular Employee*	*Total Number*
Unskilled manual workers	80%	90%	(404)
Skilled manual workers	70	86	(587)
Foremen	60	82	(158)
Clerical personnel	70	84	(98)
Professional and technical personnel	49	80	(460)
Office supervisors and managers	42	79	(193)

(1) Among all occupational groups, the regular employee is more likely to be granted consideration than the probationary employee.

(2) Among manual workers there is little distinction between regular and probationary employees; the overwhelming majority of these respondents apparently believe that probationary employees should be protected against discharge by a boss who "doesn't like his personality."

(3) Among higher-level and professional employees, there is a more striking differential between the rights accorded the probationary and regular employee. About 80 per cent would protect the regular employee in the situation described, whereas less than half would protect the probationary employee.

This pattern of responses probably reflects the belief that personality has an important effect on professional and managerial performance. On the other hand, apparently many higher-level employees conclude that there is a large risk of arbitrary treatment in the assessment of personality and that this risk ought to be borne by the probationary rather than the regular employee. Moreover, the same respondents who tend to choose a nonstatus definition of fairness (recognition of individual abilities) are sensitive to the special right of the regular employee. To this extent, then, even among the more merit-oriented employees, status is recognized as a criterion of fair treatment.

Among the lower-level respondents, the evident unwillingness to discriminate strongly between probationary and regular employees is no doubt partly due to the belief that having a personality liked by the boss is not a valid criterion of judgment. For these workers, elimination during the probationary period, if justified at all, should be based on purely technical standards of ability and performance. Nevertheless, if the status of "being a regular employee" were truly important to the lower-level workers, there ought to have been a greater willingness to discriminate against the probationary employee. That this was not so suggests that under present conditions lower-level employees do not base their claims of right on the fact of organizational membership. Rather, appeal is to the rights of the person, entitled as such to the equal protection of the laws.

The Scope of Authority

The modern employment relation is more limited, more sharply defined, than the old relation between master and servant. There is wide recognition of the employee's right to a private sphere of life of which manage-

TABLE 11   Employees Who Feel It Is Not Right to Discharge an
Employee for Something He Did off the Job,
by Occupational Category

Occupational Category	Per Cent	Total Number
Unskilled manual workers	87%	(406)
Skilled manual workers	83	(602)
Foremen	75	(160)
Clerical personnel	75	(102)
Professional and technical personnel	71	(480)
Office supervisors and managers	61	(202)

ment may disapprove but in which it has no legitimate interest. What a man does after leaving the plant is, in principle, no concern of the employer. As we have seen (page 168), this perspective is one contribution of grievance arbitration to emergent law.

Grievance arbitration fully recognizes management's right to direct the workforce and to expect capable and dependable performance. But the scope of managerial authority is limited and the worker's private sphere of life is protected. What is truly private depends, however, on the type of business in which the employer is engaged and the kind of work the employee does. This point of view is adopted by most employees in our sample. Although the more detailed issues raised by the arbitration decisions could not be explored, we did ask the extent of agreement with the following hypothetical statement: "It would be all right for a supervisor to fire an employee for something he did outside working hours and away from the company."

As is shown in Table 11, the large majority of employees in every occupational category feel that such action would be unjust. Office supervisors, managers, and professional and technical personnel, however, are somewhat less likely to express disagreement with the statement. This result corresponds to a finding of the 1958 study that "staff specialists" (professional and technical personnel) are more likely to recognize managerial control outside the worksite.[8]

In our 1958 interviews with personnel executives of San Francisco Bay Area firms, it was found that a majority of these companies subscribe to the view that they have a legitimate concern with the outside activities of employees under certain conditions.[9] One such condition is the nature of the company's main product or service:

[8] Howard M. Vollmer, Employee Rights and the Employment Relationship (Berkeley and Los Angeles: University of California Press, 1960), 119.
[9] See above, 106f.

Outside activities of employees are not considered the company's concern in this company. But whether outside activities become the concern of the company or not depends upon the nature of their product. For example, if a firm were making Bibles, then this kind of off-duty activity might be related to an employee's work and the company's reputation. (*Paper products*)

If a man were a policeman, for example, his behavior on and off duty would be related. But in this kind of case, there would be an understanding about this at the time of employment. It would be similar for a minister or a schoolteacher. But in the case of an ironworker, for example, so long as he reported properly for work, the company would have no concern for his off-duty behavior. (*Shipyard*)

Another variable is the size of the community:

We have had some cases where we were concerned with off-duty offenses. Many smaller places are more or less company towns along the railroad. Our policy in such cases would be to call the man in first and see what he has to say about his behavior. If necessary, we could fire a man in such cases in order to protect the company's reputation. We could do this under the company rule stating that people of "poor moral quality" need not be retained as employees. (*Railroad*)

We have members of minority groups who seem to alternate and spend every other weekend in jail. This is mostly the case in the canning industry. The union sends us help from the hiring hall and we take them on as they come, so we can't be very particular. In most places, we don't care what they do on Saturday night, just so they get to work sober on Monday morning. But in a small town a firm would certainly be concerned with how its employees acted off the job. We have small town operations of this type. This would not be the case in a metropolitan area, however. (*Food processing and packing*)

A third condition is the occupational category of an employee within the enterprise. Managerial and professional employees are more likely to be subject to censure for what they do away from work than are manual workers:

The reputation of a company is not related to what hourly workers do outside a plant. This would be different, however, for the personnel director or some other management person. In this case, the offense might be reported in the paper along with the individual's title. (*Automobile assembly*)

If the employee were working as a laborer in a construction job, say, without public contact, and he wasn't fouling up his work detail, the company would be harsh if it took this action. On the other hand, if he were in a position of some kind of public trust, as in a bank, then management would have some reason to discipline him. (*Banking*)

> Whether management were right [in disciplining the employee] would depend upon the position of the employee in the company. Generally, what a man does in his spare time is beyond the purview of company interests. If he were a production worker in a reasonably large community, his behavior off the job would not reflect on the company. On the other hand, if he had a job concerned with an important safety item and his reputation was one of being drunk every Saturday, this would be another type of problem. In this latter case, however, management would have to *prove* that this behavior affected company interests. (*Aircraft maintenance*)

We have already seen from Table 11 that occupational differences are important, although it should be remembered that even most supervisory and professional employees favor the principle of limited managerial authority. Higher-level employees are more likely to be involved in their work (see Table 6); they are also, apparently, more likely to recognize that this personal commitment may carry with it responsibilities to the employer that extend beyond the worksite.

Occupational Identity

Another status-claim in the emerging law of employment is the asserted right to a protected occupational identity. In modern industrial society, as in earlier ages, the division of labor can create a sense of belonging and identification, a blending of the person and the job. This assumes that the job is specialized enough to encompass distinctive skills, training, experience, and ways of working; but it should not be so specialized as to eliminate a personal factor or the possibility of developing an occupational identity. Thus the principle emerges: a skilled or professional employee may assert a claim to the protection of his occupational identity. (See above, pages 110 f., 171.)

Grievance arbitration has probably not been the major influence in establishing the integrity of crafts in American industry. Spheres of jurisdiction of the various crafts have long been spelled out in the collective contracts and work-rules of many unions. But arbitration has recognized this right when the contract has been silent, permitting craftsmen to accept a temporary layoff rather than an unsuitable assignment.

In our survey, an attempt was made to assess employees' opinions of the principle of occupational identity by asking them to respond to the following hypothetical situation:

> Suppose there is not much work available in some kind of highly skilled work, but there is a need for persons to do unskilled work. Suppose

management asked a highly skilled employee to do this unskilled work for a few weeks at his regular rate of pay, but the employee refused, saying he would rather take a layoff without pay for a while. What do you think management should do about it? (1) Fire him for not doing what he was told to do, or (2) give him a temporary layoff without pay.

Table 12 shows that a large majority of the employees studied, in all occupational categories, believe that the highly skilled worker should be given the option of a temporary layoff rather than be fired for refusing to accept another work assignment. A slightly lower proportion of office supervisors and foremen recognized this right, probably because managerial personnel are more likely to recognize that the protection of occupational identity limits flexible managerial control.

In the 1958 study, however, only 25 per cent of the forty-four personnel directors indicated that their companies would respect a principle of occupational identity for highly skilled employees, another 25 per cent were undecided or ambiguous on the subject, and 50 per cent rejected the principle. Those who rejected the principle of occupational identity usually did so on the ground that work assignment is a management prerogative.

> Management is always within its rights to offer an employee other work, and no employee has a right to tell the company what he will or will not do. The company has a right to discharge a man if it goes this far. It is a basic right of management to assign work. We once fired a union president because he refused to perform a certain work assignment. (*Petroleum products*)

Others pointed out that an understanding may be reached at the time of initial employment defining an employee's rights in this matter:

> If a company fired a man under these circumstances [refusal to take a less skilled position], then there would be good grounds for him to file a grievance on the basis of his understanding that he was hired in a particular job classification. However, if the reassignment were within this job classification, then discharge under these circumstances would be justified. (*Shipyard*)

TABLE 12 *Employees Who Favor Recognition of the Occupational Identity of Highly Skilled Employees, by Occupational Category*

Occupational Category	Per Cent	Number
Unskilled manual workers	83%	(406)
Skilled manual workers	79	(602)
Foremen	71	(160)
Clerical personnel	79	(102)
Professional and technical personnel	80	(480)
Office supervisors and managers	68	(202)

> We hire our employees to do any work available, under our understanding with the industrial union. Then a man has no recourse if he is told to do another job, except where there are special craft union agreements involved. Under the industrial union situation, a man would have to take the assignment to other work, even at a lower rate of pay. (*Can manufacturing*).

Those who favored the recognition of occupational identity often mentioned that it is required in their collective labor agreements and yet emphasized that their policy in this matter would probably be the same regardless of whether or not the matter was covered in collective contracts:

> I don't believe the company would be within its rights in firing a man under these circumstances. Our agreements for trades and crafts would not allow this sort of thing. Employees must be given the option of a temporary layoff. Yet even if a contract were not specific on this matter, we would be very shortsighted to fire a man simply because he refused to take a less skilled job—skilled people are not easy to get. (*Steel*)

> Most contracts provide that a man must be retained in the field for which he was hired and paid accordingly. This is particularly true for skilled workers. But even if the contract is silent on this point, the man should have the option of a temporary layoff. I might point out that this principle is recognized in the case of the United States Unemployment Compensation Law—an unemployed man does not have to accept a job at a lower skill than his normal trade. (*Electronics equipment*)

As more professional and technical personnel enter the labor force, the principle of occupational identity should gain wider recognition and acceptance by management. This will not be a simple capitulation to pressure from below or a hard-won collective bargain, but a realistic assessment of management's need to find new approaches and new modes of decision in a technical society. The expertise of the workforce summons something more than unrestricted managerial authority. It requires a complementary expertise on the part of management.

Seniority Rights

If we except entrepreneurial ownership, it is probably fair to say that seniority is the most pervasive status-claim in industrial life. It has been noted that "the idea of seniority is as old as the employer-employee relationship"[10] and consequently predates collective bargaining by some centuries. Certainly the view that men who have given valuable years of service to an employer are deserving of some special consideration is not

---

[10] John A. Lapp, *How to Handle Problems of Seniority* (New York: National Foreman's Institute, 1946), 2.

novel to employers or arbitrators. One study reported that 95 per cent of the nonunionized firms surveyed used seniority as a criterion when deciding who should be laid off when work shortages occur.[11] The decisions of arbitrators are influenced by the ". . . rather general feeling that a worker who has spent many years on his job has some stake in that job and in the business of which it is part and that this interest should not be lightly cast aside."[12] Of course, seniority under a collective bargaining contract is something more than a "feeling." Under such an agreement a senior employee usually has the right to be kept at work while other, less senior employees are laid off. He may also have the right to insist on preference in promotion, recall, transfer, or work shift and assignment. Seniority rights can be substantial, and their loss through discharge is a more severe deprivation to the senior than to the junior employee. They are a kind of property that creates a preferred status.

The protection of seniority, as a proprietary and status interest, is sharply revealed in the handling of discipline cases under grievance arbitration. As we have seen in the preceding chapter (page 170), seniority is an important criterion in the assessment of managerial decision, especially in discharge cases. According to this trend of arbitration decisions, long tenure does not bar management from punishing misconduct. Rather, seniority is a mitigating factor in the determination of just punishment. In imposing a penalty for misconduct, especially when the penalty is discharge, employers may be required to consider the equity the employee has in the job as well as the nature of the offense—even at the expense of apparent uniformity in the administration of justice. Of course, so long as all persons similarly situated (e.g., of equal seniority) are treated alike, it can be argued that the principle of equal protection is being upheld. This assumes, however, that there is a rational basis, acceptable to the plant community, for treating some classes of employees better than others.

Turning again to our survey, Table 13 provides a crude view of the extent to which employees favor the use of seniority as a criterion in personnel decisions. Employees were asked to indicate: (1) whether temporary layoffs ought to be based primarily on length of employment (with the company or the department) or primarily on management's judgment of "who are the poorest workers"; (2) whether promotions to job openings at higher rates of pay ought to be offered first to the employee at the

---

[11] John J. Speed and James J. Bambrick, *Seniority Systems in Nonunionized Companies,* Studies in Personnel Policy No. 110 (New York: National Industrial Conference Board, 1950), 5.
[12] Myron Gollub, *Discharge for Cause* (State of New York, Department of Labor, Special Bulletin No. 221, 1948), 40.

TABLE 13   *Opinions of Employees About Seniority in Layoffs, Promotions, Disciplinary Discharge, and Special Privileges*

	Layoffs	Promotions	Disciplinary Discharge	Special Privileges
Favor seniority	39%	8%	47%	53%
Do not favor seniority	60	91	52	46
No answer	1	1	1	1
Total (1,991)	100%	100%	100%	100%

next lower rate of pay who has been employed at the company longest or to the employee at the next lower rate of pay who has "the best training and experience for the job"; (3) whether an employee who "had a good record at a company for twenty years," but then was caught stealing company supplies, should be discharged for this offense, "like a new employee might be," or should be given a lighter form of discipline, and (4) whether or not an employee with high seniority in his line of work ought to be given any "special privileges."

Considered as an undifferentiated group, our respondents showed overwhelming sentiment against seniority as a criterion for promotions, and most were opposed to governing layoffs on that ground. Of course, a different wording of either question might well have produced other percentages, but the relative weakness of the seniority principle, particularly in promotions, was striking nonetheless.

Since only 8 per cent of the respondents favored seniority in promotions, we shall not report further on that issue, except to say that the percentage differences followed closely the pattern of variations on the question of layoffs.

The more evenly divided views on discipline and special privilege are more suggestive. We shall analyze the contrast between responses on seniority in layoffs and in discipline at a later point, but let us consider first variations in beliefs about layoffs.

Table 14 indicates the pattern of responses when the employees were classified according to various characteristics that might be expected to influence beliefs regarding seniority. For layoffs, the pattern was clear and not very surprising. Union membership, as expected, strongly influenced commitment to the seniority principle. The highest "vote" for seniority in layoffs was cast by manual workers who were members of a union. Further analysis indicated that this proportion (66 per cent) varied little when union members were subclassified by educational background, length of employment, degree of anxiety about job security, or orientation toward a career in their present organizations or lines of work. In other words, union

TABLE 14   *Employees Who Favor Seniority in Layoffs, Promotions, and Disciplinary Discharge, by Selected Characteristics*

	Layoffs	Promotions	Disciplinary Discharge	Total Number
*Union membership**				
Are now members of a union	66%	16%	47%	(565)
Have been members of a union	41	11	44	(247)
Have never been members of a union	38	8	46	(179)
Occupational category†				
Unskilled manual workers	41%	9%	43%	(194)
Skilled manual workers	39	10	46	(232)
Foremen	37	7	40	(134)
Clerical personnel	24	8	51	(88)
Office supervisors and managers	23	2	48	(192)
Professional and technical personnel	19	1	53	(449)
Highest educational level attained				
Did not complete 8th grade	53%	18%	35%	(66)
Some high school	53	16	42	(510)
High school graduate	45	9	48	(527)
Some college	31	9	50	(528)
College graduate (4 years or more)	21	1	54	(334)
Age category				
Under 30 years	30%	7%	51%	(385)
30 to 39 years	39	7	46	(622)
40 to 49 years	42	9	47	(565)
50 years or over	46	13	48	(411)
Length of employment				
Less than 1 year	25%	4%	52%	(219)
From 1 to 5 years	31	7	49	(569)
From 5 to 9 years	45	8	48	(489)
From 10 to 14 years	46	10	44	(386)
15 years or more	51	13	46	(320)

* For manual workers only.
† For nonunion members only.

affiliation appeared to have an independent effect on the beliefs of union members. Most of the union members were employed under collective contracts specifying seniority as a major consideration in layoffs.

The distributions in Table 14 also confirm common-sense expectations regarding the influence of occupational level, age, length of employment, and, perhaps, education. Among nonunion employees, the proportion favoring seniority in layoffs was inversely related to occupational level, declining steadily from unskilled manual workers (41 per cent) at one end of the scale to professional technical personnel (19 per cent) at the other. Presumably this reflected a greater dependence upon seniority rules, with respect to layoffs, at the lower occupational levels, and a greater interest, at the upper levels, in recognition of achievement.

Although it is not obvious why education as such should weaken sentiment for seniority, we do expect the inverse relation between occupation and support for seniority in layoffs to be reflected in the data on education. And indeed, the higher the educational level, the lower was the proportion favoring seniority in layoffs. Occupation and education each appeared to exert some independent influence, however. When attitudes toward seniority in layoffs were more closely analyzed, it was found that preference for conducting layoffs primarily according to seniority still tended to be relatively more prevalent among less educated employees, regardless of occupational category, and among manual workers and foremen, regardless of educational level.

Further analysis also showed that neither occupational nor educational variations in attitudes toward seniority in layoffs could be explained by association with other factors, such as varying lengths of employment, degree of anxiety about job security, or career orientation. Apparently educational background and occupation were both important in shaping attitudes toward seniority. These conclusions suggest that, as white-collar and better educated employees become an increasing proportion of the labor force, sentiment for seniority in layoffs may progressively weaken. At least some of the conditions for this outcome will be present, even though they may be offset by other factors, such as economic insecurity or the influence of collective bargaining.

Table 15 shows the effect of work orientations and job anxiety. Employees who indicated in response to survey questions that they preferred to remain employed with their present firm, even if they had to take a cut in pay, and expected to remain employed with their present firm for at least the next ten years were designated as *company-oriented;* those

TABLE 15 *Employees Who Favor Seniority in Layoffs and Disciplinary Discharge, by Career Orientation and Degree of Job Anxiety*

	Layoffs	Disciplinary Discharge	Total Number
Career orientation [*]			
Company-oriented	36%	45%	(439)
Occupation-oriented	43	45	(104)
Security-oriented	56	51	(352)
Degree of Job Anxiety			
High	55%	46%	(80)
Medium	40	48	(1,743)
Low	29	47	(168)

[*] Employees with a mixed orientation or with no determinate orientation are not shown in this tabulation.

who indicated that they preferred to remain in their present line of work, even if they had to take a cut in pay, and who expected to continue in this line of work either with their present employer or another employer for the next ten years were classified as *occupation-oriented*; employees who indicated that they valued keeping "any good job" they could get at their present rate of pay over remaining with a particular firm or in a particular line of work and that they valued "having a steady job I can depend on" over "trying to get ahead in a job" were designated as *security-oriented*.

There was a marked relation between work orientation and preference for basing layoffs primarily upon seniority. Security-oriented employees were most likely (56 per cent) to believe that seniority should govern layoffs, whereas company-oriented employees were least likely (36 per cent) to express this preference. Perhaps many company-oriented employees aspire to managerial positions. If so, preferences upholding management judgment and rejecting rules that limit its authority may reflect "anticipatory socialization."

Job anxiety was measured by the degree to which employees reported that they worried very often about losing their jobs and that it would not be very easy for them to get similar jobs elsewhere. Such respondents were classified as having "high job anxiety." Table 15 shows that 55 per cent of such employees favor basing layoffs on seniority, compared to 29 per cent of those showing low job anxiety. As might be expected, we found that job anxiety was inversely related to both education and occupational level. Nevertheless, education did not "wash out" the relation between job anxiety and preference for seniority in layoffs. As may be seen in Table 16, this association persisted at all four educational levels.

Layoff and discipline. Tables 13, 14, and 15 show a striking difference between attitudes toward seniority in layoffs and in disciplinary discharges. Where discipline was at issue, in contrast to layoffs, there was no discernible pattern of variation by union membership, occupational level, length of employment, or even job anxiety. Thus the associations we found between preference for seniority in layoffs and the independent variables did not show up, with respect to disciplinary discharge, *except for amount of education*.

Furthermore, preference for seniority in layoffs and in discipline were apparently unrelated to each other (see Table 17). On the basis of our data one could not predict whether an employee would favor applying seniority as a mitigating factor in disciplinary discharge from knowledge of his attitude toward seniority in layoffs.

TABLE 16   *Employees Who Favor Seniority in Layoffs, by*
Educational Level and Degree of Job Anxiety

Highest Educational Level Attained	Degree of Job Anxiety	Layoffs	
		Per Cent	Total Number
Did not graduate from high school	High	61%	(38)
	Medium	53	(499)
	Low	44	(39)
High school graduate	High	56%	(25)
	Medium	45	(476)
	Low	42	(26)
Some college	High	43%	(14)
	Medium	32	(460)
	Low	24	(54)
College graduate (4 years or more)	High	33%	(3)
	Medium	22	(283)
	Low	15	(48)

Thus we appear to have two distinct approaches to the seniority principle. One of these, to the extent that it is accepted at all, loses strength as we go up the educational and occupational ladders; it gains support with union influence, length of service, job anxiety, and concern for security. That is the picture with regard to layoffs and promotions. The second approach is associated only with education, but here the association is positive rather than negative. The higher the educational level, the greater the proportion of those willing to allow an appeal to seniority in mitigation of punishment. As may be seen in Table 14, the proportion of male employees favoring the use of seniority in layoffs decreased steadily from 53 per cent at the lowest educational level to 21 per cent at the highest. Conversely, with increasing education the proportion of

TABLE 17   *Degrees of Mutual Association* Among Employees'*
Attitudes Toward Seniority in Different Situations

	(2)	(3)	(4)
Preference for seniority in			
(1) Layoffs	+.45	0	+.02
(2) Promotions		+.07	−.04
(3) Disciplinary discharges			+.25
(4) Special privileges			

* Expressed in terms of Wallis and Roberts' "h" coefficient of mutual association. The coefficient varies between +1.00, indicating that values on one variable are always associated with similar values on the other variable, and −1.00, indicating that values on one variable are always associated with opposite values on the other variable. See W. A. Wallis and H. V. Roberts, *Statistics, A New Approach* (New York: Free Press, 1956), 282–284.

male employees favoring the use of seniority in disciplinary actions rose steadily from 35 per cent to 54 per cent.[13]

It is interesting that union membership, while important in affecting responses on layoff, did not seem to have a corresponding effect where discipline was the issue. Union members were about as likely to favor seniority in discipline as other employees. One might expect that the great emphasis on seniority in collective bargaining would produce a generalized disposition among union members to favor that principle. This may be so, but it is not evident from our data. Although the respondents showed considerable support for seniority in discipline, this appeared to reflect influences other than union membership, especially for the more educated employee.

Another impressive datum is the percentage of employees with low anxiety who favored seniority in discipline (see Table 15). Forty-seven per cent of these workers supported seniority in discipline, compared with only 29 per cent who favored it in layoffs. This suggests that attitudes toward seniority are not necessarily or solely related to a direct concern for job protection. Many employees who are not worried about their jobs, and many of those who have least cause for worry (in the case of better educated employees), nevertheless recognize that seniority has a place in the organization of industry. But they discriminate sharply between rules affecting layoff and rules affecting discipline.

How shall we interpret these varied patterns of commitment to the principle of seniority? Our data do not tell us directly just what rationale, if any, lies behind the preference expressed by any given category of employees. However, some interpretations, plausible on other grounds, are at least consistent with the data.

First, some employees may feel that it is indeed appropriate to give special consideration to employees of long standing *on the assumption* that the individual is otherwise qualified to make an effective contribution to the work of the firm. Seniority may be seen as an important part of the status system of the enterprise, affecting a whole set of decisions, for example, priority in vacation scheduling, not directly related to standards of performance on the job. These are matters that do not affect the composition of the workforce. On the other hand, if the question is, who shall compose the workforce if it must be cut, then other criteria are invoked. Thus a lack of interest in seniority as governing layoffs does not

---

[13] This pattern of association holds more consistently for younger employees (under age 40) than for older employees.

necessarily preclude support for seniority where employees feel that status considerations, rather than performance, are appropriate.

Second, less educated employees may be relatively more inclined to favor simple and straightforward rules of fairness applied universally to all employees. Conducting layoffs according to reverse order of seniority alone is simpler than attempting to introduce considerations of individual ability or accomplishment along with seniority. On the other hand introducing seniority as a mitigating factor in discipline complicates application of the general principle in discipline that offenders be treated equally, regardless of status. Increased sophistication may dispose the better educated workers to accept the more complex solution—a solution that takes into account the characteristics of the offender as well as the characteristics of the offense.

Third, all categories of employees, but especially the better educated, probably have a considerable commitment to the values of individual skill and company requirement. They may reason that seniority in discipline does not harm the enterprise; indeed, more equal treatment might result in the loss of capable and experienced employees. Thus special consideration for senior employees, when their technical qualifications are not called into question, may be perceived as good business, besides being fair to the worker who has invested much of his life in the company.

The future of seniority.   The survey findings reported here suggest that there may be a significant gap between the subjective preferences of many employees and the rules by which they are governed. Nor can this be understood in a simple way as management resistance to employee demands. On the question of seniority in layoffs, it may be, indeed, that the "system" is more concerned about status rights than the employees themselves. If there is such a gap, it may reflect two quite different historical trends.

(1) The exigencies of rule-making in large enterprises, combined with the pressure of trade unions, produce an institutional commitment to seniority in handling layoffs. But this need not directly reflect the attitudes of employees. For administrative reasons, management may accept the principle of seniority even when there is no direct union demand. Therefore it might be argued that many employees have simply not "caught up" with the "progressive" personnel policies under which they live.

(2) On the other hand, it is possible that a stress on seniority rather than merit looks backward to a time of greater insecurity when the protection of "simplified" status rights seemed the surest and most direct way to industrial justice. If this is so, then employee attitudes in defense of

merit may stiffen, and the foundations of support for seniority, with respect to layoffs and promotions, may weaken.

Of course, both of these trends may be operative, with uneven support among various classes of employees. However, there is a clear-cut inverse relation between educational level and support for seniority in layoffs. Therefore, in the light of changes now taking place in the composition of the labor force, the second hypothesis may have a claim to respectful attention.

It should be emphasized that the alternative to seniority is not an absence of rules. Most of our respondents want to work in a rule-governed environment. But given their attitudes toward seniority in layoffs and promotions, it seems reasonable to conclude that many would prefer rules that stress evaluation of qualification and performance rather than rules based only upon length of service. Where evaluation of qualification and performance is not a real alternative, stronger support for seniority appears, as indicated by our data on disciplinary discharge.

The widespread application of the principle of seniority, especially in conducting layoffs, might well be taken as part of the living law of modern industrial life. This may be so. But our analysis suggests that today's industrial practice will not truly foretell our legal future unless it reflects the fundamental nature of modern enterprise and the enduring aspirations of employees.

Chapter 6 | *Public Policy and the Employment Relation*

IN OUR QUEST FOR INCHOATE AND EMERGENT LAW, WE have thus far touched mainly on the "inner order" of industrial organization—rational administration, collective bargaining, and the aspirations of employees. Although each aspect reflects a broader social and legal context, our stress has been on an internal, evolutionary logic. A more clearly external source of legal development is the elaboration of government policies affecting employee rights and managerial discretion.

One aspect of public policy has already been considered in our discussion of collective bargaining. American labor law, we saw, has been facilitative rather than prescriptive. It drew from the spirit of contract a principle of legal self-restraint. The law would not say what the employment relation should be; the parties would design their own institutions.

Now we consider another set of government programs, which have had a more direct and explicit interest in regulating the conditions of employment and spelling out the rights and duties of employer and employee. To use a distinction we mentioned earlier (page 121), we now turn from "labor law" to the "law of employment." Whereas the former was primarily aimed at controlling industrial strife, the latter has grown out of different concerns, especially welfare, civil rights, and the regulation of industries affected with a public interest.

Although two branches of public policy have emerged, each with its own purposes and its own impact on employment, the line between them is by no means sharp. There are important continuities of policy, perspective, and institutional outcome. Although labor law encouraged the parties

212

to govern themselves, it also fostered an emergent law defining specific rights and duties. Conversely, regulatory public policy sought a more immediate influence on the standards and conditions of employment; yet it has been profoundly affected by the same spirit of voluntarism and governmental self-restraint that inspired labor law.

In the United States, there has not been a systematic effort to regulate employment in the light of public interest. European and Latin American legislation has approached the employment relation in a more direct and prescriptive way: regulating in detail the terms of employment, including the conditions of layoff and discharge; relying more heavily on government initiative in the enforcement of legal standards and the administration of welfare; and more closely integrating the collective agreement with government policy, especially by "extending" the terms of such agreements to all employers and employees of an industry or geographical area.[1]

The American aversion to prescriptive regulation is partly accounted for by the resistance of labor and industry. For a long time these protagonists insisted on defining their problems as "private" matters to be settled among themselves. In addition, the tendency to resist prescription reflects a strong historical commitment to limited government.

Until the late thirties employment legislation was hampered by a constitutional philosophy that saw government as a threat to private rights rather than as a positive instrument for the realization of social values. The doctrine of "substantive due process" was used to nullify legislation "unreasonably" interfering with freedom of contract:

> The general right to make a contract in relation to his business is part of the liberty of the individual protected by the Fourteenth Amendment of the Federal Constitution. . . . The right to purchase or to sell labor is part of the liberty protected by that amendment. . . . The question necessarily arises: is this a fair, reasonable, and appropriate exercise of the police power of the State, or is it an unreasonable, unnecessary, and arbitrary interference with the right of the individual to his personal liberty or to enter into those contracts which may seem appropriate or necessary for the support of himself and his family?[2]

---

[1] On this procedure in continental Europe, see Otto Kahn-Freund (ed.), *Labour Relations and the Law: A Comparative Study* (London: Stevens & Sons, 1965), 11–12, 73–76, 78–83, 96–98, 114–115, 122–123.

[2] *Lochner* v. *New York*, 198 U.S. 45 (1905), at 53. This perspective was forcefully reasserted in the 1923 *Adkins* case, which invalidated a District of Columbia statute establishing minimum wage standards for adult women employees. *Adkins* v. *Children's Hospital*, 261 U.S. 525 (1923). Similarly, the constitutionality of workmen's compensation was for a while held in doubt, at least in so far as the statutes extended their coverage beyond the narrow category of extra-hazardous occupations. See: *Ives* v. *South Buffalo Ry.*, 201 N.Y. 271 (1911). This threat was removed by the Supreme Court in

With such language the Supreme Court struck down a New York statute limiting the hours of work in bakeries to sixty per week and ten per day.

Only when government intervention was confined to specially hazardous occupations, or to the labor of women and children, could the police power —the power to promote "the health, morals and welfare of the public"— be invoked.[3] Thus the dangers and injustices routinely associated with employment were placed beyond the reach of public control.

The restrictions imposed by the doctrine of "substantive due process" were not fully overcome until 1937, when the Parrish decision reversed prior interpretations and the constitutionality of a state minimum wage statute was upheld.[4]

In addition to constitutional due process obstacles, which limited state as well as federal legislation, the powers of the federal government were significantly narrowed by restrictive interpretations of the commerce clause. The Federal Employers' Liability Act of 1906, intended to cover *all* employees of carriers engaged in interstate commerce, was held unconstitutional;[5] a new statute had to be passed in 1908, with coverage limited to those employees of the interstate carriers who were injured while actually engaged in interstate commerce.[6] Similarly the scope of the Fair Labor Standards Act of 1939 was carefully restricted to employees engaged in interstate commerce or in the production of goods for such commerce.[7] Such limitations kept federal law from reaching interstate industries as a whole, thus reducing the possibilities of systematic administrative en-

---

1917. See *New York Central RR.* v. *White*, 243 U.S. 188 (1917); *Hawkins* v. *Bleakly*, 243 U.S. 210 (1917); *Mountain Timber Co.* v. *Washington*, 243 U.S. 219 (1917). But the *Ives* case had already prompted many states to settle for fragmentary or voluntary compensation plans.

[3] See, for example, *Holden* v. *Hardy*, 169 U.S. 366 (1898), which upheld the constitutionality of a Utah statute forbidding the employment of women in underground mines, smelters, and refineries for more than eight hours daily. Also, *Muller* v. *Oregon*, 208 U.S. 412 (1908), which found regulation of women's hours compatible with due process.

[4] *West Coast Hotel Co.* v. *Parrish*, 300 U.S. 379 (1937). The constitutionality of regulations of hours of work had earlier been recognized in *Bunting* v. *Oregon*, 243 U.S. 426 (1917).

[5] 34 Stat. 232, c. 3073 (1906); invalidated by *Howard* v. *Illinois Central RR.*, 207 U.S. 463 (1908).

[6] 35 Stat. 65 (1908); upheld in the Second FELA Cases, 223 U.S. 1 (1912). This restriction was later eased by a 1939 amendment which extended coverage to employees whose duties in any way further or affect interstate commerce. 53 Stat. 1404 (1939).

[7] 52 Stat. 1060 (1938). An early attempt by the federal government to regulate child labor had been struck down in 1918 as beyond the limits of interstate commerce; the statute prohibited interstate shipment of goods manufactured under substandard child labor conditions. See *Hammer* v. *Dagenhart*, 247 U.S. 251 (1918). The FLSA relied upon the same technique for the enforcement of its child labor provisions: its constitutionality was upheld in 1941, in *United States* v. *Darby* (312 U.S. 100) which overruled the *Hammer* decision.

forcement, and compelling greater reliance upon the complaints of individual employees. The implementation of the law was thus made more problematic, dependent on the resourcefulness and initiative of aggrieved employees and their unions.[8]

These constitutional limitations have considerably eased in recent years, reflecting the more active posture of modern government and the changing balance of federal and state powers. Nevertheless, they have left a continuing imprint on the character of public policy affecting employment. Given the obstacles to direct prescriptive regulation, the government was compelled, whenever it was under pressure to act, to use less direct and less clearly prescriptive methods. Two main strategies emerged: (1) although employment could not be regulated directly, it could often be reached through indirect action, as an incident of government programs that were more clearly authorized; (2) government programs were so framed as to underscore private initiative and participation, and to diminish the visibility of public intervention.

Regulation by Indirection

American legislation has dealt with the problems of employment mainly by indirect action, incidental to programs that were aimed at other purposes. This preference for indirection is revealed in (1) the use of government procurement to impose standards on industries that enter contracts with public agencies, and (2) regulation developed as a by-product of legislation or administrative policy directed primarily toward other problems, such as civil rights or the control of industries affected with a public interest.

Whatever substantive results may have been accomplished in this way, the strategy of indirection has had its own impact on the character of public policy. First, the concern for employment has remained tangential, secondary to other objectives. This reflects the precariousness of the government's commitment to industrial justice: the latter would have to

---

[8] The point is discussed in John R. Van de Water and Harold C. Petrowitz, "Retailing Activities Under the Fair Labor Standards Act," 31 *Southern California Law Review* 248 (1958): "The wage and hour provisions [of the FLSA], and to a somewhat lesser extent the child labor provisions, do not deal with an entire business establishment or a whole industry or group of industries as such. Coverage is specified in terms of each individual employee and therefore the application of the act depends on the nature of the duties of the particular employee concerned and not on whether he is working in any particular plant or type of industry. If the acts of a particular employee are within the definitions of the act for covered persons, then the employer must observe the requirements of the act with respect to that employee and others like him who are also covered."

yield in case of conflict with more clearly recognized aims. Second, the indirect approach could sustain only *ad hoc,* fragmentary interventions: discrete issues were dealt with as opportunities arose and circumstances demanded. This prevented government from considering systematically the problems of employment and evolving a firm conception of its responsibility for industrial justice.

Regulation by contract.   Because it is a major factor in economic life, government procurement is a potent instrument of indirect regulation. Like any contracting party, government may set the terms under which it will do business with industry; contract can thus become a convenient instrument for imposing standards. At first, concern for labor problems in procurement reflected a narrow interest in the quality and continuity of supply. Government agencies might intervene in labor disputes that threatened to interrupt production; they sometimes found it necessary to impose minimum standards of wages and hours as a phase of quality control. To this end, special clauses were written into procurement contracts.[9]

Later it became apparent that procurement could be systematically used to accomplish many government aims for which there was no other legal authorization. During recent decades administrative and statutory regulations have greatly proliferated, requiring insertion in government contracts of clauses designed to secure compliance with a wide array of public policies.[10] One reason for this growth, as it bears on labor policy, is discussed in a leading case interpreting the Walsh-Healey Act of 1936, which established minimum wage standards to be imposed in public contracts:

> By statute and regulation, government contracts must go to the lowest responsible bidder. Until the Walsh-Healey Act was passed, it followed that the government, though it urged industry to maintain adequate wage standards, was often compelled to undermine them by contracting with low-wage concerns. The Walsh-Healey Act sought to support standards by withholding contracts from such concerns.[11]

Partly under pressure from industrial concerns in high-wage areas, partly out of concern for the depressing effects of competitive bidding on labor standards, minimum standards were imposed on all public contracts. But

---

[9] For an account of early War Department practices during World War I, see Stephen N. Shulman, "Labor Policy and Defense Contracts: A Matter of Mission," 29 *Law and Contemporary Problems,* No. 1, *Government Contracts,* Part I (Winter, 1964), pp. 244–247.

[10] For a brief discussion of the variety of policies government contracts have come to serve, see Arthur S. Miller, "Government Contracts and Social Control," 41 *Virginia Law Review* 27 (1955); see also Arthur S. Miller, "Administration by Contract," 36 *New York University Law Review* 957 (1961).

[11] *Mitchell* v. *Covington Mills,* 229 F 2d. 506 (1953), at 508.

what was initially a means of protecting established standards, could easily be made to justify enlarging government policy. This is clearly suggested in the following interpretations of what Walsh-Healey was about:

> This Act's purpose was to *impose obligations* upon those favored with Government business and to obviate the possibility that any part of our tremendous national expenditure would go to forces tending to depress wages and purchasing power, and offending fair standards of employment . . .[12]

> [The Act's] purpose is to use the leverage of the Government's immense purchasing power to *raise* labor standards.[13]

Regulation by contract was a welcome innovation, in view of the severe constitutional restrictions on the exercise of rule-making powers. What government was unable to do directly it could accomplish by indirection and through a process that maintained the outward form of voluntarism.

The attractiveness of contract as a regulatory technique lay in the great freedom government enjoyed. As we have seen, the purposive contract is a way of establishing *legally unsupervised* relationships.[14] In the classical doctrine of liberty of contract, each party is free to set the conditions under which he will undertake contractual obligations; having assented, he is bound by the agreement and has no right to complain of its provisions. Applied to public contracts, this doctrine left government, like any citizen, free to set the terms under which it would enter agreements with private firms. The latter had no standing to challenge the legality of regulations: Either a firm was not actually party to a contract and was thus not legally affected by the rules, or it had duly contracted and was duly bound.[15]

This doctrine has been undermined as the use of procurement for regulatory purposes has become more extensive. Transactions with government tend to lose their contractual character, especially when they serve as instruments for establishing long-term collaboration and coordinating complex activities. Regulation becomes a continuing feature of the relationship:

> [I]ndustry personnel have found themselves in the unique, unenviable and undersirable position of attempting to negotiate their contracts at the regulation-making table. . . . To regard the defense contract as merely a special kind of sales contract or a special kind of employment contract is

---

[12] *Perkins* v. *Lukens Steel Co.*, 310 U.S. 113 (1940), at 128. (Emphasis supplied.)
[13] *Endicott Johnson Corp.* v. *Perkins*, 317 U.S. 501 (1943) at 507. (Emphasis supplied.)
[14] See above, 131.
[15] See *Perkins* v. *Lukens Steel Co.*, 310 U.S. 113 (1940), at 128.

to misunderstand its true character. Not only does the contract set forth the description and performance requirements of the article or system being purchased, the compensation to be paid the producer, and the mode of payment; but in addition it spells out the many restrictions on the activities of the defense contractors. For example, they are required to pay their employees a specified minimum wage, not to discriminate in employment because of race, creed, color, or national origin, to use only materials of domestic origin, and to favor small business concerns. in making purchases. The contract also spells out the management decisions which may require approval of, or initiation by, the government— such as decisions to change the specifications of the article being produced, to "make or buy," or to enter into subcontracts. Many defense contracts also differ substantially from the ordinary commercial contract in the power that they give the government to adjust the compensation both during the performance of the contract and afterwards, as well as to examine the books and operations of the defense contractor in connection with such power.[16]

Accordingly, new rationales for "regulation by contract" have been suggested, stressing the growing integration of public and private enterprise. Since "business is no longer merely a supplier but a participant in the management and administration of a public function," then it must "ultimately become accustomed to close supervision with the resulting investigations, audits, and other paraphernalia that accompany the spending of taxpayers' money."[17] On the other hand, as the regulatory features of procurement are more clearly acknowledged, there has been a trend toward extending to government contracting at least some of the usual legal restraints on the exercise of rule-making powers. One writer argues that "the powers of [administrative] agencies to achieve unrelated social goals through contract provisions should be circumscribed by the restrictions normally applicable to government regulations, such as the Administrative Procedure Act."[18] This would limit the freedom of government to act as just another contractor, able to set whatever conditions it likes.

Yet the regulatory power of government contracts should not be overestimated. Although in theory a potent range of penalties may be invoked —specified damages; termination of the contract for failure to perform;

---

[16] Sumner Marcus, "Studies of the Defense Contracting Process," 29 *Law and Contemporary Problems,* No. 1, *Government Contracts,* Part I (Winter, 1964), p. 29.

[17] Stefan J. Dupre and W. Eric Gustavson, "Contracting for Defense: Private Firms and the Public Interest," *Political Science Quarterly,* 77 (1962), 176.

[18] Sumner Marcus, *op. cit.,* 30. The Walsh-Healey Act was amended in 1952 to provide for court review of administrative regulations affecting the making and supervision of government contracts. 41 U.S.C. Sec. 43(a) (1952). Some recent decisions have also recognized the right to challenge the legality of administrative regulations of contract clauses. See *Greene* v. *McElroy,* 360 U.S. 474 (1959).

barring the violator from eligibility for future contract awards—the effectiveness of these weapons is doubtful. There is some question how far the courts would go in enforcing regulatory contract clauses. Government contracts, it is claimed, are contracts of adhesion, in which bargaining is quite limited and there is no genuine consent to many of the terms imposed; antipathy toward this kind of contract may lead the courts to restrict their enforcement.[19]

More important is the often tangential relevance of regulatory clauses to the specific purposes of the contract. Legally, it is argued, violation of such clauses might not constitute a "material breach"; hence the more extreme legal sanctions for breach of contract would be foreclosed.[20] There are serious practical problems underlying the legal issue. The immediate purpose of the contract often carries more weight than extraneous policy aims. The ability of an agency to insist upon compliance with regulatory clauses is conditioned by the bargaining power it enjoys in its dealings with private contractors. An agency dependent upon the specialized skills of a particular firm may have to accommodate resistance or even give up some of the regulatory clauses. Conflicting policy commitments often make the enforcement of such clauses quite problematic:

> The defense contracting official must decide in a given case, whether his principal purpose is to accomplish a particular program in the aerospace field at the lowest cost to the government, or to be certain that government regulations are being fully observed in the expenditure of public money, or to help accomplish a broad national aim, such as economic growth or the maintenance of competition, or to make certain that no firm realizes excessive profits, or to insure the survival of a viable defense industry, or something else.[21]

An official of the Department of Defense concluded:

> Any study of labor policy and defense contracts must start with one fundamental fact: the mission of the Department of Defense . . . is neither labor policy nor contracting. . . . The mission of the Department of Defense is the defense of the nation. No more, no less. . . . Labor policy is the mission of other government agencies. . . . Because other government departments and agencies are primarily concerned with labor policy, the basic philosophy of the Department of Defense is and has always been to leave labor matters to the interested civilian agencies.[22]

---

[19] See Arthur S. Miller, "Government Contracts and Social Control," 41 *Virginia Law Review* 27 (1955).
[20] *Ibid.*
[21] Sumner Marcus, *op. cit.*, 24.
[22] Stephen N. Shulman, *op. cit.*, 238, 239, 242.

Therefore only "when labor problems threaten the defense of the nation" does the Department become directly concerned with labor policy: "Remission to the civilian agencies must then withstand pragmatic appraisal."[23]

The precarious commitment of contracting agencies has been apparent in the history of efforts to use government contracts as vehicles for banning racial discrimination in employment. In 1941 President Roosevelt, under threat of a March on Washington and in the context of preparation for war, issued an Executive Order requiring the insertion of non-discrimination clauses in defense contracts and establishing a Fair Employment Practice Committee.[24] The Committee had only a small staff and no power to seek judicial enforcement of its orders; it had to work through the operating agencies of the federal government. Although the FEPC was strengthened by President Roosevelt in 1943, Congressional resistance forced its termination in 1946.[25] A *legal residue remained*, however, in the unenforced requirement that there be no discrimination in government contracts.[26] A study committee set up by President Truman in 1951 found the non-discrimination provision "almost forgotten":

> In case after case, agency after agency, and region after region, the study uncovered evidence of patent discrimination and government acquiescence. "On several occasions contracting agencies to which cases were referred stated they felt a sufficient inquiry had been made by sending a representative to the plant to ask what apparently amounted to a simple question—'Are you discriminating against Negroes?' When the obvious answer 'No' was recorded, the inquiry was considered closed by the agency."[27]

In 1953 President Eisenhower created a Committee on Government Contracts, which was largely ineffectual but did reaffirm the public policy. The Committee relied on voluntary compliance and referral of individual complaints to operating agencies. When it became clear that these procedures were impotent to correct discrimination patterns in firms and unions, the

---

[23] *Ibid.*, 242.

[24] On the history of fair employment policies in government contracting, see Paul H. Norgren, "Government Contracts and Fair Employment Practices," 29 *Law and Contemporary Problems*, No. 1, *Government Contracts*, Part I (1964), pp. 225–237; Michael I. Sovern, *Legal Restraints on Racial Discrimination in Employment* (New York: The Twentieth Century Fund, 1966), Chap. 5; Arthur E. Bonfield, "The Origin and Development of American Fair Employment Legislation," 52 *Iowa Law Review* 1043 (1967); Timothy L. Jenkins, "Study of Federal Effort to End Job Bias: A History, a Status Report, and a Prognosis," 14 *Howard Law Journal* 259 (1968).

[25] See Will Maslow, "FEPC: A Case History in Parliamentary Maneuver," 13 *University of Chicago Law Review* 407 (1946).

[26] In 1943 the scope of the ban was extended from defense contracts to all government procurement.

[27] Michael I. Sovern, *op. cit.*, 254.

Committee asked the operating agencies to initiate inspection programs and make more use of the penalties provided in the contracts. But the keynote remained "education" and "conciliation": no contract award was withheld or canceled, nor was the threat of such sanction often used, for "the CGC preferred to avoid compulsion as a matter of principle."[28]

Under President Kennedy the CGC was succeeded by a President's Committee on Equal Employment Opportunity.[29] This board had more extensive powers and exercised more aggressive leadership. More reliance was placed on compliance reports and other forms of pressure. Voluntarism remained dominant, however, and much emphasis was placed on a program of "Plans for Progress," which invited government contractors to sign voluntary pledges of affirmative action to overcome the effects of past discrimination by recruiting and training minority group members.[30] In 1965 President Johnson issued a new Executive Order assigning responsibility for supervision of contract compliance with respect to job discrimination to the Department of Labor.[31] Although the Order seemed to have teeth, its administration has been attacked as "an inexcusable record of bureaucratic betrayal."[32]

Incidental regulation. To a large extent, public policy has reached the employment relation tangentially, as an incident of other purposes and programs. Thus "fair employment" has been sought, not for its own sake, but as part of a larger "civil rights" policy. The purpose was not to raise standards of fairness in the employment relation, but to redress the grievances of racial and ethnic minorities. Similarly, government policy in the field of welfare has not been motivated by a direct concern for the employment relation. Rather, the aim was to solve social problems affecting underprivileged groups, such as the protection of health or the guarantee of minimum income for the disabled, the unemployed, and the elderly.

---

[28] Paul H. Norgren, *op. cit.*, 231.

[29] On the Kennedy committee, see N. Thompson Powers, "Federal Procurement and Equal Employment Opportunity," 29 *Law and Contemporary Problems* 468 (1964).

[30] Michael I. Sovern, *op. cit.*, 116 ff., credits Plans for Progress with some success.

[31] Executive Order No. 11246, 30 Fed. Reg. 12319 (1965). An Office of Federal Contract Compliance was established within the Department of Labor.

[32] Herbert Hill, National Labor Director, National Association for the Advancement of Colored People, "The Journey to Johannesburg?" (mimeo.; excerpts from an address, National Conference on Civil and Human Rights, National Education Association, Washington, D.C., February 14, 1968), 7. Mr. Hill adds: "Since that Order was issued in September 1965, not a single contract—not one—has been cancelled for reason of noncompliance. . . . Few contracts have ever been held up, even in cases of overt, proven documented discrimination. Companies which have been cited for discrimination by the Equal Employment Opportunity Commission or state FEPC's, or against whom the Department of Justice has brought action under Title VII of the Civil Rights Act of 1964, continue to benefit from federal contracts in flat contravention of the Order."

The regulation of employment was a way of reaching the relevant clienteles, who were mostly wage-earners. Employment was a criterion of eligibility, a test of applicability, rather than an immediate object of government policy. Unemployment insurance and social security were justified as ways of preventing massive poverty and avoiding depressions by placing a floor under income and consumer expenditures. Even workmen's compensation, which today appears so closely connected with the law of employment, was originally seen as distinct from issues of fairness between employer and employee. The following comment by members of the early California Industrial Accident Commission shows how strongly this separation was made:

> When the state enacts a compensation law, it does so, not primarily to establish justice between an employer and his injured employee, but to safeguard itself against a prolific source of poverty which may become a burden to the state.[33]

The history of government policy pertaining to transportation and public utilities provides a striking example of how regulation of employment may emerge as an incident of other commitments.[34] By the Transportation Act of 1920, Congress gave the Interstate Commerce Commission power to regulate the consolidation of railroads. When the ICC orders a merger or the abandonment of a railroad, it necessarily jeopardizes many jobs as well as the job rights acquired by employees through collective bargaining. Despite pressures from organized labor, the agency at first took the position that the needs of the "public" ought to be the sole criterion in deciding consolidation cases. The growth of union power, and the consequent threat of strikes and costly interruptions of service, however, made it increasingly difficult for the ICC to sustain this posture. The issue remained in doubt until 1933, when the Emergency Transportation Act, which conferred special temporary powers on a Federal Coordinator of Transportation, specified that no employee of a railroad could be dismissed or suffer a reduction in pay as a result of consolidations ordered under the Act. Following this path, the ICC itself agreed, in a 1934 consolidation case, to provide for the protection of affected employees, on the ground that the idea of "public interest" is "broad

---

[33] California Legislature, Appendix to the Journals of the Senate and Assembly, 40th Sess., 1913, Vol. 1, No. 21, *First Report of the Industrial Accident Board*, 1911–1912 (Sacramento, 1913), p. 5.
[34] The following discussion is based primarily on Allison W. Brown, Jr., "Employee Protection and the Regulation of Public Utilities," 63 *Yale Law Journal* 445 (1954).

enough to comprehend every public interest and the interest of every group or element of the public."[35]

The power of the ICC to impose protective conditions in merger plans was upheld by the Supreme Court in 1939.[36] The Court ruled that, since the public interest can be affected by "the injurious effects on morale and labor strife of mergers," it is within the discretionary powers of the Commission to require provisions for the protection of employees. This decision was soon made obsolete by the Transportation Act of 1940 which made it a requirement, and no longer a matter of discretion, for the ICC to consider and protect the interests of employees affected by mergers. The Commission's interpretation of this mandate was at first quite restrictive. In 1942 the Supreme Court overturned an ICC policy that its power to regulate the protection of employees was confined to merger cases. It was held that the public interest and the intent of Congress required extension of this power to abandonment cases.[37] Soon afterward the Commission departed from its practice of imposing protective conditions only when adverse effects on employees were proven. Adverse effects were to be presumed and protective provisions incorporated into the merger or abandonment order.[38]

The experience of the Civil Aeronautics Board under the Civil Aeronautics Act of 1938 closely parallels that of the ICC. The CAB first asserted its authority to protect employees' rights in a 1947 route transfer case, relying on the Supreme Court decisions in ICC cases and the "public interest that labor disputes will not paralyze airlines."[39] In 1950, the CAB assumed responsibility for integrating the seniority lists of the companies involved in a route transfer.[40]

---

[35] *St. Paul Bridge and Terminal Ry. Control*, 199 ICC 588 (1934). When the powers of the Federal Coordinator expired, representatives of railroad management and unions negotiated the Washington Job Protection Agreement of 1936, which sought to protect employees against the adverse effects of mergers. The agreement provided for dismissal compensation, covering wage losses over a period of one to five years depending upon seniority, and for a displacement compensation, covering wage differences and losses from the sale of home and moving expenses, and for arbitration of disputes. 80 Cong. Rec. 7661 (1936).

[36] *United States* v. *Lowden*, 308 U.S. 225 (1939).

[37] *ICC* v. *Railway Labor Exec. Assoc.*, 315 U.S. 373 (1942).

[38] *Chicago, Burlington and Quincy Abandonment*, 257 ICC 700 (1944). The rules devised in that case, known as the "Burlington Formula," incorporated provisions similar to those of the Washington Agreement of 1936 (see fn. 35). These protections have been applied in subsequent railroad merger and abandonment cases, and in 1951 the Commission extended them to motor carriers. *Hudson Bus Line Purchase*, 58 MCC 73, 133 (1951).

[39] *United-Western Acquisition of Air Carrier Property*, 8 CAB 298 (1947) and 11 CAB 701 (1950).

[40] *North Atlantic Route Transfer*, 12 CAB 124 (1950).

The remedy thus offered went well beyond financial compensation for job loss or displacement. By requiring the adoption of a seniority list, the CAB gave specific protection to the rights each group of employees had previously acquired in the affected airlines:

> We think it is completely inequitable that American Overseas and American personnel taken over by Pan American should be treated as if they were completely new employees just coming to work for this company. Any such policy . . . would fail to recognize the equities in favor of American Overseas and American personnel who had devoted hard work and in some cases a good part of their careers to building up the operations which Pan American was taking over.[41]

The Board did not rest its decision on the collective contract provisions under which employees acquired their seniority rights. The seniority protections were to apply to both union and nonunion employees. Later the Board made it clear that its power was in no way limited by the conditions established by contract; it was merely required to take those conditions into account in setting its own standards as to what would be just and reasonable.[42] In 1953 a Federal Circuit Court affirmed the authority of the CAB to impose the integration of seniority lists, and upheld the order of the Board that the parties "refrain from making any labor contract in the future which will not conform to" the standards set by the agency:

> A private contract must yield to the paramount power of the Board to perform its duties under the statute creating it . . . only under such terms as it determines to be just and reasonable in the public interest.[43]

These decisions tend to change the nature of seniority rights, from contractually defined benefits that may be bargained away and that expire with the end of the agreement, into publicly protected rights that emerge from and remain incident to participation in the enterprise.[44]

In addition to the trends just discussed, other regulations impose even more direct restrictions on the discretion of employers in regulated industries. The Interstate Commerce Act limits the hours of work on railroads; the Motor Carriers Act of 1935 empowers the ICC to establish

---

[41] *Ibid.*, 424.
[42] North Atlantic Route Transfer, 14 CAB 910 (1951).
[43] *Kent* v. *CAB* 204 F. 2d 263 (2d Cir. 1953), at 266.
[44] Following the path of federal law, state public utilities commissions have also assumed jurisdiction over the protection of employees in consolidation and abandonment cases. See California Public Utilities Commission, *Richmond and San Raphael Ferry and Transportation Co.*, Termination of Service, Application No. 33942, Decision No. 48045, 48112, 48315 (1952–1953).

maximum hours for certain employees of interstate motor carriers; the Civil Aeronautics Act authorizes regulation of the work schedules of pilots and co-pilots, qualifications of skilled personnel, standards for the size and composition of the crews, and many other working conditions. In the shipping industry, the Coast Guard establishes rules as to minimum numbers and qualifications of officers and crews, licenses the personnel, and prescribes a variety of health and safety standards.

The regulation of job rights and conditions of work in such industries does not mean, for the most part, that there is a special commitment to employee welfare. The justification is usually some other goal, such as protection of public safety in rail or air transportation. Accordingly, the regulatory agencies are likely to be relatively passive, adapting their policies to the emergent demands and powers of the unions, sometimes waiting for the courts to lead the way. Often the rights they granted were already recognized in collective agreements. In this context, the government is less a creator of standards than a vehicle for endowing private rules with a new source of authority. To a limited extent, the employee's rights are made less dependent on contract and on the relative power of the parties.

Voluntarism and Passivity

The American law of employment has placed a high value on the initiative and assent of private interests. Even when public regulation is fairly explicit, as a phase of welfare administration or of the extension of civil rights, there has been a search for strategies that would diminish the visibility of government intervention. The preferred role of government is more responsive than affirmative. Administration should proceed by responding to claims, not by systematic regulation and surveillance. Enforcement should aim at voluntary compliance, and public purposes should be redefined to accommodate the special interests of private groups.

This voluntarist motif is apparent in the tendency to turn enforcement agencies into passive recipients of privately initiated complaints. The agency then acts as a "neutral" judge or mediator. The focus is more on settling disputes than on affirmative action aimed at realizing public goals.

This orientation pervades the administration of fair employment legislation. The federal government and a number of states have created special agencies to implement laws against discrimination in employment.[45]

---

[45] This legislation should be distinguished, of course, from the anti-discrimination clauses in government contracts, discussed above. On the federal act, see Comment, "Enforce-

Although some of these agencies have broad powers to initiate action and fashion remedies, all have exhibited considerable timidity in using their authority. Despite the ignorance, apathy, and fear that may prevent aggrieved persons from filing complaints, most "fair employment practice" (FEP) commissions have preferred to avoid acting on their own initiative. A study of the New Jersey Division of Civil Rights concluded:

> . . . one critical weakness of the Division was its insistence on having a "real live" complainant before it would investigate, conciliate, or otherwise enforce the laws against discrimination. The Division simply did not initiate investigations looking to enforcement on its own motion. This overtly procedural decision to await complainants kept the enforcement activities of the Division at a minimum level and meant that these activities were carried on in a haphazard manner, depending on the chance pattern of complaints. . . .
> By awaiting complaints instead of initiating enforcement activities, the Division has failed to develop interpretations and techniques for dealing with patterns of discrimination by unions or employers.[46]

Moreover, only a few of the Commissions allow civil rights organizations to file complaints, even though group advocacy might make a decisive difference in the representation of passive constituents. Such agencies apparently fear that a too committed advocacy would thwart their ability to make needed accommodations.[47]

Fair employment commissions have indeed been marked by an overriding concern for persuasion and compromise. The very procedures under which the agencies operate attest to the ingenuity with which the law has sought to avoid the "last resort" of compulsory orders and enforcement. Instead of a trial ending in an authoritative ruling, the proceedings usually provide for: (1) a preliminary investigation of complaints, ending in a finding of "probable cause," followed by (2) informal proceedings of conciliation; (3) if the latter fail, the agency may decide to initiate formal proceedings; (4) only then may the case be officially heard and a final order obtained; and (5) even this order may not be enforced without further proceeding in court, which may reconsider the evidence and issue a new decision. Some statutes provide penal sanctions for willful violations of Commission orders, but those penalties have rarely been

---

ment of Fair Employment under the Civil Rights Act of 1964," 32 *University of Chicago Law Review* 430 (1965). A survey of the state legislation may be found in Michael A. Bamberger and Nathan Lewin, "The Right to Equal Treatment: Administrative Enforcement of Anti-Discrimination Legislation," 74 *Harvard Law Review* 526–589 (1961).
[46] Alfred W. Blumrosen, "Antidiscrimination Laws in Action in New Jersey: A Law-Sociology Study," 19 *Rutgers Law Review* 218, 234 (1965).
[47] See Bamberger and Lewin, *op. cit.*, 528–532.

applied.[48] The federal Equal Employment Opportunity Commission has no jurisdiction beyond the conciliation stage; it may only recommend to the Attorney General that he intervene in a claimant's action when the case involves a pattern of discrimination of public importance.[49]

In view of this reluctance to take initiative, it is hardly surprising that FEP commissions have seldom used the full measure of their legal powers, especially in cases involving social reform rather than limited individual grievances. It is relatively easy to order the reinstatement of an arbitrarily discharged employee. It is another matter to challenge the general policies or practices of a firm or union in such areas as recruitment and membership requirements, training and apprenticeship, promotion and election of officers, all of which involve difficult political problems for the affected firms and unions. As emphasis shifts from recognized individual rights to policy issues and social reform, the agencies are under pressure to maintain a posture of accommodation and compromise.

Similar patterns are evident in welfare law. In the administration of the federal Fair Labor Standards Act, the technique used to uncover violations is not "continuing detailed federal supervision or inspection of payrolls. . . . Rather . . . [Congress] chose to rely on information and complaints received from employees seeking to vindicate rights claimed to have been denied."[50] An employee may either bring suit in court or file a complaint with the Secretary of Labor, who then conducts an investigation and may introduce an action against the employer before the courts. Programs like workmen's compensation, which were inspired by the idea of a public responsibility for the welfare and rehabilitation of industrial accident victims, have been entrusted to private employers and insurance carriers, on the assumption that employers and employees would, with their own resources and under the spur of self-interest, see to the accomplishment of legislative aims. Administrative action would center on the resolution of private controversies, rather than on positive social action, regulation, and surveillance.[51]

---

[48] On this point and generally on the enforcement of state FEP laws, see Michael Bamberger and Nathan Lewin, *op. cit.*, 540–557; Morroe Berger, *Equality by Statute* (Garden City, N. Y.: Anchor Books, 1968), 169–214; Leon H. Mayhew, *Law and Equal Opportunity* (Cambridge, Mass.: Harvard University Press, 1968), 120–151.

[49] 78 Stat. 259 (1964) par. 705–706. It would seem also that a claimant cannot proceed in court without first having applied to the Commission for relief; and it is the policy of the Act that state and local remedies must have been exhausted before the Commission may be asked to intervene.

[50] *Mitchell v. DeMario*, 14 Wage and Hour Cases 418 (1960).

[51] This point is discussed in Philippe Nonet, *Administrative Justice: Advocacy and Change in a Government Agency* (New York: Russell Sage Foundation, 1969) 149–159.

These administrative patterns no doubt bespeak an uncertain political commitment and consensus. But they also reflect the larger orientations of American public law. The whole thrust of the developing administrative law has been toward making the administrative process more responsive to, if not dependent on, the initiative of the private parties it governs. The emphasis on adversariness, on opportunities for participation and scrutiny by affected citizens, the search for procedural guarantees, the insistence on limited discretion, all support this tendency.

When government looks to the initiative and participation of affected parties, there is a serious risk that the aims of public policy will be redefined and public purpose attenuated. This erosion is apparent in the history of social insurance programs, which have followed a pattern of substituting private insurance plans for government sponsored programs. The growth of welfare legislation in the 1910's stimulated a number of private businesses to develop their own welfare plans. In this way, it was hoped, further government intrusion would be forestalled. Organized labor itself was initially hostile to social insurance, public or private. Such benefits were perceived as precarious gratuities that would eventually weaken labor's independence and assertiveness. This attitude began to change in the late thirties and especially during World War II. As a result of the severe restrictions imposed by government on wage increases in the war economy, union demands in collective bargaining turned to "fringe benefits." Private welfare plans have ever since become firmly established in collective contracts. The gross (and often intended) inadequacy of statutory benefits provided sufficient incentive for the growth of voluntary programs. Indeed some legislation, such as the California law providing for temporary disability benefits to employees injured off the job, encourages the substitution of private plans for state benefits when "the rights afforded to the covered employees are greater than those provided for" under the state program.[52] But however well protected the beneficiaries of such plans may be, the more general outcome of this substitution is to diminish the capacities and resources of public welfare. A major purpose of social insurance was to create, out of contributions from employers and employees, a special fund government might use to extend the guarantee of a minimum income to the disabled and the unemployed. This purpose is frustrated when contributions are diverted into private programs that serve only the interests of a special group. Government loses the power to redistribute those funds in accordance with larger social needs.

---

[52] California Unemployment Insurance Code, Sec. 3251–3271.

Private Law and Public Policy

Regulation by indirection, and the commitment to voluntarism, point to major limitations of government action. Compared to more clearly prescriptive systems, such as those of France and West Germany, the American approach reflects a relative weakness and lack of purpose in the regulation of employment. The main symptom of this weakness is that labor policy in the United States has served mostly the interests of unionized workers; to a large extent it has been unable to reach the great majority of the unorganized.

To underscore those limitations is not to say that the influence of public policy has been small or unimportant. Rather its influence has been of a special kind. The very conditions that undermined the prescriptive role of government helped fashion another—the creation of opportunities. Instead of imposing a systematic set of regulations, public policy has made available an inchoate variety of ideas and resources that employers and employees could use creatively in furthering their interests. The passivity of government defined its programs as *potentials to be developed rather than as benefits to be received*. Public policy did not offer a fully defined or clearly bounded scheme; its scope and import remained open-ended.

Privatization of public policy. It followed that public policy would develop less through an accumulation of regulations than through a process by which the parties invoked the authority of public purpose in support of new demands and claims of right. The latter would be treated as private controversies to be resolved by negotiation and adjudication. Public policy became a resource labor and industry would appropriate and adapt to their own needs. Instead of being handed down as a product of governmental authority, public policy would grow in conjunction with the parties' pursuit of their own interests, in the course of bargaining and litigation. In this process, an external constraint is "internalized": Rules emerge from the parties' own needs and sense of right, and hence can, at least potentially, be more fully accepted and built into the "living law" of their relationship.

Public policy has thus been privatized.[53] Ideas and standards originally intended as guides for governmental action became principles to govern the "private" relations of employer and employee. Benefits that were to be dispensed under the authority and discretion of government, were trans-

---

[53] A similar point is made with respect to anti-discrimination laws in Leon H. Mayhew, *Equal Opportunity and the Law* (Cambridge, Mass.: Harvard University Press, 1968), 272–274.

formed into recognized private rights and duties. Privatization was revealed in three main ways, two of which have already been considered.

(1) *Self-administration*. Initiative in the implementation of public policy was transferred from public officials to private actors. We have commented before on the tendency to recoil from active and committed modes of administration. Behind this preference for sitting back and awaiting complaints was an assumption that public policy could be self-administering: self-interest would spur the parties themselves to set in motion the processes of enforcement and elaboration. The stage was thereby set for the parties to make public policy an affair between themselves, an aspect of their private relation. It followed that the reach of government action would remain uneven; the extent of enforcement would vary with the capacities and aspirations of the parties.

(2) *Erosion of public purpose*. Public aims were redefined to accommodate the special interests of private groups. Dependence on voluntary participation brought continuing pressure on government to make policy adaptive to the demands of the parties. Administration would have to rely on private arrangements to implement its programs, thus leaving greater discretion for bargaining and accommodation. We have already indicated how this process affected the evolution of public welfare plans. The pressure for accommodation has tended to undermine the integrity and competence of government programs; at the same time it has made them more responsive to the special needs of particular groups.

(3) *Public policy as a source of private law*. The blurring of public and private aims facilitated an assimilation of public policy to the law of employment. Instead of constituting two distinct and institutionally separated bodies of ideas and standards, private law and public policy came to overlap and merge into a relatively unified system of legal thought. The vehicle of this evolution was a process of legalization, in which public policy was subjected to legal elaboration in the light of concepts drawn from the more established branches of private law. In this process, some major ideas of public policy were also absorbed into the common law of employment. The effect of this evolution was to remove public policy from the realm of administrative discretion, and to transform it into a source of vested rights.

Formation of private law.   In their early stages, government programs insisted on drawing a sharp line between public policy and the private law of employment. Welfare law was viewed as an instrument of public action, rather than as a system of rules defining private rights and duties. Efforts were made to detach the new legislation from the context of the employment relation, in part by entrusting its administration to specialized agencies protected from judicial control and "legalistic" doctrines and procedures. Such efforts were especially prominent in the regulation of safety, which had been traditionally linked to the law of employers' liability. The older safety statutes simply established presumptions of negligence in case of accident following a violation of the statutory requirements by the employer; those private-law statutes were replaced in the 1910's by new legislation that severed this connection of safety to the law of employment and established independent administrative machinery for making and enforcing safety standards. In its early years, workmen's compensation was conceived "not [as] an issue between the employer and his injured employee," but as a means of social action "against a prolific source of poverty which may become a burden to the state."[54] This segregation of private law and public policy had two advantages. First it protected the new agencies from partisan claims and reduced the threat of legal obstacles to administrative action. The agencies could more freely pursue their welfare aims without controversy and undue "legalism." In addition, the separation helped preserve the integrity of the new policies by guarding them from the influence of older ideas in the law of employment.

The wished-for segregation was never fully realized, however. In the course of its own efforts to establish welfare standards, government encouraged the participation of labor and industry, not as clients or objects of administration, but as claimants and defendants. Programs designed in the spirit of social welfare, for the purpose of providing services and distributing benefits, were transformed into legal resources for pressing claims of right and formulating new obligations. The reliance on complaints, instead of administrative initiative, was especially conducive to this change. Petitions to government agencies took on the aspect of demands or grievances addressed by the employee to his employer. Hence public policy was invoked less as a mandate for the agency to provide services than as a source of authoritative standards for the adjudication of contested claims. The growth of adversariness in the administrative process affected the orientations of the agencies themselves, undermining their commitments to service and social action, and redefining their role as responding to claims and giving recognition to new rights and duties.

As a result, legal modes of reasoning and procedure, initially seen as irrelevant to the task at hand, were increasingly brought to bear on the making and implementation of public policy. This change initiated a proc-

---

[54] See above, 222.

ess of elaboration in which the more fully developed intellectual resources of received law were used to explore the legal implications of public policy. Advocacy and adjudication, with the accumulation of legal arguments and interpretations, were the means by which private law and public policy were fused. This legalization had the effect of (1) transforming the benefits of public welfare into vested rights, ingredients of the legal status of employee; and (2) fostering doctrinal changes in the law of employment, as common law conceptions were influenced by the new perspectives of public policy.

The role of public policy as a source of private rights may be illustrated by the case of workmen's compensation. Under the classic law of employment, an employee injured on the job had no remedy beyond that offered by the law of torts: he had to show that his master had been negligent and sue him for damages. The posture of the law was to treat employer and employee as unrelated strangers: The servant had no more right against his master than any member of the public.[55] Workmen's compensation introduced a radical change. The injured employee was guaranteed a limited compensation, including medical treatment and indemnity for temporary and permanent disability, in all cases of injury "arising out of and in the course of employment," regardless of negligence.[56]

This policy was originally regarded as part of a government welfare program, aimed at raising standards of public health and well-being and looking to relief and rehabilitation. In some countries indeed, as in France, workmen's compensation has been built into the organization of social

---

[55] If anything, employment weakened even those limited rights. Thus, although an employer was normally liable for injuries caused by the fault of his employees, a special rule barred employees from recovering damages when the injury resulted from the negligence of a "fellow servant." In addition, employees were harshly affected by the application of two principles in the law of torts. Applying the doctrine of "contributory negligence," an employee lost his right to recovery when it could be proved that his own negligence helped cause the accident. He was similarly deprived of a remedy when it was shown that he had "assumed the risk" of accident by knowingly exposing himself to the dangers involved. On the common law of employers' liability, see. H. G. Wood, *A Treatise on the Law of Master and Servant* (2nd. ed.; San Francisco: Bancroft-Whitney Co., 1886), 670–914.

The first efforts of government in this area were devoted to removing these restrictive applications of the law of torts. During the first decade of the century, most states and Congress enacted "employers' liability acts" which restricted or removed the employer's "common law defenses" against negligence suits by employees. This legislation did not affect the basic principle of liability based on negligence, but it did recognize the distinctive nature of the employment relation.

[56] On workmen's compensation laws generally, see: Arthur Larson, *The Law of Workmen's Compensation* (New York: Matthew Bender and Co., 1952); Walter F. Dodd, *The Administration of Workmen's Compensation* (New York: The Commonwealth Fund, 1936); Herman and Anne R. Somers, *Workmen's Compensation* (New York: John Wiley & Sons, 1954).

security: the claims of injured employees are administered by a public agency and paid out of a public insurance fund financed by contributions assessed on employers. The issues that arise are not between the employee and his employer, but between the employee and a government service.[57] In the United States, however, workmen's compensation was based on a liability of the employer to the employee. Although special agencies were created to implement the program, the preservation of the idea of liability opened a door for private litigation. An infusion of advocacy changed what was initially conceived as a welfare program, into a set of legal principles for determining the property rights and liabilities of master and servant. In this way, a policy that was meant to establish a responsibility of government was redefined as the source of a duty owed by the employer to his employee. It was thereby absorbed into the law of employment, bringing considerable change to legal conceptions of the employer's duties that might have remained unaffected by a distant program of public welfare. Instead of being a stranger, as he was under the law of negligence, the employee would be entitled to special treatment as a member of the enterprise.

The legalization of public welfare is reflected in the changing legal doctrine concerning private welfare plans. Under the contractual law of employment, the benefits an employer voluntarily provided were legally defined as gratuities "devoid of consideration" that gave the employee no enforceable right.[58] This accounts in part for the objections organized labor had to welfare programs, both public and private. Left to the paternalistic authority of management, welfare plans tended to increase the dependence of the employee, strengthen his loyalty and compliance, and prevent unionization.[59] The growth of public welfare has made employees less dependent on managerial goodwill, however. It has often brought private welfare plans, such as wage guarantees, unemployment or disability

---

[57] A striking feature of French labor law is the sharp separation it maintains between the *droit du travail*, which governs the conditions of employment and labor-management relations, and the *droit de la securité sociale*, which governs public social insurance programs. One has its roots in private law, the other in public and administrative law; they are administered by different institutions, subject to different procedures; they have given rise to different bodies of legal doctrine, and are taught as distinct topics in law schools. For a brief discussion of this separation, see Roger Jambu-Merlin, "Securité sociale et droit du travail," in *Melanges offerts a Pierre Voirin* (Paris: Librairie Generale de Droit et de Jurisprudence, 1967), 408–422.

[58] For the evolution of legal theories concerning private welfare benefits, see Benjamin Aaron, *Legal Status of Employee Benefit Rights under Private Pension Plans* (Homewood, Ill.: Richard D. Irwin, Inc., 1961), 4–20.

[59] On labor's hostility to welfare, see Benjamin Aaron (ed.), *The Employment Relation and the Law* (Boston: Little, Brown and Company, 1957), 693.

insurance, under the scrutiny of public agencies; for example, government may be called upon to rule on whether and under what conditions such plans are to be treated as supplements to or substitutes for state compensation.[60] More generally, the legalization of public policy has facilitated the extension of a legal perspective to welfare benefits. The notion of welfare as a gratuity has tended to give way to the idea that such benefits are part of the terms of employment and can be claimed as legally protected rights.[61] In 1948, the NLRB was asked to decide whether private pension plans are among the "conditions of employment" with respect to which employers have a duty to bargain collectively under the Wagner Act. The Board answered affirmatively and its decision was upheld by the courts.[62] Since then, private welfare has increasingly been removed from the unilateral control of management and brought under the scope of collective contract and the grievance procedure.

In addition to creating new private rights, the legalization of public policy has entailed a process of doctrinal elaboration, in which statutory policies were examined, criticized, and often profoundly transformed in the light of private-law doctrines. As used in the early welfare legislation, such concepts as "employment," "wages," "injury," "disability," were common sense, unsophisticated ideas, the interpretation of which was a matter of administrative discretion. Even though they were often meant to be more inclusive than parallel common law concepts, they were usually construed in a relatively restrictive and mechanical way. Advocacy brought public policy under legal scrutiny and helped qualify and extend its interpretation. Private law concepts and doctrines often provided useful tools of legal analysis and elaboration. In administrative practice, the "wages" on the basis of which welfare benefits are computed were likely to be confused with payroll statements, without inquiry into what other income might have been earned from employment. Although agencies might have been asked to evolve their own concept of "wages," geared to the special purposes of welfare policy, they were pressed to abide by legal definitions of the income "contractually due" to the employee. Similarly, to show that a disability was compensable as "caused" by employment required demonstrating an almost visible link between events at the time and place of work and the fact of injury. The more subtle concepts of the law of torts helped extend the meaning of "injury" and "causation," and the

---

[60] See Aaron, *The Employment Relation and the Law*, 639–640.
[61] See above, fn. 57.
[62] *Inland Steel Co.* v. *NLRB*, 170 F 2d. 247 (7th Cir. 1948), cert. denied, 336 U.S. 960 (1949).

legal idea that linked employment to the authority of the master made it possible to enlarge the scope of compensation beyond the time and place of work to any situation where an element of duty and subordination could be identified. More generally, private law supplied intellectual resources and bases of argument for analyzing and extending the public policy.

But this process has not left private law unchanged. The common law of employment, infused with some of the ideas and values that inspired government programs, has drifted away from contract and given greater recognition to the interests of the employee as a person. Some aspects of this evolution are suggested in the following paragraphs.

Under the common law, employment was distinguished from other legal relations, such as agency, by the so-called "power of control" test. An employment contract was known by the employer's legal authority, established by contract, to direct the employee in the performance of his duties.[63] The development of welfare legislation led to a reexamination of this concept in an effort to include among the beneficiaries of public policy all the persons that were meant to be included.[64] It was necessary, for instance, that so-called independent contractors be considered employees for the purpose of welfare policy, if their actual economic situation made their alleged independence an illusion and warranted extending benefits to them. In 1930 a New York Court of Appeals had this to say about a milk salesman:

> The contract is adroitly framed to suggest a different relation, but the difference is a semblance only . . . Much of his apparent freedom is in truth apparent only. . . . If he does anything at variance with the will of his employers, its policy or preference, he knows that his contract of employment may be ended overnight. He is bound hand and foot as long as he works the route at all, his freedom an illusion, and his independence but a name.[65]

The underlying problem was discussed in a 1947 United States Supreme Court opinion on the meaning of employment in the Social Security Act:

> As the federal social security legislation is an attack on recognized evils in our national economy, a constricted interpretation of the phrasing by the courts would not comport with its purpose. Such an interpretation

---

[63] See above, 132. On the right of control and its origins, see Wigmore, "Tortious Responsibility," 7 *Harvard Law Review* 315 (1893); T. B. Smith, "Master and Servant: Further Historical Outline," *Juridical Review* 215 (1958).

[64] For a review of this subject, see Don W. Sears, "The Employment Status in Social Legislation," 23 *Rocky Mountain Law Review* 392 (1951); *The Employment Relation and the Law*, 3–53.

[65] *Gliolmi v. Netherland Dairy Co.*, 254 N.Y. 60, at 62–63 (1930); 171 N.E. 906, at 906–907 (1930).

would only make for a continuance, to a considerable degree, of the difficulties for which the remedy was devised and would invite adroit schemes by some employers and employees to avoid the immediate burdens at the expense of the benefits sought by the legislation . . .[66]

Manipulations of wording in a formal contract should not, it was argued, be given great weight. What matters is the "economic reality" of the relation. The same opinion referred to an earlier case involving the National Labor Relations Act:

> The word "employee," we said, was not there used as a word of art, and its content in its context was a federal problem to be construed "in the light of the mischief to be corrected and the end to be attained." We concluded that, since that end was the elimination of labor disputes and industrial strife, "employees" included workers who were such *as a matter of economic reality*.[67] (Emphasis supplied.)

Some decisions seem to suggest the rudiments of a new criterion of employment. In a case under the Fair Labor Standards Act, the Supreme Court affirmed a decision which had held some alleged independent contractors to be employees on the ground their work was "part of an integrated unit of production."[68] The case involved a contract between a slaughterhouse and its meat boners; in characterizing this relation, the court said, one should take account of "the circumstances of the whole activity:"

> We agree with the Circuit Court of Appeals . . . in its characterization of their work as *part of an integrated unit of production* task were employees of the establishment. Where the work done, in its essence, follows the usual path of an employee, putting on an "independent contractor" label does not take the worker from the protection of the Act. . . .
>
> Viewed in this way, the workers did a specialty job on the production line. The responsibility under the boning contract without material change passed from one boner to another. The premises and equipment of [the employer] were used for the work. The group had no business organization that could or did shift as a unit from one slaughterhouse to another. The managing official of the plant kept close touch on the operation. While profits to the boners depended upon the efficiency of their work, it was more like piecework than an enterprise that actually depended for success upon the initiative, judgment or foresight of the typical independent contractor. Upon the whole we must conclude that these meat boners were

---

[66] *United States* v. *Silk; Harrison* v. *Greyvan Lines, Inc.,* 331 U.S. 704.
[67] *Ibid.* The case to which the decision refers is *Labor Board* v. *Hearst Publications,* 322 U.S. 111 (1944).
[68] *Rutherford Food Corporation* v. *McComb,* 331 U.S. 722 (1947).

employees of the slaughtering plant under the Fair Labor Standards Act. (Emphasis supplied.)[69]

Of special interest in this decision is the shift of concern from contract "labels" to the character of membership in the organization. The immediate reason for the change is to vindicate a legislative purpose: Reliance on explicit contractual arrangements would leave too much room for the parties to maneuver themselves out of the scope of the act. The change has a broader significance, however. It contributes to a conception of employment, not as an artifact of contractual will, but as a mode of participation in a going concern.

A broadened concept of employment is also reflected in a line of decisions concerning what injuries may legally be considered as "arising out of employment," and thus compensable under workmen's compensation. Must the injury occur during and as a direct result of the performance of the duties undertaken by the employee, as a contractual conception of employment would suggest? This is the view the courts tended to adopt in the early years of workmen's compensation. In 1916, the California Supreme Court ruled that accidents occurring as a result of playful activities of fellow employees are not compensable:

> [It is] clear that the accident did not arise out of [the injured worker's] employment. That the act of his fellow servant was but momentary and without malice and not in excess of the usual intercourse between servants makes no difference.[70]

The California Industrial Accident Commission had taken the opposite view:

> It is inevitable that when human beings are associated together there will be a certain amount of departure from the work in hand, and certain thoughtless acts of employees, not at all evilly disposed, will result in injury. We think that, up to a certain standard, such risks may properly be regarded as risks of the occupation and a proper charge against the industry.[71]

To the Commission, "employment" meant more than the performance of a determinate contractual service; it encompassed all the conditions normally associated with the social situation of a worker in an enterprise. A compensable injury is one that is traceable to such conditions. The California Supreme Court ultimately adopted the same position, reversing itself in 1945.[72]

---

[69] *Ibid.*, 730.
[70] *Coronado Beach* v. A. J. *Pillsbury,* 172 Cal. 682 (1916).
[71] Quoted in *ibid.*, 683.
[72] *Pacific Employers Insurance Co.* v. IAC, 26 Cal. 2d 286 (1945).

Welfare legislation also raised new issues as to the meaning of "work" and the nature of "wages" under the contract of employment. Legal problems arose regarding what constitutes "work" for the application of wage-and-hour regulations. Are such activities as dressing, preparing tools and equipment, traveling from the plant gate to the work place, or waiting around for calls or assignments, to be considered compensable work and included in the computation of hours? The answer was formerly governed by the employment contract, and in practice depended largely on managerial fiat. As an incident of regulation, the issues have come under the jurisdiction of government, to be examined in the light of public policy. This point is made quite clear in the following excerpt from a regulation of the Wage and Hour Division of the United States Department of Labor. The regulation dealt with a provision of the Portal to Portal Act of 1947, which had sought to restrict the range of activities to be treated as compensable work for the application of the Fair Labor Standards Act:

> Under section 4 of the Portal Act, an employer who fails to pay an employee minimum wages or overtime compensation for or on account of activities engaged in by such employee is relieved from liability or punishment therefor if . . . (1) They constitute . . . activities "preliminary" or "postliminary" to the "principal activity or activities" which the employee is employed to perform; . . . The term "principal activities" includes all activities which are an integral part of a principal activity. . . . Such preparatory activities, which the Administrator had always regarded as work and as compensable under the Fair Labor Standards Act, remain so under the Portal Act, *regardless of contrary customs or contract* [emphasis supplied]. (c) Among the activities included as an integral part of a principal activity are those closely related activities which are indispensable to its performance. If an employee in a chemical plant, for example, cannot perform his principal activities without putting on certain clothes, changing clothes on the employer's premises at the beginning and end of the workday would be an integral part of the employee's principal activity. On the other hand, if changing clothes is merely a convenience to the employee and not directly related to his principal activities, it would be considered as a "preliminary" or "postliminary" activity rather than a principal part of the activity. However, activities such as checking in and out and waiting in line to do so would not ordinarily be regarded as integral parts of the principal activity or activities. . . .[73]

Similar issues have arisen in the determination of wages. Under what conditions and to what extent should such benefits as meals, dress, living accommodations, profit-sharing allowances, employer contributions to wel-

---

[73] U.S. Department of Labor, Wage and Hour Division, Interpretive Bulletin, 29 C.F.R. Pt. 790 (1949). For a survey of problems of coverage and interpretation arising in connection with wage-and-hour legislation, see Aaron, *op. cit.*, 395–527.

fare funds, and other discretionary or contractually determined bonuses, be treated as wages? These problems come up whenever a standard or benefit depends on wages received, as in minimum-wage legislation, social insurance, and workmen's compensation.

By removing such issues from the constricting influence of contract doctrine, welfare policy has done its modest bit to bring the law to a more realistic assessment of the nature of employment. The result is a somewhat more secure legal basis for limiting managerial authority and recognizing the rights and duties that inhere in the employment relation.

The themes of this chapter identify another phase of legal development —the contribution of public policy to a law of employment. That policy has been inchoate, open-ended, and weakly implemented. Legal development has occurred, but it has been largely left to advocacy, bargaining, and the adjudication of private claims. In such a setting, public policy serves as a resource and to some extent as a spur; it is something less, however, than an effective exercise of public will.

There is much to be said for the voluntarist strategy. The very conditions that narrow and diminish the competence of government—indirection, passivity, self-limitation—may encourage the assimilation of public policy to the operative private law. By insisting on voluntarism, the parties themselves are pressed into service as agents of legal development. They provide the energy, they make the claims, they specify the rights. Implementation occurs, not as alien edict from above, but as part of a living relationship, reflecting the social realities of aspiration and of power. This hoped-for advantage may explain why contractualism is still so highly valued in industrial law and policy.

Moreover, the private-law approach makes a contribution to the political community by defusing controversy in the larger arena of legislation and ideology. The political process continues, but it is narrowed to the parties concerned and muted by the piecemeal, self-limiting responsiveness of the common law. Policy commitments fashioned in the political arena are kept ambiguous and tentative; hence they remain open to redefinition in the course of private controversy. Provision is made for extensive participation in legal and administrative decision-making, thus opening up the legal process to an alternative mode of political change. Acceptance of that process is facilitated because opportunities are available to make the now "legalized" policy responsive to special needs and circumstances.

These benefits of voluntarism carry a heavy cost, however. The system depends on participation, but *effective* participation requires resources of organization, skill, and political consciousness. These resources are unevenly distributed, and many who cannot form effective constituencies are excluded from the law's reach and benefit. (It is hardly surprising, therefore, that the American law of employment has served mainly the interests of organized labor.) Unless affirmative steps are taken to enlarge effective participation, the blurring of law and politics tends to diminish the ability of the legal system to control and correct the balance of power.

Even more important is the danger that the privatization of public policy may weaken the political community. The fate of the law depends on the play of special interests who need not take account of more comprehensive needs and aspirations. The result, as we have suggested, is an erosion of public purpose. The law of employment, in remaining very much a "private" law, has been little inspired by larger ideals of democracy and freedom. The meaning of justice in industry has therefore remained impoverished. To overcome that weakness a more direct approach is needed —one that may bring issues of governance into sharper legal focus.

Part Three | *The Emergent Law*

Chapter 7 | *Private Groups and the Law of Governance*

IN PART TWO WE HAVE SKETCHED THE MAIN SOCIAL foundations of industrial justice—the transformation of management, the impact of collective bargaining, the expectations of employees, and the context of public policy. (We have not studied the broader cultural changes that lend support to legal and democratic values and that undermine claims to managerial prerogative.) None of these social changes—or all of them together—can guarantee industrial justice. Their influence is uneven and in many respects precarious; and ideals are achieved through commitment and action, not by any automatic process. What we have pointed to, however, is a *receptive institutional setting* within which further legal change may take place.

This chapter considers the legal implications of the pattern we have traced. Our concern is not for detailed rules of law, nor for any specialized machinery of adjudication. Rather, we are interested in the posture of the legal system, its conceptual readiness to seize what we take to be an emergent historical opportunity.

The legal issues are broadly issues of administrative law, the law of bureaucracy. But administrative law should look beyond the agencies of public government; it should address itself to the similar institutions of the private sector. For the basic problem is the same, in both spheres: "how executive power can be controlled by law and also, so to speak, colonized by legal principles of fair and proper procedure."[1] In this chapter, there-

---

[1] H. W. R. Wade, *Administrative Law* (Oxford: Clarendon Press, 1967), 6. Wade speaks of the "great objective" of administrative law as "the improvement of administration by transfusion of the legal standards of justice" (p. 8).

fore, we return to the issue posed at the outset of Chapter 2: Can we justify, within the framework of legal theory, the application to private organizations of principles hitherto restricted to public government?

Public Law and Private Law

The conventional distinction between public law and private law seems simple enough. Public law has to do with the organization of government and with the relation between government and the individual. Private law, on the other hand, encompasses the legal relations among individuals and groups outside the government. The great branches of public law are constitutional law, criminal law, and administrative law. Contract, tort, and property are classic private-law subjects. On this view, public law is the law of the sovereign. It contains the rules whereby the lawful sovereign organizes and regulates himself, and it spells out the powers which he may exercise over those within his jurisdiction. All else is private law.

For the political and legal philosophy of nineteenth-century liberalism, the separation of public and private law was more than an academic exercise. It had a special salience, for it was a corollary of the distinction between state and society. Freedom, it was thought, required that the powers of the state be clearly bounded, and this objective would be served by maintaining the integrity of private law.

At the same time, in English legal thought there is a well-known tradition of resistance to the segregation of private law and public law. This tradition has done its part to frustrate the development of a public-law jurisprudence. In 1914 Ernest Barker pointed out that "in England, where there is no separate administrative law, separately administered, and where all the law that there is is administered by the ordinary courts as they stand. . . . We have no distinction between private law and public law; because our ordinary judges administer all the law that there is, that law is one body. There is not one law for acts of public authority, and another law for acts of private citizens."[2] This recalls Dicey's suspicion of the separate *droit administratif* in France. Dicey thought it essential to the rule of law that governmental powers be subject to common-law principles, that the ordinary courts apply the law equally to all men, including government officials.[3]

[2] Ernest Barker, "The Rule of Law," *The Political Quarterly* (May, 1914), 116.
[3] See A. V. Dicey, *Introduction to the Study of the Law of the Constitution* (10th ed. London: Macmillan and Co., Ltd., 1959), Chap. XII. The revision of Dicey's views is discussed in E. C. S. Wade's introduction to this edition.

The resistance to public law as a special category was a way of defending the historic victories of the English judiciary:

> An essential feature of the revolutionary settlement of the seventeenth century was to ensure that the judges were independent of the power of the Crown. Henceforth there was to be one system of law to which all would owe obedience; and the only prerogatives permitted to the King would be those recognized by the law. This conception of an indivisible system of law and a single judicature commanding universal obedience from public authorities and citizens alike, seemed to be threatened not only by the emergence of administrative tribunals but also by the mere recognition of a separate body of public law even though it were subject to the jurisdiction of the ordinary courts.[4]

This background helps explain why the concept of public law has received little systematic development in common-law countries; it may also explain the tardy development of administrative law as a distinct subject.

The underlying issue is somewhat obscured by the equation of legal categories and jurisdiction. The administration of justice by courts of general jurisdiction may well put some barriers in the way of a sharp separation of public and private law, if only because there will be a strain toward consistency in procedure, whoever the parties may be. Moreover, there will be a tendency to carry over the more general categories of private law to situations that involve government agents. Common-law courts use the materials they have at hand and are not anxious to create new categories which might commit them in unforeseeable ways. A special system of courts, having a distinct mission and responsibility, will more readily develop a coherent subsystem of the law. But this is only to say that separate agencies are likely to create their own thoughtways, uniquely adapted to their special problems and opportunities. It does not follow that the ordinary courts are unable to develop distinct categories and principles for application to public-law situations.

There are, however, additional and more contemporary sources for the blurring of the distinction between private and public law. Among these is the decline of sovereignty as a compelling political doctrine. For a great many years, the idea of sovereignty offered a heady symbolism in support of the assertion that government was unique among human institutions. This uniqueness consisted in more than a monopoly of the rightful use of violence—a view still generally accepted. Rather, sovereignty suggested a commanding presence, a whole system of privileges and immu-

---

[4] W. A. Robson, "Administrative Law," in Morris Ginsberg (ed.), *Law and Opinion in England in the Twentieth Century* (London: Stevens and Sons, Limited, 1959), 200.

nities, an inviolate status among the lesser ranks of organized groups. As long as the word "sovereign" retained persuasive power, a mystique was lent to public law, strengthening its distinctive identity, reinforcing the separation between public and private spheres. But today sovereignty has lost its hold on the political and legal imagination. As a symbol, sovereignty has lost much of its glitter and in many quarters is not quite respectable. The writings of the political pluralists did much to produce this change. They helped to "secularize" the state, urging that, whatever its special functions and powers, the state is to be understood as one association among others. As a result, it is easier to question the conventional belief that public law is uniquely identified with government.

The most important source of the weakness of public-law jurisprudence is the great growth of large-scale organization, both public and private. A striking feature of this development is the convergence of governmental and nongovernmental forms of organization and modes of action. A great deal of government activity is similar to that carried on by private groups. Government today includes many activities and agencies that have little to do with the distinctive functions of a sovereign and to which, therefore, the traditional logic of public law may not properly apply. At the same time, discussions of the modern corporation and trade union, in many ways the representative institutions of industrial society, have increasingly stressed their "quasi-public" status. It is asked quite seriously whether such institutions are really so different from large public enterprises. In attempting to fix the responsibilities of leadership in large organizations, in and out of government, the distinction between what is public and what is private becomes hazy. This raises the question whether we have a theory of public law adequate to deal with the group structure of modern society.

This problem has been dealt with in an extensive and somewhat anguished legal literature on the liability of government for the torts of its agents.[5] There is a strong feeling that government should be responsible for harms done to individuals, in cases where negligence can be shown. At the same time, it is recognized that some form of immunity is required if legislative and administrative discretion, so often harming some persons while benefiting others, is not to be made subject to liabilities inconsistent with the very process of government. The problem is to find a defensible classification of activities or harms, one that will produce the needed balance between immunity and responsibility.

One effort to classify activities rests on a distinction between "govern-

---

[5] See K. C. Davis, *Administrative Law Treatise* (St. Paul: West Publishing Co., 1958), Vol. III, Chap. 25.

mental" and "proprietary" functions.[6] The tendency of the law is to hold the government responsible as a proper defendant in a tort suit when it can be shown that the harm occurred while government agents were carrying on "nongovernmental" activities. Various efforts have been made to distinguish the "uniquely governmental" function, but no really settled and authoritative doctrine has as yet emerged. One suggestion would hold the government liable for decisions made at the "operational" level but would allow immunity when the decision producing the harm was made at the level of policy or planning.[7] A related idea is that government immunity should be restricted to the consequences of "legislative" decision.[8] These suggestions properly shift attention from *kinds of institutions* to *kinds of decision*.

According to Kelsen, the key to the difference between public law and private law is found in the "principle of autonomy."[9] In private law, the individual obligates himself by his own voluntary action. The state is present, to be sure, but only to enforce the legal consequences of an act that the individual undertakes voluntarily. *If* a man makes a contract, or infringes another's protected right to person or property, *then* a legal obligation is created. "In civil [private] law the principle of autonomy prevails, according to which nobody can be obligated against, or even without, his own consent. This is . . . the decisive difference between private and public law."[10] On the other hand, when a citizen is subject to taxation, an obligation arises without his consent. Private law would then include the law of voluntary transactions, including those entered into by government. Public law fixes the obligations of and to a constituency.

Kelsen recognizes that the principle of autonomy or consent does not satisfactorily explicate all the relations that have usually been included within the ambit of private law. Thus he notes that in family law obligations are created, such as the duty of filial obedience, without the consent of the person obligated.[11] More generally, Kelsen stresses the difficulty of distinguishing between public and private law. "In all modern legal orders, the State, as well as any other juristic person, may have rights *in rem* and rights *in personam*, nay any of the rights and duties stipulated by 'private law.' . . . The difficulty in distinguishing between public and private

---

[6] *Ibid.*, 459 ff.
[7] *Ibid.*, 479 ff.
[8] Dissenting opinion of Justice Jackson, *Dalehite* v. *U.S.*, 346 U.S. 15, 59 (1953).
[9] Hans Kelsen, *General Theory of Law and the State* (Cambridge, Mass.: Harvard University Press, 1949), 201 ff.
[10] *Ibid.*, 142.
[11] *Ibid.*, 206.

law resides precisely in the fact that the relation between the State and its subjects can have not only a 'public' but also a 'private' character."[12]

Another approach looks to the *purpose* of law rather than to the nature of obligation as forced or free, compelled or discretionary. Radbruch, for example, saw public law as the "law of subordination," performing the public task of meting out distributive justice to classes of individuals by elevating some interests and giving a lesser priority to others.[13] Private law, on this view, is "coordinating," treating all interests as on the same plane, merely adjusting rights in the light of factual circumstances. This approach has the merit of suggesting that anyone who is in a position to apply a "law of subordination" should be considered as administering public law—a theory that brought Radbruch to the view that the employment relation was "in the nature of public law."[14]

A related theory looks to the idea of "status" as in some special sense a concept of public law. The point was made by Vinogradoff[15] and more recently Graveson[16] has offered a more extended analysis. We shall return to the concept of status later; at this point we wish only to note its implications for the concept of public law. Status is a .defined condition or role with which rights and duties are associated, such incidents being to some extent independent of the consent of one who occupies the status. Status may emerge out of what was originally a contractual relation,[17] but if it does, it will be associated with duties that are set by public interest and not only as a result of free bargaining. More characteristic examples of status are marriage, infancy, legitimacy of birth, and the special status of a convicted felon. Graveson also discusses incorporation as a representative form of status.[18]

Status does indeed have a peculiar relation to public law, but it does not follow that all legal ascriptions of status are propositions of public law. The legal incapacity of an infant defines a status; one who acquires real property by prescription has a status; a soldier has a status; a defendant in court has a status; so too has a public official. These are not negotiated

[12] *Ibid.,* 202.
[13] See *The Legal Philosophies of Lask, Radbruch, and Dabin* (Cambridge: Harvard University Press, 1950) 152 ff. This is a translation by Kurt Wilk of Gustav Radbruch's *Rechtsphilosophie* (3rd ed.; 1932). See also Roscoe Pound, *Jurisprudence,* I, 261–262.
[14] *Op. cit.,* 152, fn. 1.
[15] Paul Vinogradoff, *Collected Papers* (London: Oxford University Press, 1928), II, 230–231.
[16] R. H. Graveson, *Status in the Common Law* (University of London: The Athlone Press, 1953), 6, 44.
[17] See above, 62.
[18] *Ibid.,* 72 ff.

rights and duties. They accrue by operation of law when certain conditions have been fulfilled. To equate public law and status is to create a vast residual category in which practically everything outside the law of contract, and some of that too, becomes part of public law.

It is *citizenship*, not status in general, that helps fix the ambit of public law. Citizenship is a special kind of group membership. It is known by the public rights accruing to the individual who occupies that status. These are, minimally, the right to a civic identity and to civic participation. For many centuries, citizenship as a status was closely bound to other statuses, especially those created by kinship, race, sex, and the ownership of property. By the twentieth century citizenship had been largely disentangled from those contexts. The peculiar blending of public law and private law, so striking a feature of feudalism, was gradually eliminated.

But the disentanglements of the modern era have proved unstable and transitional. The historic mission of post-feudal society was to dissolve the "natural" freedom-stifling continuities of social, economic, and political participation. The post-modern world, founded in organization and interdependence, reasserts those continuities in its own way. One outcome, not always benign, is the reintegration of public and private law. Its most important manifestation, full of promise and of peril, is the enlargement of civic participation.

In our time, the meaning of citizenship is being enlarged in three ways: (1) by new expectations of what public government should do, including the opportunities it should create for individual betterment and self-esteem; (2) by the notion that "full citizenship" means effective participation in an entire opportunity structure, social and economic, as well as in the formal political process; and (3) by the recognition that private relationships decisively affect the achievement of full citizenship. In the United States, the most dramatic and consistent exemplar of these trends is the recent evolution of public policy on racial discrimination.

Citizenship cannot be understood apart from the theory of polity. To be a citizen is to belong to a political community, to be a member of a polity. But if, as we argued in Chapter 1, polity is emergent, then citizenship too must be a changing thing. The meaning of citizenship may be quite limited in a primitive polity; it will be fuller and more elaborate when polity is mature. *As the status of citizenship evolves, the scope of public law is also altered.*

With this perspective, we can return to the traditional concept of public law and yet transcend it. The relation between government and the individual has long been taken as the touchstone of public law. A theory of polity and citizenship at once broadens and narrows that conventional view. It is broadened insofar as "polity" goes beyond the meaning of "government" (a) by opening the door to the identification of plural polities as private or special-purpose institutions become to some degree political communities,[19] and (b) by taking account of the ways private relationships affect participation in the larger community. It is narrowed as we recognize that not everything in the relation between government and the individual has to do with participation in the polity. A vast number of ordinary transactions involve government and the individual at some point, yet this does not bring them within the scope of public law.

Due Process as the Law of Governance

In American jurisprudence, perhaps the cardinal principle of public law is "due process." For the rationale of due process rests directly on the ideal of legality itself. The rules of due process may be thought of, indeed, as *the positive law of legality*—the working concepts of right and duty that give effect to the more general ideal. Due process is thus a critical part of the law of governance. Wherever men govern, due process has its say. Its distinctive contribution is the development of guiding ideas and practical rules for the limitation of arbitrary power.

Thus, as a public-law idea giving definite form and substance to legality, an examination of due process may help us to find a way of extending the rule of law to areas hitherto controlled only by concepts of private law. Given the meaning of due process, as it has actually developed in our positive law, must we say that it is inescapably and exclusively attached to government as we ordinarily understand it? Or can we, without undue strain, apply it in a broader field? Our task, it should be remembered, is the exploration of fundamental principles and not the assessment of specific rules.

As a basic principle, due process has a special combination of weakness and strength. This is so because the phrase is something more than a jurist's invention, a construct of legal cognition. The words are built into our written constitution. This gives them greatly added strength, as a source of positive law. On the other hand, as a part of enacted law, albeit constitutional enactment, they are vulnerable to demands that their meaning be fixed. Not less important is the drawback that the idea of due process, so explicitly part of the law of *the* constitution, will be insulated

---

[19] See above, 41 ff.

from other branches of the law, such as labor law or the law of torts, and will not be able to build on their experience.

But due process is more than a phrase in a constitutional clause. It is an *inherently* constitutional idea, a device for protecting the basic aims of the constitution itself. An element of due process is "a fundamental principle of liberty and justice which inheres in the very idea of free government, and is the inalienable right of a citizen of such a government."[20] If a procedure is so fundamental, and states that sort of a right, it is so whether or not a written constitution is available to sustain it. "If due process of law has any meaning," it has been said, "it is that there is no sovereign unless he conform to the principles of legality . . . this provision is primarily a guarantee of legality itself, legality not of the formal or superficial kind, but of the fundamental, inherent form which is based upon tested principles of constitutional government."[21] A principle of constitutional government may, perhaps happily, be incorporated in a constitutional document. But its status as such a principle, available to judicial and administrative notice, does not depend on that event.

The American attempt to enact so basic a principle, by way of an obscure and oracular phrase, has apparently met with little favor abroad.[22] It may be that we have tried to have the best of both worlds, treating a natural-law concept as if it were positive law, thus gaining for it a double authority, at some cost to the reputation of our courts.

However that may be, a fairly broad and authoritative recognition of the inherently constitutional status of due process has led to an emphasis on the general and flexible character of the principle.[23] "What is due process of law depends on the circumstances. It varies with the subject matter and the necessities of the situation."[24] More broadly, in the language of Justice Frankfurter, the meaning of due process "unfolds," presumably as history offers new possibilities for the application of legal ideals.[25] It is "not a stagnant formulation of what has been achieved in the past but a

---

[20] *Twining v. State of New Jersey*, 211 U.S. 78, 106 (1908).
[21] Rodney L. Mott, *Due Process of Law* (Indianapolis: The Bobbs-Merrill Company, Inc., 1926), 589, 604.
[22] Wallace Mendelson, "Foreign Reactions to American Experience with 'Due Process of Law,'" 41 *Virginia Law Review* 493 (1955).
[23] For a review of the debate between "fixity" and "flexibility" in the interpretation of due process, see Sanford H. Kadish, "Methodology and Criteria in Due Process Adjudication—A Survey and Criticism," 66 *Yale Law Journal* 319, 321–328 (1957).
[24] Edward S. Corwin (ed.), *The Constitution of the United States of America*, Senate Doc. No. 170, 82d Cong. (Washington, D.C.: Government Printing Office, 1953).
[25] See *Joint Anti-Fascist Defense Committee v. McGrath*, 341 U.S. 123, 162–163 (1951).

standard for judgment in the progressive evolution of the institutions of a free society."[26]

This approach properly retains for due process the status of a legal principle.[27] A principle *generates* rules of law, as circumstances may require or permit. Principles are legal instruments for devising rules and for criticizing them. Therefore they should not be confused with the rules themselves. On the other hand, rules do not flow from principles in any necessary or immanent way. Principles alone cannot justify rules. To them must be added a specific historical warrant; and there must be an appropriate accommodation of any new rule to the existing system of positive law.

Due process is a governing or "master" ideal. As such, no set of rules can fully exhaust its meaning. Therefore due process functions as a *residual restraint* on government. It offers an appeal beyond current positive law to an authoritative principle whose force is not completely spent no matter how elaborate the system of rules generated by it may be. It does not follow, of course, that the logical and human meaning of due process, as distinguished from its embodiment in positive law, must remain unspecified.

The special ideals of due process may be formulated as follows:

1. Governance should be restrained by a proper regard for all legal interests affected.[28] A problem of due process arises because governors, in carrying out their duties, inevitably inflict deprivations on those who are governed. The citizen is punished, taxed, drafted, and in a great many ways affected by legislation, adjudication, and administration. Deprivations must occur, but the manner of their infliction, as well as their quality and extent, must take account of the right infringed. The act of governance should be so fashioned as to protect all legal interests affected—so far as may be consistent with the attainment of its own purposes. Such a view leaves plenty of room for maneuver, but it is not without point and authority. A government contemptuous of due process pursues its aims without counting social costs. Such an accounting is precisely what due process demands.

This ideal has a peculiar legal effect: *It commands inquiry.* The interplay of government objective and affected right is to be scrutinized, not ignored. Whether a given procedure is necessary to the public objective, or should be modified to protect a highly regarded interest, is always open

---

[26] 324 U.S. 401 (1945).
[27] See above, 26 ff.
[28] See Frank C. Newman, "The Process of Prescribing 'Due Process,'" 49 *California Law Review* 218 (1961), where it is argued that "life, liberty, or property" should be treated as a description of *all legal interests,* with the qualification, however, that this "does not mean that all interests therein merit identical protection."

to question. That military organization is necessary, that it has its distinctive requirements of training and discipline will be readily granted. But the result is not untrammeled power. A system of military justice, a distinction between lawful and unlawful commands, and a nondiscriminatory personnel policy, reflect the working out of due process ideals in the special military context. This development is guided by an essential demand—that faithful and honest attention be given to the accommodation of military necessity and civil right.

At the level of positive law, it has been held that only certain definitely recognized legal interests need be taken account of, that only these can invoke the protection of due process. Thus at one time it was denied that government employment was a constitutionally protected right[29] within the ambit of "life, liberty, or property." In more recent years, these terms, like due process itself, have been given a wider legal meaning. But it cannot be denied that many other human and social interests, having but weak recognition in the law, will receive small consideration when balanced against the competing necessities of government. The positive law, however, should not be confused with the legal ideal. The latter has a broader compass and a greater simplicity. It insists on the principle of restraint and it looks toward an ever-widening recognition by positive law of what is essential to human freedom and well-being.

2. The making and the application of law should affirm reason. This ideal accounts for much in the positive law of due process. It restates the essential notion that whatever is arbitrary is offensive to legality. Rule-making that is based on evident caprice or prejudice, or that presumes the contrary of clearly established knowledge, violates due process. Procedure cannot be "due" if it does not conform to the canons of rational discourse or if it is otherwise outside the pale of reasoned and dispassionate assessment. Thus legislative classification of persons or groups may be struck down as arbitrary and against reason if they have no defensible connection with, or inherently frustrate, the professed aims of the legislation. Similarly a host of administrative actions, though they may enjoy large grants of discretion, are subject to this ultimate appeal.

This injunction, that reason be affirmed, can easily lead to an abuse of judicial authority. Nevertheless, it is inescapable if legality is to be upheld. Applied with caution, as a guiding ideal, it demands only a gradual conformity with the rational consensus of the community. By its own logic, the process of affirming reason may well recognize the absence of secure

---

[29] Note, "Due Process and the Right to a Job," 46 *Virginia Law Review* 323 ff. (1960).

knowledge, including the fact that relative ignorance is the normal state of human affairs. Given that ignorance, much must be left to common-sense problem-solving and to politics rather than to the judicial process.

3. A reliable assessment of legal fact should be assured.   Although this ideal is logically subsumable under that just discussed, it has a special significance and authority. Even if we did not accept the governing status of the more general ideal, this one would still be effective. The injunction is simple: Where official power may be used against him, every man has the right to such protection as the truth may give him.

Historically, this right has been recognized in an elaborate body of law embodying special assumptions regarding how truth is to be determined within the legal process. These assumptions include: (a) The idea that *ex parte* proceedings should be extraordinary at best. An affected party should have notice of an impending or tentative assessment of facts that may lead to a judgment against him, with the corollary, of course, that he may then present his own version of the facts. All necessary steps should be taken to make him a true party to the proceedings, and to this end the right of counsel is protected. (b) The exclusion of such material offered in evidence as may be deemed especially unreliable, given the apparent limitations of a court, including its use of a lay jury. (c) Protection of the adversary principle as a high road to reliability in the assessment of legal fact. (d) The maintenance of judicial integrity, including freedom from external pressures, personal corruption, and the more evident sources of bias.

Clearly, this body of law rests upon assumptions regarding what the courts can do and what are the standard sources of unreliability in reportage and assessment. These assumptions may well be questioned as legal institutions develop new capabilities.

4. The legitimacy of authority should be assured.   It is elementary that governance according to due process is governance according to the "law of the land." This is more than an adventitious association of historic phrases. Legal process presumes a proper tribunal or officer acting within a defined scope of authority and in accordance with accepted principles of legitimacy. Thus the positive law of due process deals with problems of jurisdiction, with the conditions under which commands should be accepted as lawful.

An appeal to the "law of the land" is not necessarily limited by the specific rules of positive law enunciated for the control of governing authority. Rather, this appeal may be to the legal principles, not always explicitly formulated, which give shape and direction to a particular legal order. Therefore the raising of questions of legitimacy—by what right do you rule?—is often a harbinger of creative legal development.[30]

5. A basic minimum of rights of personality should be protected. Although a general ideal of due process is to take account of all legal interests, there is a more specific concern for rights of personality. This is sometimes put as insuring respect for the dignity of the individual.[31] Clearly the idea of a "basic minimum" is an invitation to flexibility and growth. As government develops competence and sophistication, it may be held to higher standards of respect for the integrity of personality. Just what "dignity" or "integrity" may mean remains obscure, but there is probably consensus on the right to be heard on one's own cause and on elimination of the more extreme forms of punishment, especially where they involve public degradation or self-abasement. Beyond this minimum, it may be demanded of government that certain substantive rights of personality be given a special place in defining due process. These may include a right to minimal privacy and to the pursuit of a lawful occupation. These or similar rights are not only to be taken account of as legal interests–they may also determine the limits beyond which government action cannot go, perhaps also the affirmative responsibilities of government.

The basic nature of personal right stems in part from its relation to the role of reason in legality and due process. Thus Roscoe Pound has said:

> But the most important phase of the social interest in individual self-assertion, from the standpoint of modern law, is what might be called the social interest in freedom of the individual will—the claim or interest, or policy recognizing it, that the individual will not be subjected arbitrarily to the will of others. This interest is recognized in an old common-law policy which is declared in the Fifth and Fourteenth Amendments. If one will is to be subjected to the will of another through the force of politically organized society, it is not to be done arbitrarily, but it is to be done upon some rational basis, which the person coerced, if reasonable, could appreciate. It is to be done upon a reasoned weighing of the interests involved and a reasoned attempt to reconcile them or adjust them.[32]

The right to be treated fairly is, in one vital meaning, the right to be judged according to rational principles, without whim or caprice or disregard of consequence. This essential personal right is precisely that which the law of due process is designed to serve. Therefore the ideals of affirming reason and of protecting minimum rights of personality are intimately related.

---

[30] See above, 30 f.
[31] See Kadish, *op. cit.*, 347.
[32] Roscoe Pound, "A Survey of Social Interests," 57 *Harvard Law Review* 34–35 (1943).

If it is correct to think of due process as a summary term for the principles just stated, then it seems clear that we must expect an ever-present interplay of procedural and substantive rights. "Substantive due process" is an unlovely phrase, not well respected. But whatever the terminology, the conclusion cannot be avoided that substantive rights are involved when the legality of governmental action is tested. It would be difficult indeed to determine whether a set of procedures fulfills the requirements of due process without answering the questions: What rights are placed in jeopardy here? How much protection do they need or merit? If the rules of due process vary from one setting to another, as is generally granted today, this is in part because the weight we give to a substantive right determines how much procedural nicety will be required. Substantive rights are not absolute. The weight they receive depends in part on their intrinsic merit, in part on how seriously they are threatened, and in part on the competing social interests to be served. Thus the interplay of substance and procedure has a distinctive outcome for the administration of criminal justice. The right to a jury trial is more important in criminal cases than in civil suits, and a number of other procedural safeguards, such as the exclusion of illegally obtained evidence and protection against self-incrimination, are especially valued where imprisonment or worse may be threatened. In other settings, a less rigorous approach to "procedural due process" may be in order. If the harm to be done is more tolerable, a greater risk of acting unfairly may be taken.

The interplay of substance and procedure is especially manifest where procedure includes *intellectual* processes. Judicial reasoning is a kind of procedure. In principle, it is subject to appraisal according to objective standards. Yet this procedure has the most serious consequences for the definition of substantive rights. Any procedure, such as lawful interrogation, may affect the allocation of substantive rights, but some procedures determine the rights themselves. At that point, the relation between substantive and procedural aspects of due process becomes intimate indeed.

We have already noted that due process, as "a fundamental principle of liberty and justice," has a warrant beyond the terms of a written constitution. In this sense, it is a common-law principle, deriving its authority from our intellectual appraisal of what is necessary to the establishment and maintenance of free government. What we have developed is a *common law of governance*, helped along historically by the existence of key words in an authoritative document, but not ultimately dependent on that phraseology or on that document. This point is important to a proper assessment of how the ideals of due process can be given legal effect outside the conventional sphere of public law.

There are two main reasons for believing that due process should be understood as a common-law idea. First, the *grounds* of legal development in this field suggest that conclusion. The rules of due process are not *ad hoc* expressions of legislative will. They are based on assessments of the conditions that must be met if the rule of law is to be achieved. Given an initial commitment to the establishment of a legal order, and given purported understanding of human weaknesses under known social conditions, a set of conclusions follows regarding safeguards to be set up for protecting the integrity of the legal process. It is arguable that these assessments fall within the special competence of the courts and are therefore prime prospects for judicial legislation.[33]

Second, the principles of due process spring from a legal tradition that is older and more broadly relevant than the United States Constitution. The classic argument for legal recognition of a right of privacy starts from the familiar premise: "That the individual shall have full protection in person and in property is a principle as old as the common law."[34] Thus we are reminded that no legislative or constitutional mandate is needed for the identification and restraint of wrongful invasions of personal right. More specifically, the common-law idea of "natural justice" has similar connotations and authority.[35]

---

[33] "Several of the common objections to an enlarged judicial review lose much of their persuasiveness, however, where the challenge is not to remake substantive policy but to supervise the procedures through which laws are enforced upon individuals. The objection that judges lack the expertise and background to make competent judgements of policy falls short of the mark when the policy concerns procedural matters. The main business of courts, after all, has historically been the process of adjudication—applying rules of law to the concrete setting of a case. It is unlikely that any other organ of government will have greater insight into procedural problems." Kadish, *op. cit.*, 358. Perhaps the self-confidence of the courts in this area—their sense of legitimacy—is more important than expertise as such in encouraging judicial assessment and creativity.

[34] S. D. Warren and L. D. Brandeis, "The Right to Privacy," 4 *Harvard Law Review* 55 (1890).

[35] Wade, *op. cit.*, 154: " 'Natural justice' is the name given to certain fundamental rules which are so necessary to the proper exercise of power that they are projected from the judicial to the administrative sphere. In English law the term covers two rules: first, that a man may not be judge in his own cause; and secondly, that a man may not be condemned unheard. These rules . . . should apply to all administrative acts in so far as the nature of the case admits. For all power ought to be exercised fairly, both in appearance and in reality. It is the universality of this ideal of justice which leads to its being called 'natural.' . . . Just as the broad constitutional guarantee of 'due process of law' has proved of such importance in the United States for the imposition of general standards of justice, so in England the concept of natural justice should provide the legal foundation on which administrative procedure should rest." For a broader canvas, see Barna Horvath, "Rights of Man: Due Process of Law and *Excès de Pouvoir*," 4 *American Journal of Comparative Law* 539 (1955); also Frank C. Newman, "Natural

This argument does not rest on a distinction between judge-made or unwritten law on the one hand and statute on the other. That dichotomy is really irrelevant. The legal order as we know it is produced by statute as well as by judicial creativity. We should follow Pound's lead[36] in advocating the blending of common law (in the sense of judge-made law) and such legislation as offers "a principle from which to reason." The result is an integral body of general law which may be called, as we do here, simply "common law." This seems justified because there has always been at least some integration of "landmark" statutes into traditional common law and because it is a method of reasoning and a kind of growth, rather than a particular source or form, that seems most important to the idea of a common law.

Pound outlines four alternatives available to the courts when confronted by legislative innovation:

(1) The courts might receive the innovation fully into the body of the law as affording not only a rule to be applied but a principle from which to reason, and hold the principle so established superior in authority to judge-made rules on the same general subject as being a later and more direct expression of the general will. Accordingly, they might reason from the legislatively introduced precept by analogy, that is, might reason from its principle in cases not within its purview to add to reasoning from a pre-existing judicially established principle. . . .

(2) The courts might receive the legislative innovation fully into the body of the law, to be reasoned from by analogy the same as any other legally established proposition; regarding it, however, as of equal or co-ordinate authority as a basis for reasoning with the judicially established precepts on the same subjects. Thus there might be a choice between competing equally authoritative starting points for legal reasoning, something which happens not infrequently as between principles of the common law and is the chief source of difficulty when new questions come before the courts.

(3) The courts might refuse to receive the legislative innovation fully into the body of the law, and instead give effect to the legislative enactment directly only. That is, they might refuse to reason from it by analogy, but nevertheless give it a liberal interpretation to cover the whole field it may reasonably be made to cover.

(4) Or finally, the courts might not only refuse to reason from the legislative provision by analogy and insist upon applying it only directly as a rule rather than as giving a principle, but they might also give it a strict

and narrow interpretation, holding it down rigidly to the exact cases which it clearly covers expressly.[37]

Commenting on these alternatives, Pound adds:

This fourth hypothesis represents the orthodox common-law attitude in the nineteenth century toward legislative innovations. Probably the third hypothesis represents more nearly the attitude toward which the course of decision has been tending in the present century. The second and first hypotheses in the past appealed to the common-law lawyer as absurd. He has seemed unable to conceive that a rule of statutory origin may be treated as part of the permanent body of the law except in the case of certain landmarks or old legislation which have been incorporated into the traditional element of our law. It is submitted, however, that when the growing point of a legal system shifts definitely to legislation, the legal system must come at least to the method of the second hypothesis.[38]

Thus a proper perspective avoids counterposing legislation to common law. Rather, we are encouraged to see the contribution legislation can make to the evolution of a legal order. With this approach, we can draw the followng conclusions:

(1) Any legislation, including constitutional legislation, can be the source of general concepts and principles. These are the authoritative materials, starting-points of legal reasoning, available for the guidance of both judges and legislative draftsmen.

(2) Legal principles encourage reasoning by analogy. They provide a logical basis for applying concepts and conclusions developed in one area of human experience to other areas having similar characteristics.

Of course, these considerations cannot of themselves determine whether a contribution to common law, in the broad sense used here, has indeed occurred. Each possibility must be examined and judged on its own merits. But it is suggested here that the principles of due process are and properly ought to be considered part of our common law. *And this determines the route by which public-law principles, including the ideals of due process, may be legally applied to private settings.*

The Concept of Private Government

If there is a "law of governance," to what should it be applied? Clearly it should apply wherever the social function of governing is performed, wherever some men rule and others are ruled. The question remains, however, whether one can properly speak of "government" apart from

---

[37] *Ibid.,* 656–658.
[38] *Ibid.,* 658–659.

the state itself. If there are "private" governments, how can we recognize them so that the law of governance may be summoned to play its authoritative role in fixing responsibilities and protecting rights?

To approach these issues, we must disentangle three related ideas. The first of these asserts that private groups are "governmental" insofar as they act for, or fulfill the responsibilities of, the official or public government. The second holds that autonomous groups in modern society often have very considerable social effects; therefore they should assume corresponding "public" responsibilities. Finally, it may be argued that some private groups exercise distinctively governmental functions, on their own account and apart from any connection with public government, and therefore should be subject to the rules of just governance.

1. Private action as state action. In American constitutional law, the question of private government is closely bound to the doctrinal and policy quandaries that beset the interpretation of the Fourteenth and Fifteenth Amendments, adopted after the Civil War. In 1875 Congress passed a Civil Rights Act, prohibiting racial discrimination by "any person"[39] in places of public accommodation and amusement. In 1883, however, the Supreme Court declared these provisions unconstitutional, insisting that the language of the Amendment[40] meant that the civil rights guaranteed therein could be asserted only against public government. "It is State action of a particular character that is prohibited. Individual invasion of individual rights is not the subject-matter of the amendment."[41] Sixty-five years later, in a controversial opinion that greatly expanded the meaning of "state action," the Court reaffirmed that "since the decision of this Court in the *Civil Rights* cases . . . the principle has become firmly embedded in our constitutional law that the action inhibited by the first section of the Fourteenth Amendment is only such action as may fairly be said to be that of the States. That Amendment erects no shield against merely private conduct, however discriminatory or wrongful."[42]

In applying this doctrine, the Court has looked closely at the agencies of discrimination. Where a clear public responsibility is at stake, as in the administration of elections,[43] the modern Court has pierced the shield of

---

[39] Sec. 2 of the Civil Rights Act of 1875 (18 Stat. 335) provided that any person who violated Sec. 1 was guilty of a misdemeanor.

[40] "No State shall . . . deprive any person of life, liberty, or property, without due process of law; nor deny to any person within its jurisdiction the equal protection of the laws."

[41] *Civil Rights Cases*, 109 U.S. 3, 11 (1883).

[42] *Shelley* v. *Kraemer*, 334 U.S. 1, 13 (1948).

[43] Here the context is the Fifteenth Amendment: "The right of citizens of the United States to vote shall not be denied or abridged by the United States or by any State on account of race, color, or previous condition of servitude."

privacy. The 1935 Court upheld a procedure by which the Democratic party of Texas, purporting to be a private organization with inherent power to determine its own membership, excluded Negroes from participation in the party's primary election.[44] Nine years later the Court changed its mind,[45] arguing that the Democratic party's activities were too intimate a part of the election process to be other than a public function, even though no direct action by the legislature or public officials was involved. Finally, in *Terry* v. *Adams*,[46] the Court declared illegal a device by which a private group, the Jaybird Association of Fort Bend County, Texas, which excluded Negroes, sponsored sure winners in the Democratic party's primary election.

Other decisions have struck at private action when the government itself is in some way implicated. For example, if a state agency provides a public facility, a private operator of the facility will be held to Fourteenth Amendment standards.[47] If a pattern of private violation of individual rights involves state officials, including the courts, as abettors, the Amendment may be brought into play.[48] In a recent case the Court asserted that the "involvement of the State" need be neither exclusive nor direct. "In a variety of situations the Court has found state action of a nature sufficient to create rights under the Equal Protection Clause even though the participation of the State was peripheral, or its action was only one of several co-operative forces leading to the constitutional violation."[49]

In these cases, the Court's main purpose has been to hold public government to a constitutional responsibility undiluted by the use or intervention of private agencies. Thus understood, the search for state action has not been "misleading."[50] But the Court has had another concern: The constitutional *values* of due process and equal protection should be given effect even when they are infringed by private agencies. The recognition of "peripheral" state action, and the broad extensions that have been given to the meaning of that phrase, testify to the Court's anxiety. This approach, however, with its dependence on state action as the constitutional lever, turns attention away from the realities of private power. The result may be a tortuous formalism that may sacrifice the Court's credibility in the interests of short-run legitimacy.

[44] *Grovey* v. *Townsend*, 295 U.S. 45 (1935).
[45] *Smith* v. *Allwright*, 321 U.S. 649 (1944).
[46] 345 U.S. 461 (1953).
[47] *Burton* v. *Wilmington Parking Authority*, 365 U.S. 715 (1961).
[48] This is one reading of *Shelley* v. *Kraemer*, 334 U.S. 1 (1948).
[49] *U.S.* v. *Herbert Guest* et al., 383 U.S. 745, 755, 756 (1966).
[50] Cf. Harold W. Horowitz, "The Misleading Search for 'State Action' under the Fourteenth Amendment," 30 *Southern California Law Review* 208 (1957).

2. Monopoly and governance. Beyond public officials and their special responsibilities, we may find a weak form of "government" in monopoly situations where issues of arbitrary exclusion arise. If an individual or group controls access to public accommodation or other necessary services, or to employment, or to education, it may be said that a social responsibility emerges. Where important segments of the public are affected, there is a duty to exercise *de facto* power without arbitrary exclusion. This duty does not depend on the Constitution, or even on a statute. It is founded in a principle that goes back to common-law rules regarding the responsibilities of innkeepers.[51] A modern case is *James* v. *Marinship Corp.*, in which the California Supreme Court held that closed-shop contracts may not be enforced in the absence of an open union. If a union controls access to employment, it may not exclude workers on the basis of race; and full membership rights must be available to all. The court leaned on the idea that a union, especially if it has a closed-shop agreement, occupies a "quasi public position":

> In our opinion, an arbitrarily closed or partially closed union is incompatible with a closed shop. Where a union has, as in this case, attained a monopoly of the supply of labor by means of closed shop agreements and other forms of collective labor action, such a union occupies a quasi public position similar to that of a public service business and it has certain corresponding obligations. It may no longer claim the same freedom from legal restraint enjoyed by golf clubs or fraternal associations. Its asserted right to choose its own members does not merely relate to social relations; it affects the fundamental right to work for a living.[52]

Here the values of particularistic or personal choice are subordinated to the civil right of equal access. That subordination is made easy by the evidently impersonal and instrumental character of the association.

Granted the emergence of a public responsibility, it does not follow that the imagery of *government* is very helpful in these cases. "Equal access" certainly has echoes of "equal protection"; and the exercise of impersonal authority suggests an official posture. But acts of exclusion do not necessarily establish, or depend upon, a relation of ruler and ruled. It takes some stretching to think of the excluding innkeeper or merchant as a "governor," even if his power is very great.

Is not the protection of potential union members against arbitrary exclusion simply another in the continually expanding system of rights and

---

[51] And others, such as common carriers, who served the public. For contemporary relevance, see Matthew O. Tobriner and Joseph R. Grodin, "The Individual and the Public Service Enterprise in the New Industrial State," 55 *California Law Review* 1247 (1967).
[52] *James* v. *Marinship Corp.*, 25 Cal. 2d 721, 731 (1944).

duties that characterizes modern industrial society? Why should not such exclusion be recognized as an actionable wrong, with its own sufficient justification as an unacceptable interference with the rights of individuals to work wherever they can get employment suitable to their qualifications? *One* way to make unions and other private groups socially responsible is to insist that their admission practices be consistent with the rights of persons freely to engage in competition for employment unhindered by arbitrary discrimination. This does not seem to require that private groups be clothed with any special "governmental" or even "public" status. The legislation on fair employment practices, affecting the hiring policies of business organizations, does not presume such a status.

For both individuals and groups, the law enforces responsible conduct by demanding that the actor restrain his decisions by taking account of the consequences of what he does for the rights of others. Usually this means that consequences for defined classes of individuals are to be assessed, for example, customers, applicants, creditors, potential accident victims, contractual obligees, and the like. We may speak of a broader "social" responsibility when private groups are asked to consider the effect of what they do on the general state of public health or economic well-being, the integrity of the democratic process, international relations, educational opportunity, or on some other set of values or community needs. In either case, however, there is no substitute for working out specific rules and principles defining responsible conduct with respect to whatever individual rights or social outcomes may be at issue. The entire body of law bears the burden of enforcing responsibility. That is not a peculiar function of any single branch of law or special legal doctrine.

The theory of private government is not a general justification for enforcing responsibility. It is but one route among many others toward that end. *If there is governance,* then a special set of legal ideas may be brought into play. As a result, the responsibility of actors *in their capacity as governors* will be upheld. The same men, acting in other capacities, will be subject to many other legally defined standards of acceptable conduct— including standards that speak to the effect of private power on equality of opportunity.

3. Governance proper. In a number of different contexts, the courts have brought private government into sharper focus. Thus in *Marsh* v. *Alabama*[53] a member of Jehovah's Witnesses was prosecuted for refusing, after a warning, to leave the street of a company town. The Gulf Ship-

---

[53] 326 U.S. 501 (1946).

building Corporation, which owned the town and rented stores on a "business block," had posted a notice forbidding vending or solicitation without written permission. This privately established rule was applied to bar the Witness from distributing religious literature on the company-owned sidewalk.

The Supreme Court held that application of the state's criminal trespass statute in these circumstances violated the First and Fourteenth Amendments. But this finding of unconstitutional state action was based on an assessment of the private conduct. The majority opinion was clear that the corporation was being permitted "to govern a community of citizens." The Court reasoned that residents of the town were entitled to uncensored information, on the same terms as residents of other towns. Therefore the town managers should be held to the same standards as other municipal officials. The latter may not "completely bar the distribution of literature containing religious or political ideas on its streets, sidewalks and public places or make the right to distribute dependent on a flat license tax or permit to be issued by an official who could deny it at will."[54]

A company town, said the Court, is still a town. He who governs a town must assume his distinctive responsibilities. The responsibility flows from the function. To apply the Constitution, and thus bring to bear the federal power, might require a finding of state action, such as the state's "permitting" the corporation to govern, but the underlying social and legal reality is the process of governing by a private group.

As we have seen in Chapter 4, the Supreme Court has leaned heavily on the idea of private government in its attempt to understand and guide the evolution of labor-management relations.[55] A related concern is the authority and responsibility of union leadership. In *Steele* v. *Louisville & Nashville Railroad Co.*, the Court drew some implications for union responsibility from the legislatively supported system of collective bargaining. When a union is given statutory authority to act as exclusive bargaining representative for a class of employees, that authority carries a duty "to represent non-union or minority union members of the craft without hostile discrimination, fairly, impartially, and in good faith."[56] Here the Brotherhood of Locomotive Firemen & Enginemen, chosen as bargaining representative under the provisions of the Railway Labor Act, negotiated an agreement that was flagrantly discriminatory against Negro firemen. The latter were excluded from the union but included in the

---

[54] *Ibid.*, 504.
[55] See above, 153.
[56] *Steele* v. *Louisville & Nashville Railroad Co.*, 323 U.S. 192, 204 (1944).

bargaining unit. The Court found a "breach of statutory duty," arguing that the role of representative, conferred by the statute, could not be interpreted as a grant of unfettered authority to the union. As a representative, the union is obliged to deal fairly with all members of the bargaining unit. Its powers are "comparable to those possessed by a legislative body." Thus the Court spoke to the issue of governance proper, without relying on the Constitution.[57]

In 1959 the Congress passed a Labor-Management Reporting and Disclosure Act (Landrum-Griffin) which specified the rights of union members, especially freedom of speech and political opposition, and required minimum standards of due process in disciplinary proceedings. The statute takes for granted that unions are political institutions, and that union officers are deeply involved in governance. Thus, so far as the reach of federal labor law is concerned, many long-standing issues regarding the nature of union membership, for example, as contractual or as founded in property right, were set aside.[58] During the preceding decades, state courts were moving toward similar conclusions.[59] They were protecting rights of political controversy within the union, at least for non-Communists, and insisting on due process standards. This evolution required that the courts attenuate or ignore the contract model even as they gave lip-service to it. For example, the conception of the union constitution as a contract could not be sustained when the constitution itself, in explicit terms, restrained political activity within the union. The state courts invoked "public policy" to uphold the democratic rights of opposition groups and to require notice

---

[57] In a concurring opinion, Justice Murphy chided the Court for "remaining mute and placid as to the obvious and oppressive deprivation of constitutional guarantees." "While such a union is essentially a private organization, its power to represent and bind all members of a class or craft is derived solely from Congress. The Act contains no language which directs the manner in which the bargaining representative shall perform its duties. But it cannot be assumed that Congress meant to authorize the representative to act so as to ignore rights guaranteed by the Constitution. Otherwise the Act would bear the stigma of unconstitutionality under the Fifth Amendment in this respect. For that reason I am willing to read the statute as not permitting or allowing any action by the bargaining representative in the exercise of its delegated powers which would in effect violate the constitutional rights of individuals." *Ibid.*, 208–209. The majority opinion looked to the inherent duties of a representative, public or private; the concurring opinion would have invoked the Constitution (a) by interpreting the statute consistent with upholding its constitutionality; and (b) by viewing the union as exercising "delegated powers," thus subject to the constitutional restrictions on public government. The first aspect (a) is consistent with the majority's reasoning, for it simply gives added weight to the Court's interpretation of the statutory duty, while (b) asserts a different ground.

[58] See above, 69 f.

[59] See Clyde W. Summers, "The Law of Union Discipline: What the Courts Do In Fact," 70 *Yale Law Journal* 175 (1960).

and hearing in disciplinary cases.[60] This approach maintained the contract model by invoking the principle that courts may nullify contract provisions that are "contrary to public policy." Clearly, however, the courts based this finding of public policy (a) on their sense that the values of political freedom and due process are important ingredients of the legal order, and (b) on the conclusion that decision-making in trade unions is governmental in fact. It should also be noted that nullification of contractual terms, as repugnant to public policy, could not be an adequate basis for specifying the *affirmative* obligations of union officials.

Another context for the evolving law of governance is the academic community. In the case of *public* institutions, the courts have little difficulty in recognizing the exercise of governmental powers. Public colleges are assimilated to administrative agencies, and the main question has been whether students have a legal interest sufficient to make due process standards mandatory. For many years, on the theory that student status is a privilege, the courts upheld administrative discretion to restrict constitutional rights. More recently, in line with decisions affecting the rights of public employees, the range of administrative discretion has been narrowed. Thus in *Dixon v. Alabama*, the expulsion of demonstrating students without notice or hearing was at issue. A United States Court of Appeals answered yes to the question "whether due process requires notice and some opportunity for hearing before students at a tax-supported college are expelled for misconduct." The Court held that "the State cannot condition the granting of even a privilege upon the renunciation of the constitutional right to procedural due process.[61]

The rights of students attending *private* institutions are more ambiguous. Without a finding of state action, the courts may fall back upon the prerogatives of private ownership and the importance of autonomy for institutions of higher education. In 1967 a United States District Court upheld the dismissal without notice or hearing of disruptive students at Howard University.[62] The Court explicitly denied that the rule in *Dixon v. Alabama* was applicable, on the ground that Howard University is a private corporation and therefore beyond the reach of the Bill of Rights. The Court refused to find state action in the fact that a large part of the University budget is derived from Congressional appropriations:

It would be a dangerous doctrine to permit the Government to interpose any degree of control over an institution of higher learning, merely because

---

[60] *Ibid.*, 180.
[61] *Dixon v. Alabama*, 294 F. 2d 150, 156 (1961).
[62] *Greene v. Howard University*, 271 F. Supp. 609 (1967).

it extends financial assistance to it. . . . Surely it should not be held that any institution by entering into a contract with the United States for the conduct of some project of this sort and receiving funds for that purpose, has placed its head in a noose and subjected itself to some degree of control by the Federal Government. Such a result would be intolerable, for it would tend to hinder and control the progress of higher learning and scientific research. Higher education can flourish only in an atmosphere of freedom, untrammeled by Governmental influence in any degree. The courts may not interject themselves into the midst of matters of school discipline. Such discipline cannot be administered successfully in the same manner as governs the trial of a criminal case or a hearing before an administrative agency.[63]

It is by no means clear that public institutions have a lesser need for "an atmosphere of freedom" or that judicially imposed standards of due process are an intolerable interference with institutional autonomy. The decisions affecting public colleges have been careful to specify only minimum standards, leaving a great deal of room for variations in form to take account of the academic context. Thus in *Dixon* v. *Alabama* the Court held that a "hearing" should provide "an opportunity to hear both sides in considerable detail," but this "is not to imply that a full-dress judicial hearing, with the right to cross-examine witnesses, is required. Such a hearing, with the attending publicity and disturbance of college activities, might be detrimental to the college's educational atmosphere and impractical to carry out. Nevertheless, the rudiments of an adversary proceeding may be preserved without encroaching upon the interests of the college."[64]

The main weakness of the opinion in *Greene* v. *Howard* lies in the comment that Howard University "is not a public institution *nor does it partake of any governmental character*."[65] It is one thing to say that the autonomy of religious, educational, or economic institutions may be more easily protected if they are not classified as "public," with all that might mean for the assertion of authority by agencies of public government. It is something else to deny the sociological phenomenon itself, that is, the sense in which private authority "partakes" of a "governmental character" and therefore might be said to sound in the law of governance.

While the courts have thus far held back, a number of legal commentators have urged a blending of constitutional and common-law approaches to judicial review of disciplinary procedures in private colleges. A recent

---

[63] *Ibid.*, 613.
[64] *Dixon* v. *Alabama*, 159.
[65] *Greene* v. *Howard University*, 612–613. (Emphasis supplied.)

analysis of the law of academic freedom, in examining the nonconstitutional bases for judicial protection of student rights, suggests:

> Although a student may have no constitutional claim in a given case, the court may, in promulgating common law standards for adjudication, follow the constitutional norm, most notably in regard to procedure. Whenever a student has been found on nonconstitutional grounds to be entitled to procedural guarantees, the standard of procedural due process has invariably determined the content of those rights. Accordingly, the precise procedural standards which have been, and should be, formulated under a common law theory closely mirror those worked out by the courts under the due process clause.[66]

This argument views the Constitution as a resource for the development of standards to be applied in the course of nonconstitutional adjudication. In this way, the funded experience of the legal order, in the field of public government, may be applied to private contexts. The constitutional norms need not be applied directly, however. They may be incorporated into a common-law theory of the rights asserted. Recognition of a "law of governance," to be applied wherever the social process of governing takes place, would lean on the constitutional experience without directly invoking the Constitution and without necessarily establishing a federal jurisdiction.

Such a development would serve the end sought in the following comment:

> I think it is fair to say that although the concept of "state action" is in the process of a development that eventually may make the due-process limitations applicable to dismissal proceedings conducted by so-called "private" colleges and universities, that development has not yet come to fruition. But the federal Constitution is not the only, or even the principle, source of law. State courts have ample power both to require procedural fairness in dismissal proceedings and to limit or, if necessary, to invalidate regulations or by-laws of "private" institutions that purport to authorize summary dismissal or otherwise restrict the student's right to a fair hearing. This is an area in which I believe that, in the long run, creative judges will cautiously but surely develop the law to the end that students in "private" colleges and universities will be accorded the same safeguards as their counterparts in "public" institutions.[67]

To bring private and public institutions under the same standards, a common rubric is needed. That rubric would deny the significance of the

---

[66] "Developments in the Law—Academic Freedom," 81 *Harvard Law Review* 1045, 1143 (1968).

[67] Clark Byse, "The University and Due Process: A Somewhat Different View," *AAUP Bulletin*, 54 (June, 1968), 146.

private-public distinction, not for all matters, but for those that bear on the exercise of governing authority.

At the conclusion of a comprehensive analysis of standards to be applied in judicial review of university expulsions, it was noted that no distinction had been made between "state" and "private" colleges:

> To some this may seem strange. The distinction between the two is common to everyday language, and has long been assumed by the courts. And the characterization of an institution as "state" has been useful in extending constitutional protections. . . . But the standards here developed are based on the natures of universities and their students—and a school is as much a school whether it be named "state" or not. . . . [The] differences between state and private universities are of degree and not of kind. They do not alter the task of weighing the competing school and student interests which is necessary to provide content for the standard of reasonableness by which to judge expulsion. . . . To the extent that a school—state or private—is functionally a government, our social values demand that standards be imposed on the discretion of administrators— state or private—to protect justice and liberty in the school community.[68]

The final sentence in effect calls for a law of governance to be applied to any institution "that is functionally a government." It follows that the standards are not based solely "on the nature of universities and their students." They must also derive from the theory of governance.

Several writers have found governance in the *rule-making* activity of private associations. Thus Charles E. Merriam took as his starting point that "the problem of systems of rules, the problem of consent, and the problem of leadership are common to all units of association, whether labeled public or private."[69] And Beardsley Ruml put it this way:

> It is in no sense a figure of speech to refer to a business company as a private government. A business is a *government* because within the law it is authorized and/or organized to make rules for the conduct of its affairs. It is a *private* government because the rules it makes within the law are final and are not reviewable by any public body. Some might say that the reason a business is a private government is because it is owned by private individuals, but it seems to me that the existence of private authority is more significant than the element of ownership.[70]

---

[68] "Private Government on the Campus—Judicial Review of University Expulsions," 72 *Yale Law Journal* 1362, 1409 (1963).
[69] Charles E. Merriam, *Public and Private Government* (New Haven: Yale University Press, 1944), 3.
[70] Beardsley Ruml, "Corporate Management as a Locus of Power," *Social Meaning of Legal Concepts*, No. 3, New York University School of Law, 1950, p. 220.

These ideas clearly imply that governance is something more specific than the mere existence of power to influence men and events. It is not how much power it has but how the group is organized that creates the distinctive function of government. On this view a small organization with but little effect on community life can be just as surely self-governing as any large and powerful association.

If we are indeed speaking of a special mode of organization, this must affect our understanding of "rule-making" and "authority." In a broad sense, there are rules of conduct in every human group, and leadership of some sort, while not universal, is hardly uncommon. Yet we would not wish to apply the idea of government to an informal social clique. A stronger criterion is needed. Government presumes *a special form of human association*. We may approach an understanding of this by reviewing again the nature of associational membership, which we have discussed at various points in preceding chapters.[71]

Two basic modes of belonging have long occupied the interest of social analysts: contract and kinship. In the contractual model group membership is based on reciprocity, on arms-length contact, on limited and defined commitments. On the other hand, in the "primary group" model, which applies most closely to friendship and kinship, personal ties and satisfactions are paramount. This is the realm of intimacy, diffuse obligation, and unlimited commitment.

The governmental model stands between these polar types. The term "association" may suggest its essential elements. An association is a group organized for defined and public ends. Known and acknowledged purposes provide the basis of adherence and discipline. Given such ends, rational criteria may be developed to assess the means used to attain them. Thus membership in an association is a way of participating in a system of rationally coordinated activities. Objective and impersonal standards, determined by the requirements of that system, may be invoked for the assessment and control of association members. The members in turn may claim the protection of those same rational criteria.

As in the contract model, formal obligation and impersonal assessment are essential to the idea of association. Indeed, a weakly developed association may be little more than a complex contract where each member participates on the basis of an individual agreement to make certain specific contributions in consideration of definite rewards. On the other hand, even when the commitment of the individual deepens and his participa-

---

[71] See above, 51 f., 67 ff., 117 ff.

tion can no longer be accounted for on a contract theory, the element of formality is not lost. It takes on new dimensions and rests on new foundations.

Beyond formality, however, is the meaning of membership for the individual. This varies considerably, both within a given organization and from one type of organization to another. But we may suggest here that a distinctive characteristic of association membership is *the creation and formalization of status*. This takes a little explaining, and perhaps some revision of conventional images of organization membership.

Sociologists have often emphasized the "segmental" nature of participation in organizations. By this they mean that the individual gives only a part of himself, a segment of his total energies and identity, to a group that has circumscribed goals and can make only limited claims upon him. For many associations, this is certainly an important part of the truth; and it can have decisive consequences for what the organization can do and what its role in society may be. But "segmental participation" is a gross term covering a great many variations. Participation thickens, it takes on a new dimension, as people in organizations strive for personal satisfactions and for protection against threats to their personal security.[72]

This quest for personal meaning and security encourages a process by which minimal affiliation ripens into membership. As this occurs, we see a movement from contract to status. What matters is who you are, what position you occupy, what role you play, rather than what voluntary agreements you may have entered. Nor is this only a product of personal psychology. Other forces, at least equally important, are also at work. Wherever there is an effort to create and sustain a going concern—based on continuing relationships rather than discrete transactions—a drift to status may be expected. Thus even a "customer" may become a "regular customer" and as such may be granted privileges that recognize his valued status.

Of course, the strain toward status is a universal feature of group life. It results from *the inherent instability of narrowly defined, instrumental social relations*. The more important it is to hold a group together, the more likely will be the emergence and stabilization of a system of statuses. Just what that system looks like will depend on the type of group with which we are dealing. The pattern of status in the family is one thing; in a purposive association it is another. And history may alter that pattern as the family or the association changes its role in society.

---

[72] This is the burden of a great deal of research on human relations in industry. A classic study is *Management and the Worker* by F. J. Roethlisberger and W. J. Dickson (Cambridge, Mass.: Harvard University Press, 1939).

In the association, there are both extrinsic and intrinsic sources of status. Extrinsic status arises because the association member may also be a citizen, gambler, family member, club member. Such statuses, derived from other contexts, may be recognized informally in the decision-making of a firm or trade union or college. However, we are concerned here with intrinsic status, based on the defined roles of organization members.

By itself, the allocation of an individual to specific functions within the division of labor may create only a weak form of status. A fuller status arises when a technical function defines the *social identity* of the participants. The narrower and more unskilled a job is, the greater the likelihood that an individual's status will derive from extrinsic factors, such as ethnic origin or personal quality. As the level of skill increases, or as the job becomes more generalized, the technical function becomes more capable of sustaining a social identity. There is a closer congruence of the job and the person. When this congruity becomes stabilized, and has determinate effects, we may speak with confidence of the emergence of social role and status.

We should distinguish what a man does in the division of labor from the significance of his affiliation, taken in itself. The former may not be an adequate basis for social identity, yet the latter may well provide the needed support. The distinctive social role of an ammunition carrier in an infantry squad may be weakly defined, but his status as a soldier, or even as a member of a special company or battalion, can have depth and dimension. Status based on meaningful participation depends in large part on how much the individual has at stake—how much he has invested in the association, how much it dominates his life. The investment, of course, may be emotional or financial; and his dependence will reflect the extent to which realistic alternatives are available.

With the emergence of status we may expect a claim of right. When the job (or the affiliation) confers social identity, the *person* becomes a critical unit within the system of coordination. Without the intrusion of status, rational organization may be free to coordinate "activities" or "units of energy" without taking direct account of the individual in his uniqueness and wholeness. But this theoretical ideal gives way to the pressure of human need. Recognition is claimed for the individual as a distinctive actor, as a person with legitimate aspirations and expectations. The primary demand is that the technical manipulation of persons as things be limited and controlled.

This demand can be satisfied in part without adapting the organization to the uniqueness of the participants. When status rights are recognized, and uniform rules are developed to govern the acquisition or transformation of such rights, the individual gains a large part of his demand for protection against arbitrary manipulation. At the same time, from the standpoint of the association, impersonality and the application of universalistic criteria of decision can be maintained. But the transition from an administered machine—in which human beings are deployed as fully manipulable resources—to a system of governance will have begun.

Membership becomes a form of status when the group loses the option, informally or formally, to expel an individual arbitrarily; when membership carries with it the right to some security of tenure; when the prerogatives of membership become important to the individual *as a person* and not merely as an occupant of a technical or transitory role in the division of labor. The emergence of status is, in the first instance, a matter of fact. It depends on the meaning of affiliation for the individual and on the expectations that naturally arise in the circumstances. By the same token, the enforcement of claims to status at first rests on mutual dependency and on informal social controls. But status fully established summons recognition by the legal order of the association or of the larger society.

The formalization of status, in the context of association, brings with it a certain kind of authority and a concomitant system of objective rules. Governing authority is legal and rational. It goes beyond primitive legitimacy.[73] It presumes that objective and authoritative principles of criticism are engendered regarding the proper ends of power, the scope of authority, and rightful succession; that duty and obedience, in accordance with known standards, extend to all participants; that causes are defined and remedies available for the relief of injustice.

Where these conditions are approximated, *not as a result of external constraint but as the outcome of the group's own problem-solving,* we may speak of the evolution of government. Therefore we cannot argue from an abstract ideal to an institutional prescription. The whole point is that the conditions for governance must be found in the life of the institution itself. On that basis, the law of governance may be invoked. Without that basis the law is irrelevant, its application self-defeating.

Before concluding, a brief summary of the argument in this chapter may be helpful:

1. Although there has been a blurring of the distinction between public law and private law, that distinction does have merit. Public law properly refers to a function, a kind of activity, and not to an institution. The

---

[73] See above, Chap. 1, p. 30.

process of governing is the heart of public law. Much that "governmental institutions" do is outside the purview of governance. Much that "private institutions" do lies within that purview. Our problem, therefore, is to press for a fuller understanding of governance as a generic social process.

2. In American jurisprudence "due process" is the key to the law of governance. The law of due process is, inevitably, the primary source of concepts and doctrines to be used in bringing the rule of law to new settings. However, due process has been too closely tied to a conventional public-law context and, especially, to the sphere of constitutional law. The law of due process should be seen as part of the common law, though based in part on statute. As a common-law field, comparable to the law of tort or contract, the law of due process may be applied as needed wherever the functions of governance are performed.

3. Private government should not be identified with the existence of centers of power in society. Rather, we should look to the character of the association to see whether and to what extent governance exists. This quest for governance centers upon the nature of group membership and the pattern of authority. The emergence of intrinsic status, important to the social identity of the member and grounded in the explicit aims and structure of the association, creates the private equivalent of citizenship. The minimal concomitants of citizenship are legitimate authority and objective rules. When these conditions exist, or may properly be expected, the realm of public law has been entered.

If the concept of a law of governance carries import for legal change, it is not as a deduction from abstract premises. Rather, its legal relevance and warrant derive from a specific historical trend in modern society, a trend that is changing the nature of administration, altering the claims asserted by participants, and erasing the distinction between public and private enterprise. As we move toward a "mixed economy," these trends will produce new and urgent demands for appropriate responses in legal policy and cognition.[74]

The spread of legal ideals to special-purpose institutions says more about historical opportunity, and about concomitant expectations, than it does about new forms of oppression. We have pointed to the emergence of an autonomous order in industry, helped along, to be sure, by facilitative legal change. In the development of grievance arbitration, for example,

---

[74] On the need to overcome the distinction between public and private enterprise, see Michael P. Fogarty, *Company and Corporation—One Law?* (London: Geoffrey Chapman, 1965), Chaps. 5–6.

the legal system attempts to place the burden of adjudication on the private machinery. But the significant sociological fact is that *the very existence of the internal order tends to validate external control and, at the same time, makes it feasible.* It is just when fairness is already institutionalized in much of the private sphere that an appeal to the larger political community is warranted.

If social evolution has taken place, it does not follow that legal change is not needed or expected. On the contrary, the legal order is pressed to put into practice ideals that have always had an abstract validity but which may not, in the past, have reflected the institutional competence of the society. Law works best when appropriate social foundations exist, but those foundations do not obviate the need for legal support and direction, to confirm rights and to extend them. In the contemporary American setting, the law of employment remains weakly developed. Labor law shows great strength, but the legal bases of managerial authority—in property and in the employment contract—have not been reconstructed. This will not occur until corporation law itself is remade to take account of the enterprise as a social unit, face up to the realities of authority and the separation of ownership and control, and assert the rights of employees as members.[75]

It is not our business to suggest specific legal changes. But in concluding we should call attention to a broad issue that has been implicit in our discussion: What is the larger promise of the law of governance? What is the relation between due process and democracy? Our analysis has centered on industrial *justice* fairly narrowly conceived, not on a more generous view of industrial *democracy*. That emphasis reflects our special concern for emergent law, but it also says something about our perception of the institutional realities. We can speak with far greater assurance about the social foundations for limiting arbitrary power than for sustaining democratic decision-making.[76] By the same token, it is easier to see a basis for managerial self-restraint than for affirmative social responsibility.

On the other hand, we have argued in Chapter 1 that legality has a strong affinity with the ideal of political democracy, and that a legal order should be seen as transitional to polity. It follows that there is latent in the law of governance a norm of participation. Due process strains to take account of all legal interests, provide opportunities for the offering of

---

[75] See above, 43–52.
[76] A similar view is expressed in Allan Flanders, "The Internal Social Responsibilities of Industry," *British Journal of Industrial Relations*, 4 (March, 1966), 10 ff.

proofs and arguments, and deepen the legitimacy of authority. These premises invite new forms of legal and political participation. Without yielding the position that democratic forms are not to be imposed mechanically on uncongenial institutional settings, the perspective of governance sounds a note of caution and of hope: In the end, the quest for justice may be indistinguishable from the quest for civic competence and personal autonomy.

Index

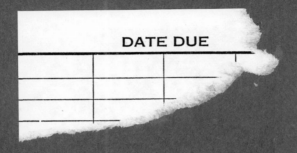

DATE DUE